4-4-18

Everyday Mathematics

Student Reference Book

The University of Chicago
School Mathematics Project

Everyday
Mathematics®

Student Reference Book

**The University of Chicago
School Mathematics Project**

EVERYDAY
LEARNING

Chicago, Illinois

UCSMP Elementary Materials Component

Max Bell, Director

Authors

Max Bell, Jean Bell, John Bretzlauf, Amy Dillard, Robert Hartfield, Andy Isaacs, Deborah Arron Leslie, James McBride (Director), Kathleen Pitvorec, Peter Saecker

Technical Art

Diana Barrie

Everyday Learning Development Staff

Editorial: Anna Belluomini, Mary Cooney, Christine Fraser, Elizabeth Glosniak, Janet Kapche Razionale
Design: Fran Brown
Production: Annette Davis, Tina Dunlap, Elizabeth Gabbard

Additional Credits

Black Dot Group, Loretta Becker, Kathleen Burke, Phil Ciciora, Lindaanne Donohoe, Lauren Harper, Herman Adler Design Group, Lucy Lesiak, Precision Graphics, Regina Thoeming

Photo Credits

Phil Martin/ Photography
US©Maslowski/Visuals Unlimited, p. 62
Mark Gibson/Visuals Unlimited, p. 74 (second right)
Mark Gibson/Visuals Unlimited, p. 74 (third right)
John Edwards/Tony Stone Images, p. 80
Leonard E. Morgan/Custom Medical Stock Photos, p. 132
Loren Santow/Tony Stone Images, p. 151
Australia, Edition 8/Lonely Planet Publications, p. 210
Doris De Witt/Tony Stone Images, p. 210 (top)
James Nelson/Tony Stone Images, p. 210 (center)
John Neubauer/FPG, p. 211
Peter Gridley/FPG, p. 212
John Lawrence/Tony Stone Images, p. 239 (right top)
Sivestre Machado/Tony Stone Images, p. 240
Will and Deni McIntyre/Tony Stone Images, p. 242 (top)
Natalie Fobes/Tony Stone Images, p. 242 (bottom)
Gene Peach/Tony Stone Images, p. 244
Pete Seaward/Tony Stone Images, p. 246
Jason Hawkes/Tony Stone Images, p. 247 (left)
Hugh Sitton/Tony Stone Images, p. 247 (center)

The maps on pages 216, 217, 219–221, and 226–237 were created using ArcView GIS version 3.2 software. Source data: ArcWorld.

The *Student Reference Book* is based upon work supported by the National Science Foundation under Grant No. ESI-9252984. Any opinions, findings, conclusions, or recommendations expressed in this material are those of the authors and do not necessarily reflect the views of the National Science Foundation.

ISBN 1-57039-911-5

Any questions regarding this policy should be addressed to:

Everyday Learning Corporation

P.O. Box 812960
Chicago, IL 60681
www.everydaylearning.com

3 4 5 6 7 8 9 QW 05 04 03 02 01

Contents

Whole Numbers   1

Decimals and Percents   23

Fractions and Rational Numbers   39

Data and Probability   61

Problem Solving 147

Calculators 159

Games 183

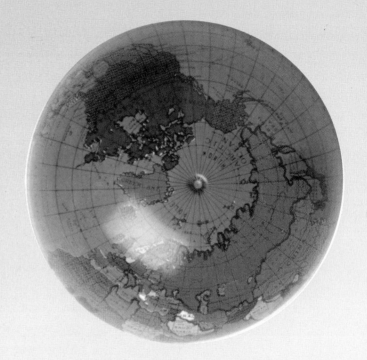

About the *Student Reference Book*

A reference book is organized to help people find information quickly and easily. Dictionaries, encyclopedias, atlases, cookbooks, even telephone books are examples of reference books. Unlike novels and biographies, which are usually read in sequence from beginning to end, reference books are read in small segments to find specific information at the time it is needed.

You can use this *Student Reference Book* to look up and review information on topics in mathematics. It consists of the following sections:

- A **table of contents** that lists the topics covered and shows how the book is organized.

- Essays on **mathematical topics,** such as whole numbers, fractions, decimals, percents, geometry, measurement, data analysis, and problem solving.

- Descriptions of how to use a **calculator** to perform various mathematical operations and functions.

- Directions on how to play some of the **mathematical games** you may have played before.

- A **glossary** of mathematical terms consisting of brief definitions of important words.

- A set of **tables and charts** that summarize information, such as a place-value chart, prefixes for names of large and small numbers, tables of equivalent measures and of equivalent fractions, decimals, and percents.

- An **answer key** for every Check Your Understanding problem in the book.

- An **index** to help you locate information quickly.

This reference book also contains a **World Tour** section. It is a collection of numerical information about people and places around the world.

How to Use the
Student Reference Book

Suppose you are asked to solve a problem and you know that you have solved problems like it before. But at the moment, you are having difficulty remembering how to do it. This is a perfect time to use the *Student Reference Book.* You can look in the **table of contents** or the **index** to find the page that gives a brief explanation of the topic. The explanation will often show a step-by-step sample solution.

In some essays you will see a small book symbol. The symbol gives page number references to essays that are related to the topic under discussion. For example, simplifying fractions involves finding equivalent fractions; so in the side-column, next to the paragraphs that discuss simplifying fractions, there is a reference to the page which contains a description of how to find equivalent fractions.

There is also a set of problems at the end of most essays, titled **Check Your Understanding**. It is a good idea to solve these problems and then turn to the answer key at the back of the book to check your answers to make sure that you understand the information presented on the page.

Always read mathematical text with paper and pencil in hand. Take notes; draw pictures and diagrams to help you understand what you are reading. Work the examples. If you get a wrong answer in the **Check Your Understanding** problems, try to find your mistake by working back from the correct answer given in the answer key.

It is not always easy to read text about mathematics, but the more you use the *Student Reference Book,* the better you will become at understanding this kind of material. You may find that your skills as an independent problem-solver are improving. We are confident that these skills will serve you well as you undertake more advanced mathematics courses.

Whole Numbers

Uses of Numbers

Try to imagine living even one day without using or thinking about numbers. Numbers are used on clocks, calendars, car license plates, rulers, scales, and so on. The major ways that numbers are used are listed below.

- Numbers are used for **counting**.

EXAMPLES   Students sold 147 tickets to the school play.

The first U.S. Census counted 3,929,326 people.

- Numbers are used for **measuring**.

EXAMPLES   Hector swam the length of the pool in 34.8 seconds.

The package is 26 inches long and weighs $2\frac{1}{4}$ pounds.

- Numbers are used to show where something is in a **reference system**.

EXAMPLES

Situation	Reference System
Normal room temperature is 21°C.	Celsius temperature scale
Tom was born on May 21, 1993.	Calendar
The time is 7:29 P.M.	Clock time
Detroit is located at 42°N and 83°W.	Earth's latitude and longitude system

- Numbers are used to **compare amounts** or **measures**.

EXAMPLES   The cat weighs $\frac{1}{2}$ as much as the dog.

There were 3 times as many boys as girls at the game.

- Numbers are used for **identification** and as **codes**.

EXAMPLES   phone number: (709) 555–1212

ZIP code: 60637   driver's license number: M286-423-2061

Kinds of Numbers

The **counting numbers** are the numbers used to count things. The set of counting numbers is 1, 2, 3, 4, and so on.

The **whole numbers** are any of the numbers 0, 1, 2, 3, 4, and so on. The whole numbers include all of the counting numbers and zero (0).

Counting numbers are useful for counting, but they do not always work for measures. Some measures fall between two consecutive whole numbers. **Fractions** and **decimals** were invented to keep track of such measures. For example, fractions are often used in recipes for cooking, and for measurements in carpentry and other building trades. Decimals are used for almost all measures in science and industry.

> **EXAMPLES** The letter weighed $3\frac{1}{2}$ ounces.
>
> The recipe called for $2\frac{3}{4}$ cups of flour.
>
> The window sill is 2 feet $6\frac{1}{2}$ inches above the floor.

Negative numbers were invented to express quantities with reference to a zero point.

> **EXAMPLES** A temperature of 10 degrees below zero is written as $-10°F$.
>
> A depth of 235 feet below sea level is written as -235 feet.

Negative numbers are also used to indicate changes in quantities.

> **EXAMPLES** A weight loss of $4\frac{1}{2}$ pounds is recorded as $-4\frac{1}{2}$ pounds.
>
> A decrease in income of $1,000 is recorded as $-$1,000.

Place Value for Whole Numbers

Any number, no matter how large or small, can be written using one or more of the **digits** 0, 1, 2, 3, 4, 5, 6, 7, 8, and 9. A **place-value chart** is used to show how much each digit in a number is worth. The **place** for a digit is its position in the number. The **value** of a digit is how much it is worth according to its place in the number.

Study the place-value chart below. As you move from right to left in the chart, the value of each place is 10 times greater.

ten thousands 10,000s	thousands 1,000s	hundreds 100s	tens 10s	ones 1s
7	2	6	0	3

EXAMPLE The number 72,603 is shown in the place-value chart above. It is read "seventy-two thousand, six hundred three."

The value of the 7 is 70,000 (7 $*$ 10,000).
The value of the 2 is 2,000 (2 $*$ 1,000).
The value of the 6 is 600 (6 $*$ 100).
The value of the 0 is 0 (0 $*$ 10).
The value of the 3 is 3 (3 $*$ 1).

In larger numbers, look for the commas that separate groups of 3 digits. The commas will help you identify the thousands, millions, billions, and so on.

EXAMPLE Last year, the U.S. Mint made 10,257,400,075 new pennies.

billions				millions				thousands				ones		
100	10	1	,	100	10	1	,	100	10	1	,	100	10	1
	1	0	,	2	5	7	,	4	0	0	,	0	7	5

Read from left to right.
Read "billion" at the first comma.
Read "million" at the second comma.
Read "thousand" at the last comma.
The number is read as "10 **billion**, 257 **million**, 400 **thousand**, 75."

CHECK YOUR UNDERSTANDING

Read each number to yourself. What is the value of the 7 in each number?

1. 27,308   **2.** 96,700,000   **3.** 52,074   **4.** 2,475,000

Check your answers on page 277.

Powers of 10

Numbers like 10, 100, and 1,000 are called **powers of 10.**
They are numbers that can be written as products of 10s.
100 can be written as 10 * 10. 1,000 can be written as
10*10*10. And so on.

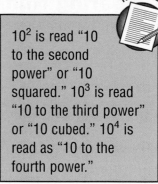

10^2 is read "10 to the second power" or "10 squared." 10^3 is read "10 to the third power" or "10 cubed." 10^4 is read as "10 to the fourth power."

There is a shorthand method for writing products of 10s.
10*10 can be written as 10^2.
10*10*10 can be written as 10^3.
10*10*10*10 can be written as 10^4.

The raised digit is called an **exponent.** The exponent tells how
many times 10 is multiplied by itself.

The chart below shows the powers of 10 from ten through one billion.

Powers of 10

Standard Notation	Product of 10s	Exponential Notation
10	10	10^1
100	10*10	10^2
1,000 (1 thousand)	10*10*10	10^3
10,000	10*10*10*10	10^4
100,000	10*10*10*10*10	10^5
1,000,000 (1 million)	10*10*10*10*10*10	10^6
10,000,000	10*10*10*10*10*10*10	10^7
100,000,000	10*10*10*10*10*10*10*10	10^8
1,000,000,000 (1 billion)	10*10*10*10*10*10*10*10*10	10^9

EXAMPLE   1,000 * 1,000 = ?

Use the table above to write 1,000 as 10*10*10.
1,000*1,000 = (10*10*10)*(10*10*10)
            = 10^6
            = 1 million

So, 1,000*1,000 = 1 million.

EXAMPLE   1,000 millions = ?

Write 1,000*1,000,000 as (10*10*10)*(10*10*10*10*10*10).
This is a product of nine 10s, or 10^9.

1,000 millions = 1 billion

Comparing Numbers and Amounts

When two numbers or amounts are compared, there are two possible results: They are equal, or they are not equal because one is larger than the other.

Different symbols are used to show that numbers and amounts are equal or not equal.

- Use an **equal sign** (**=**) to show that the numbers or amounts *are equal.*
- Use a **greater-than symbol** (**>**) or a **less-than symbol** (**<**) to show that they are *not equal.*

EXAMPLES	Symbol	=	>	<
	Meaning	"equals" or "is the same as"	"is greater than"	"is less than"
		$\frac{1}{2} = 0.5$	$7 > 3$	$2 < 4$
		$20 = 4 * 5$	$1.23 > 1.2$	$398 < 1,020$
		$3 \text{ cm} = 30 \text{ mm}$	$14 \text{ ft } 7 \text{ in.} > 13 \text{ ft } 11 \text{ in.}$	$99 \text{ minutes} < 2 \text{ hours}$
		$5 + 5 = 6 + 6 - 2$	$8 + 7 > 9 + 5$	$2 * (3 + 3) < 4 * 5$
		$2 * 4 = 7 + 1$	$3 * 6 > 24 / 2$	$100 - 1 < 99 + 1$

When you compare amounts that include units, be sure to use the same unit for both amounts.

EXAMPLE Compare 30 yards and 60 feet.

The units are different—yards and feet.

Change yards to feet, and then compare.
1 yd = 3 ft
So, 30 yd = 30 * 3 ft, or 90 ft. 90 ft > 60 ft

Therefore, 30 yd > 60 ft.

CHECK YOUR UNDERSTANDING

True or false?

1. $6 + 11 < 12$ **2.** $38 \text{ in.} > 3 \text{ ft}$ **3.** $6 * 5 = 90 / 3$ **4.** $15 + 1 > 17 - 1$

Check your answers on page 277.

Factors and Arrays

When two numbers are multiplied, the answer is called the **product.** The two numbers that are multiplied are called **factors** of the product.

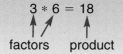 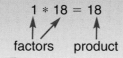 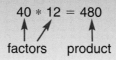

EXAMPLES	Name the factors and the products.

3 * 6 = 18   1 * 18 = 18   40 * 12 = 480

factors   product   factors   product   factors   product

An **array** is a group of objects arranged in **rows** and **columns.**

* The rows and columns of an array form a rectangle.
* Each row of the array has the same number of objects.
* Each column of the array has the same number of objects.

Arrays can be used to show all the factors of a number.

Push buttons on a telephone form a 4-by-3 array

EXAMPLE	Find all of the numbers that are factors of 6.

There are 4 different ways to make an array that has 6 objects.
A multiplication number model is shown for each array.
Each number model shows two factors of 6.

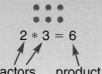   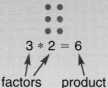   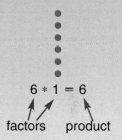

2 * 3 = 6   3 * 2 = 6   1 * 6 = 6   6 * 1 = 6

factors   product   factors   product   factors   product   factors   product

The arrays show that 1, 2, 3, and 6 are all factors of 6.
These numbers are the *only* factors of 6.

EXAMPLE	Find all the numbers that are factors of 5.

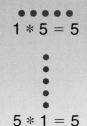

There are only 2 ways to make an array that has 5 objects.
The arrays show that 1 and 5 are the only factors of 5.
There are only 2 ways to multiply two whole numbers and get 5.
1 * 5 = 5 and 5 * 1 = 5. So 1 and 5 are both factors of 5.

1 * 5 = 5

5 * 1 = 5

1 and 5 are the *only* factors of 5.

CHECK YOUR UNDERSTANDING

Draw arrays and find all of the factors for each number.

1. 12   **2.** 15   **3.** 24   **4.** 13

Check your answers on page 277.

Kinds of Counting Numbers

The **counting numbers** are the numbers 1, 2, 3, 4, 5, and so on.

A counting number is an **even number** if 2 is one of its factors. The even numbers are 2, 4, 6, 8, 10, and so on.

A counting number is an **odd number** if it is not an even number. The odd numbers are 1, 3, 5, 7, 9, 11, and so on.

A **prime number** is a counting number that has exactly 2 factors. 5 is a prime number because the only factors of 5 are 1 and 5. All of these numbers are prime numbers:

> 2, 3, 5, 7, 11, 13, 17, 19

A **composite number** is any counting number greater than 1 that is not a prime number. Each composite number has 3 or more factors. All of these numbers are composite numbers:

> 4, 6, 8, 9, 10, 12, 14, 15, 16, 18, 20

Facts about the Numbers 1 through 20

Number	Factors	Prime or Composite	Even or Odd
1	1	neither	odd
2	1 and 2	prime	even
3	1 and 3	prime	odd
4	1, 2, and 4	composite	even
5	1 and 5	prime	odd
6	1, 2, 3, and 6	composite	even
7	1 and 7	prime	odd
8	1, 2, 4, and 8	composite	even
9	1, 3, and 9	composite	odd
10	1, 2, 5, and 10	composite	even
11	1 and 11	prime	odd
12	1, 2, 3, 4, 6, and 12	composite	even
13	1 and 13	prime	odd
14	1, 2, 7, and 14	composite	even
15	1, 3, 5, and 15	composite	odd
16	1, 2, 4, 8, and 16	composite	even
17	1 and 17	prime	odd
18	1, 2, 3, 6, 9, and 18	composite	even
19	1 and 19	prime	odd
20	1, 2, 4, 5, 10, and 20	composite	even

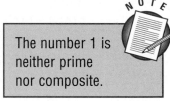

NOTE

The number 1 is neither prime nor composite.

Addition Methods
Partial-Sums Method

The **partial-sums method** is used to find sums mentally or with paper and pencil. Here is the partial-sums method for adding 2-digit or 3-digit numbers:

1. Add the 100s.
2. Add the 10s.
3. Add the 1s.
4. Then add the sums you just found (the partial sums).

EXAMPLE Solve 248 + 187 using the partial-sums method.

		100s	10s	1s
		2	4	8
		+ 1	8	7
Add the 100s.	200 + 100 →	3	0	0
Add the 10s.	40 + 80 →	1	2	0
Add the 1s.	8 + 7 →		1	5
Add the partial sums.	300 + 120 + 15 →	4	3	5

248 + 187 = 435

Larger numbers with 4 or more digits are added the same way.

Use base-10 blocks to show the partial-sums method.

EXAMPLE Use base-10 blocks to solve 248 + 187.

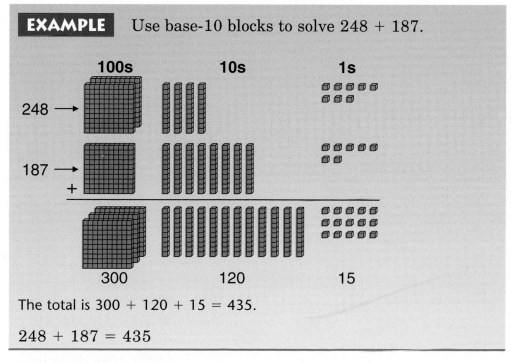

The total is 300 + 120 + 15 = 435.

248 + 187 = 435

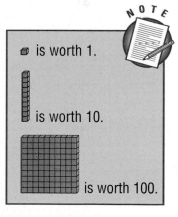

NOTE

▱ is worth 1.

▯ is worth 10.

▣ is worth 100.

Column-Addition Method

The **column-addition method** can be used to find sums with paper and pencil, but it is not a good method for finding sums mentally.

Here is the column-addition method for adding 2-digit or 3-digit numbers:

1. Draw lines to separate the 1s, 10s, and 100s places.

2. Add the numbers in each column. Write each sum in its column.

3. If there are 2 digits in the 1s place, trade 10 ones for 1 ten.

4. If there are 2 digits in the 10s places, trade 10 tens for 1 hundred.

EXAMPLE   Solve 248 + 187 using the column-addition method.

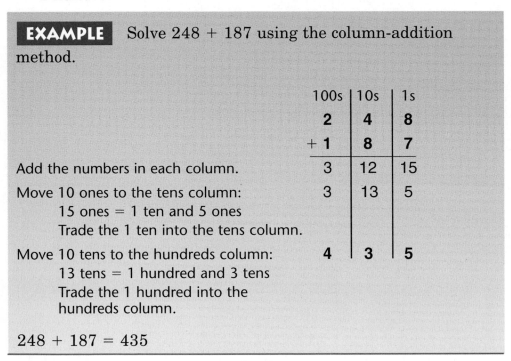

	100s	10s	1s
	2	4	8
+	1	8	7
Add the numbers in each column.	3	12	15
Move 10 ones to the tens column: 15 ones = 1 ten and 5 ones Trade the 1 ten into the tens column.	3	13	5
Move 10 tens to the hundreds column: 13 tens = 1 hundred and 3 tens Trade the 1 hundred into the hundreds column.	4	3	5

248 + 187 = 435

Larger numbers with 4 or more digits are added the same way.

CHECK YOUR UNDERSTANDING

Add.

1. 263
    + 425

2. 75
    + 38

3. 188
    + 233

4. 1,357
    + 468

5. 23
    45
    + 67

6. 43 + 39

7. 62 + 37

8. 508 + 427

9. 1,204 + 58

10. 80 + 37 + 6

Check your answers on page 277.

Subtraction Methods
Trade-First Subtraction Method
The **trade-first method** is similar to the method for subtracting that most adults were taught when they were in school.

Here is the trade-first method for subtracting 2-digit or 3-digit numbers:

- Look at the digits in the 1s place. If you cannot subtract these digits without getting a negative number, trade 1 ten for 10 ones.
- Look at the digits in the 10s place. If you cannot subtract these digits without getting a negative number, trade 1 hundred for 10 tens.
- Subtract in each column.

EXAMPLE Subtract 164 from 352 using the trade-first method.

100s	10s	1s
3	5	2
− 1	6	4

Look at the 1s place. You cannot remove 4 ones from 2 ones.

100s	10s	1s
	4	12
3	5̸	2̸
− 1	6	4

So trade 1 ten for 10 ones. Look at the 10s place. You cannot remove 6 tens from 4 tens.

100s	10s	1s
	14	
2	4̸	12
3̸	5̸	2̸
− 1	6	4
1	8	8

So trade 1 hundred for 10 tens. Now subtract in each column.

So, $352 - 164 = 188$.

Larger numbers with 4 or more digits are subtracted the same way.

CHECK YOUR UNDERSTANDING
Subtract.

1. $\begin{array}{r} 95 \\ - 58 \end{array}$ 2. $\begin{array}{r} 873 \\ - 392 \end{array}$ 3. $\begin{array}{r} 654 \\ - 205 \end{array}$ 4. $\begin{array}{r} 909 \\ - 648 \end{array}$

5. $6{,}534 - 3{,}388$ 6. $856 - 94$

Check your answers on page 277.

Base-10 blocks are useful for solving problems, but sometimes they are not available. You can draw pictures instead. The pictures sometimes used in this book to show base-10 blocks are shown in the margin.

Pictures of base-10 blocks show how the trade-first method works.

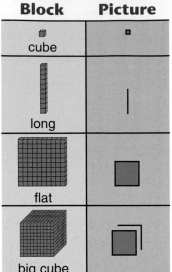

Base-10 Block	Shorthand Picture
cube	·
long	|
flat	▪
big cube	▪

EXAMPLE   324 − 167 = ?

Model the larger number, 324.
Write the number to be subtracted, 167,
beneath the block pictures.

100s	10s	1s
3	2	4
− 1	6	7

hundreds	tens	ones
⬛⬛⬛	||	▪ ▪ ▪ ▪
1	6	7

Think: Can I remove 7 cubes from 4 cubes? no
Trade 1 long for 10 cubes.

hundreds	tens	ones
⬛⬛⬛	|| →	▪ ▪ ▪ ▪ ▪▪▪▪▪ ▪▪▪▪▪
1	6	7

Think: Can I remove 6 longs from 1 long? no
Trade 1 flat for 10 longs.

hundreds	tens	ones
⬛⬛⬛	| ||||||||||	▪ ▪ ▪ ▪ ▪▪▪▪▪ ▪▪▪▪▪
1	6	7

After all of the trading, the blocks look like this:

hundreds	tens	ones
⬛⬛	| ||||||||||	▪ ▪ ▪ ▪ ▪▪▪▪▪ ▪▪▪▪▪
1	6	7

Now subtract in each column.
The difference is 157.

100s	10s	1s
3	2	4
− 1	6	7
1	5	7

hundreds	tens	ones
⬛	| ||||	▪ ▪ ▪ ▪ ▪ ▪ ▪

Counting-Up Method

You can subtract two numbers by counting up from the smaller number to the larger number.

- First count up to the nearest multiple of 10.

- Next, count up by 10s and 100s.

- Then count up to the larger number.

EXAMPLE $325 - 38 = ?$

Write the smaller number, 38.

As you count from 38 up to 325, circle each number that you count up.

Add the numbers you circled:
$2 + 60 + 200 + 25 = 287$
You counted up by 287.

```
        3 8
  +      2        Count up to the nearest 10.
        4 0
  +    6 0        Count up to the nearest 100.
      1 0 0
  +  2 0 0        Count up to the largest possible hundred.
      3 0 0
  +    2 5        Count up to the larger number.
      3 2 5
```

$325 - 38 = 287$

Left-to-Right Subtraction Method

Starting at the left, subtract column-by-column.

EXAMPLES $932 - 356 = ?$ $782 - 294 = ?$

Subtract the 100s.

Subtract the 10s.

Subtract the 1s.

```
        9 3 2                      7 8 2
      - 3 0 0                    - 2 0 0
        6 3 2                      5 8 2
      -   5 0                    -   9 0
        5 8 2                      4 9 2
      -     6                    -     4
        5 7 6                      4 8 8
```

$932 - 356 = 576$ $782 - 294 = 488$

CHECK YOUR UNDERSTANDING

Subtract.

1. $284 - 86$ **2.** $364 - 168$ **3.** $739 - 425$ **4.** $617 - 48$

Check your answers on page 277.

Partial-Differences Method

1. Subtract from left to right, one column at a time.

2. Always subtract the smaller number from the larger number.

   • If the smaller number is on the bottom, the difference is **added** to the answer.

   • If the smaller number is on the top, the difference is **subtracted** from the answer.

EXAMPLE   746 − 263 = ?

```
              7  4  6
          −   2  6  3
```

Subtract the 100s.	700 − 200 →	+ 5 0 0
Subtract the 10s.	60 − 40 →	− 2 0
Subtract the 1s.	6 − 3 →	+ 3
Find the total.	500 − 20 + 3 →	4 8 3

(The smaller number is on top, so include a minus sign.)

746 − 263 = 483

Same-Change Rule

Here is the **same-change rule** for subtraction problems:

• If you add the same number to both numbers in the problem, the answer is the same.

• If you subtract the same number from both numbers in the problem, the answer is the same.

Use this rule to change the second number in the problem to a number that has zero in the ones place.

EXAMPLES   92 − 36 = ?

One way: Add 4.

```
   9  2   (add 4)        9  6
−  3  6   (add 4)     −  4  0
                         5  6
```

Another way: Subtract 6.

```
   9  2   (subtract 6)      8  6
−  3  6   (subtract 6)   −  3  0
                            5  6
```

CHECK YOUR UNDERSTANDING

Subtract.

1. 714 − 192   2. 174 − 36   3. 483 − 164   4. 857 − 409

Check your answers on page 277.

Basic Multiplication Facts

The symbols × and * are both used to indicate multiplication. In this book, the symbol * is used most often.

A basic multiplication fact is a product of two one-digit factors. 8 * 5 = 40 is a basic fact. If you don't remember a basic fact, try one of the following:

Use Counters or Draw a Picture

To find 8 * 5, make 8 groups of counters with 5 counters in each group, or draw a simple picture to show 8 groups of 5 objects. Then count all the objects.

Skip Count Up

To find 8 * 5, count up by 5s, 8 times:
5, 10, 15, 20, 25, 30, 35, 40. Use your fingers to keep track as you skip count.

Use Known Facts

The answer to a 4s fact can be found by doubling, then doubling again. For example, to find 4 * 7, double 7 (14) and double that result (28).

The answer to a 6s fact can be found by using a related 5s fact. For example, 6 * 8 is equal to 8 more than 5 * 8. 6 * 8 = 5 * 8 + 8 = 40 + 8, or 48.

There is a **pattern** to the 9s facts:

- The 10s digit in the product is 1 less than the digit that is multiplying the 9.

  For example, in 9 * 3 = 27, the 2 in 27 is 1 less than the 3 in 9 * 3.

  In 9 * 7 = 63, the 6 in 63 is 1 less than the 7 in 9 * 7.

- The sum of the digits in the product is 9.
  For example, in 9 * 7 = 63, 6 + 3 = 9.

9s Facts
9 * 1 = 9
9 * 2 = 18
9 * 3 = 27
9 * 4 = 36
9 * 5 = 45
9 * 6 = 54
9 * 7 = 63
9 * 8 = 72
9 * 9 = 81

Extended Multiplication Facts

Numbers such as 10, 100, and 1,000 are called **powers of 10.**

It is easy to multiply a whole number, *n,* by a power of 10:

To the right of the number *n,* write as many zeros as there are zeros in the power of 10.

EXAMPLES   Notice that the number of zeros added and the number of zeros in the power of 10 are the same.

$10 * 64 = 640$	$10 * 30 = 300$	$100 * 270 = 27,000$
$100 * 64 = 6,400$	$100 * 30 = 3,000$	$10,000 * 61 = 610,000$
$1,000 * 64 = 64,000$	$1,000 * 30 = 30,000$	$1,000,000 * 8 = 8,000,000$

If you have memorized the basic multiplication facts, you can solve problems such as $8 * 60$ and $4,000 * 3$ mentally.

EXAMPLES

$8 * 60 = ?$	$4,000 * 3 = ?$
Think: 8 [6s] = 48	*Think:* 4 [3s] = 12
Then 8 [60s] is 10 times as much.	Then 4,000 [3s] is 1,000 times as much.
$8 * 60 = 10 * 48 = 480$	$4,000 * 3 = 1,000 * 12 = 12,000$

You can use a similar method to solve problems such as $30 * 50$ and $200 * 90$ mentally.

EXAMPLES

$30 * 50 = ?$	$200 * 90 = ?$
Think: 3 [50s] = 150	*Think:* 2 [90s] = 180
Then 30 [50s] is 10 times as much.	Then 200 [90s] is 100 times as much.
$30 * 50 = 10 * 150 = 1,500$	$200 * 90 = 100 * 180 = 18,000$

CHECK YOUR UNDERSTANDING

Solve these problems mentally.

1. $9 * 100$ **2.** $1,000 * 37$ **3.** $6 * 400$ **4.** $3,000 * 8$ **5.** $70 * 30$ **6.** $600 * 50$

Check your answers on page 277.

Multiplication Methods
Partial-Products Method

In the **partial-products method,** you must keep track of the place value of each digit. Each partial product is either a multiplication fact or an extended multiplication fact.

EXAMPLE 5 * 26 = ?

	100s	10s	1s	
Think of 26 as 20 + 6.		2	6	
*			5	
Multiply each part of 26 by 5. 5 * 20 →	1	0	0	extended multiplication fact
5 * 6 →		3	0	basic multiplication fact
Add these two partial products.	1	3	0	

5 * 26 = 130

EXAMPLE 34 * 26 = ?

		100s	10s	1s	
Think of 26 as 20 + 6.			2	6	
Think of 34 as 30 + 4.	*		3	4	
Multiply each part of 26 by each part of 34. 30 * 20 →		6	0	0	
30 * 6 →		1	8	0	} extended multiplication facts
4 * 20 →			8	0	
4 * 6 →			2	4	basic multiplication fact
		8	8	4	

Add these four partial products.

34 * 26 = 884

CHECK YOUR UNDERSTANDING

Multiply. Write each partial product. Then add the partial products.

1. 84 * 6   **2.** 32 * 75   **3.** 50 * 57   **4.** 33 * 33   **5.** 217 * 4

Check your answers on page 277.

Lattice Method

The **lattice method** for multiplying has been used for hundreds of years. It is very easy to use if you know the basic multiplication facts.

EXAMPLE 3 * 45 = ?

The box with cells and diagonals is called a **lattice.**

Write 45 above the lattice.
Write 3 on the right side of the lattice.
Multiply 3 * 5. Then multiply 3 * 4.
Write the answers in the lattice as shown.

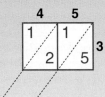

Add the numbers along each diagonal.

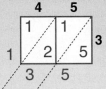

Read the answer. 3 * 45 = 135

EXAMPLE 34 * 26 = ?

Write 26 above the lattice and 34 on the right side of the lattice.

Multiply 3 * 6. Then multiply 3 * 2.
Multiply 4 * 6. Then multiply 4 * 2.
Write the answers in the lattice as shown.

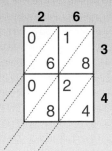

Add the numbers along each diagonal.
When the numbers along a diagonal add to 10 or more:
• record the ones digit
• add the tens digit to the sum in the diagonal above

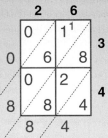

Read the answer. 34 * 26 = 884

CHECK YOUR UNDERSTANDING

Draw a lattice for each problem. Then multiply.

1. 3 * 68   **2.** 7 * 89   **3.** 44 * 25   **4.** 23 * 91   **5.** 6 * 815

Check your answers on pages 277 and 278.

Basic Division Facts

A division fact represents sharing equally or forming equal groups.

$40 / 5 = ?$ 5 people share 40 pennies.
How many pennies does each person get? 8

$40 / 5 = ?$ There are 40 oranges in all. 5 oranges are put into each bag. How many bags can be filled? 8

If you don't remember a basic fact, try one of the following:

Use Counters or Draw a Picture

To find $40 / 5$, start with 40 objects.

Think: How many 5s in 40?

Make or circle groups of 5 objects each. Count the groups.

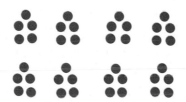

Skip Count Down

To find $40 / 5$, start at 40 and count by 5s down to 0. Use your fingers to keep track as you skip count.

40, 35, 30, 25, 20, 15, 10, 5, 0. That's 8 skips.

Use Known Multiplication Facts

Every division fact is related to a multiplication fact. For example, if you know that $5 * 8 = 40$ or $8 * 5 = 40$, you can figure out that $40 / 5 = 8$ and $40 / 8 = 5$.

> **NOTE**
> You can multiply by 0, but you cannot divide by 0. For example, $0 * 9 = 0$, but $9 / 0$ has no answer.

Extended Division Facts

Numbers such as 10, 100, and 1,000 are called **powers of 10.**

In the examples below, use the following method to divide a whole number, *n*, by a power of 10:

- Cross out zeros in the number *n*, starting at the ones place.
- Cross out as many zeros as there are zeros in the power of 10.

EXAMPLES Notice that the number of zeros crossed out and the number of zeros in the power of 10 is the same.

800 / **10** = 80~~0~~	7,000 / **10** = 700~~0~~	46,000 / **10** = 4600~~0~~
800 / **100** = 8~~00~~	7,000 / **100** = 70~~00~~	46,000 / **100** = 460~~00~~
	7,000 / **1,000** = 7~~000~~	46,000 / **1,000** = 46~~000~~

If you know the basic division facts, you can solve problems such as 240 / 3 and 15,000 / 5 mentally.

EXAMPLES

240 / 3 = ?	15,000 / 5 = ?
Think: 24 / 3 = 8	*Think:* 15 / 5 = 3
Then 240 / 3 is 10 times as much.	Then 15,000 / 5 is 1,000 times as much.
240 / 3 = 10 * 8 = 80	15,000 / 5 = 1,000 * 3 = 3,000

You can use a similar method to solve problems such as 1,800 / 30 mentally.

EXAMPLE 1,800 / 30 = ?

Think: 18 / 3 = 6	
First, try 6 as the answer:	Next, try 60 as the answer:
6 * 30 = 180, but you want 1,800 or 10 times 180.	60 * 30 = 1,800, so 1,800 / 30 = 60.
6 is *not* the answer.	1,800 / 30 = 60

CHECK YOUR UNDERSTANDING

Solve these problems mentally.

1. 3,000 / 100 **2.** 36,000 / 1,000 **3.** 24,000 / 8 **4.** 4,200 / 10 **5.** 4,200 / 70

Check your answers on page 278.

Division Methods

Different symbols may be used to indicate division. For example, "94 divided by 6" may be written as $94 \div 6$, $6\overline{)94}$, $94 / 6$, or $\frac{94}{6}$.

- The number that is being divided is called the **dividend.**
- The number by which it is divided is called the **divisor.**
- The answer to a division problem is called the **quotient.**
- Some numbers cannot be divided evenly. When this happens, the answer includes a quotient and a **remainder.**

Partial-Quotients Method

In the **partial-quotients method,** it takes several steps to find the quotient. At each step, you find a partial answer (called a **partial quotient**). These partial answers are then added to find the quotient.

Study the example below. To find the number of 6s in 94, first find partial quotients, then add them. Record the partial quotients in a column to the right of the original problem.

EXAMPLE $94 / 6 = ?$

Write partial quotients in this column.

$6\overline{)94}$ ↓   *Think:* How many [6s] are in 94? At least 10.

$- 60$ | 10   The first partial quotient is 10. $10 * 6 = 60$

34 Subtract 60 from 94. At least 5 [6s] are left.

$- 30$ | 5   The second partial quotient is 5. $5 * 6 = 30$

4 15   Subtract. Add the partial quotients.

↑   ↑

Remainder   Quotient

The answer is 15 R4. Record the answer as $6\overline{)94}^{\,15\ R4}$ or write $94 / 6 \rightarrow 15$ R4.

Whole Numbers

The partial-quotients method works the same whether you divide by a 2-digit or a 1-digit divisor. It often helps to write down some easy facts for the divisor first.

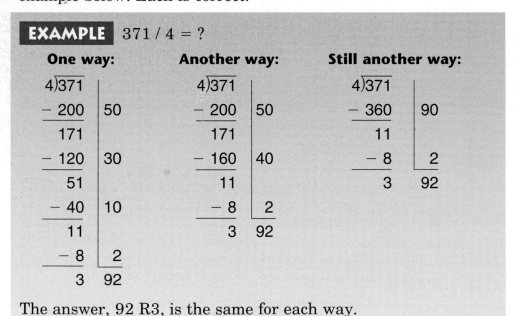

EXAMPLE 400 / 22 = ?

Some facts for 22
(to help find partial quotients):

1 * 22 = 22
2 * 22 = 44
5 * 22 = 110
10 * 22 = 220

$$22\overline{)400}$$
$-\ 220$ | 10 (10 [22s] in 400)
180
$-\ 110$ | 5 (5 [22s] in 180)
70
$-\ 44$ | 2 (2 [22s] in 70)
26
$-\ 22$ | 1 (1 [22] in 26)
4   18

Record the answer as $22\overline{)400}^{\,18\ R4}$, or write 400 / 22 → 18 R4.

There are different ways to find partial quotients when you use the partial-quotients method. Study the different ways in the example below. Each is correct.

EXAMPLE 371 / 4 = ?

One way:

$4\overline{)371}$
$-\ 200$ | 50
171
$-\ 120$ | 30
51
$-\ 40$ | 10
11
$-\ 8$ | 2
3   92

Another way:

$4\overline{)371}$
$-\ 200$ | 50
171
$-\ 160$ | 40
11
$-\ 8$ | 2
3   92

Still another way:

$4\overline{)371}$
$-\ 360$ | 90
11
$-\ 8$ | 2
3   92

The answer, 92 R3, is the same for each way.

CHECK YOUR UNDERSTANDING

Divide.

1. $2\overline{)85}$

2. 130 / 7

3. 166 ÷ 3

4. $5\overline{)694}$

Check your answers on page 278.

Decimals & Percents

Decimals

Mathematics in everyday life involves more than just whole numbers. **Fractions** name a part of a whole thing or a part of a collection. We also use fractions to make more precise measurements when we measure to a fraction of an inch.

Decimals, like fractions, can be used to name a part of a whole or a part of a collection. Decimals and fractions are ways to write numbers that are between consecutive whole numbers. Fractional parts of a dollar are almost always written as decimals. The receipt at the right shows that lunch cost between 25 dollars and 26 dollars. The "64" in the cost names a part of a dollar.

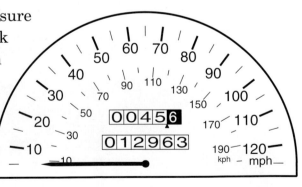

```
    THE QUAY   KEY WEST
^^^^^^^^^^^^^^^^^^^^^^^^^^

0127     Table 26  #Party 2
TOM M        SvrCk: 7 15:14 09/11/00

1 ICED TEA                     1.25
1 CALIF BURGER                 7.25
1 CHEFS SANDWICH               7.95
1 COFFEE                       1.50
2 KEY LIME PIE                 5.90

            Sub Total:        23.85
                 Tax:          1.79
09/11 15:51  TOTAL=           25.64

***********************

  WE HOPE YOU ENJOY YOUR STAY IN
         KEY WEST.


   COME BACK SOON!
```

You probably see many other uses of decimals every day.

Weather reports give rainfall amounts in decimals. The average annual rainfall in New Orleans, Louisiana, is 61.88 inches.

The digital scales in supermarkets show the weight of fruits, vegetables, and meat with decimals.

The winners of many Olympic events are often decided by times measured to hundredths, and sometimes even thousandths, of a second. Florence Griffith-Joyner's winning time for the 100-meter run in 1988 was 10.54 seconds.

Many sports statistics use decimals. In 1993, basketball player Michael Jordan averaged 32.6 points per game. In 1989, baseball player Kirby Puckett had a batting average of .339.

Cars have instruments called odometers that measure distance. The word *odometer* comes from the Greek words *odos,* which means road, and *metron,* which means measure. The odometer at the right shows 12,963 which means the car has traveled at least 12,963 miles. The trip meter above it has digits in one color that represent tenths of a mile. The trip meter at the right shows the car has traveled at least 45.6 miles.

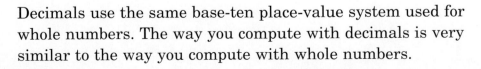

Decimals use the same base-ten place-value system used for whole numbers. The way you compute with decimals is very similar to the way you compute with whole numbers.

Understanding Decimals

Decimals are a way to write fractions that have denominators of 10, 100, 1,000, and so on.

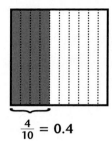

$$\frac{4}{10} = 0.4$$

$$\frac{42}{100} = 0.42$$

This square is divided into 10 equal parts. Each part is $\frac{1}{10}$ of the square. The decimal name for $\frac{1}{10}$ is 0.1.

$\frac{4}{10}$ of the square is shaded. The decimal name for $\frac{4}{10}$ is 0.4.

This square is divided into 100 equal parts. Each part is $\frac{1}{100}$ of the square. The decimal name for $\frac{1}{100}$ is 0.01.

$\frac{42}{100}$ of the square is shaded. The decimal name for $\frac{42}{100}$ is 0.42.

In a decimal, the dot is called the **decimal point.** It separates the whole number part from the decimal part. A number with one place after the decimal point names *tenths;* a number with two places after the decimal point names *hundredths;* a number with three places after the decimal point names *thousandths.*

EXAMPLE

tenths	hundredths	thousandths
$0.3 = \frac{3}{10}$	$0.23 = \frac{23}{100}$	$0.151 = \frac{151}{1,000}$
$0.7 = \frac{7}{10}$	$0.75 = \frac{75}{100}$	$0.002 = \frac{2}{1,000}$
$0.9 = \frac{9}{10}$	$0.02 = \frac{2}{100}$	$0.087 = \frac{87}{1,000}$

Like mixed numbers, decimals are used to name numbers greater than 1.

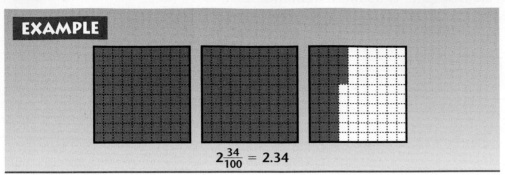

EXAMPLE

$$2\frac{34}{100} = 2.34$$

Reading Decimals

One way to read a decimal is to say it as you would a fraction. For example, $6.8 = 6\frac{8}{10}$, so 6.8 can be read as "six and eight-tenths." $0.001 = \frac{1}{1,000}$ and is read as "one-thousandth." Sometimes decimals are read by first saying the whole number part, then saying "point," and finally saying the digits in the decimal part. For example, 6.8 can be read as "six point eight"; 0.15 can be read as "zero point one five." This way of reading decimals is often useful when there are many digits in the decimal.

EXAMPLES

0.17 is read as "17 hundredths" or "0 point 17."
98.7 is read as "98 and 7 tenths" or "98 point 7."
55.05 is read as "55 and 5 hundredths" or "55 point 05."

CHECK YOUR UNDERSTANDING

Write a decimal for each picture.

1.
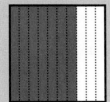

2.

3.
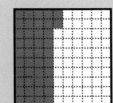

Read each decimal to yourself. Write each decimal as a fraction or mixed number.

4. 1.36　　　　　5. 0.09　　　　　6. 9.27

Check your answers on page 278.

Our System for Recording Numbers

The first systems for writing numbers were primitive. Ancient Egyptians used a stroke to record the number 1, a picture of an oxbow for 10, a coil of rope for 100, a lotus plant for 1,000, and a picture of a god supporting the sky for 1,000,000.

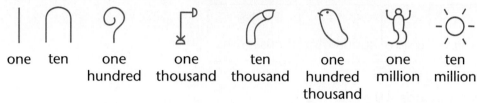

| one | ten | one hundred | one thousand | ten thousand | one hundred thousand | one million | ten million |

This is how an ancient Egyptian would write the number 43:

10 + 10 + 10 + 10 + 1 + 1 + 1

Our system for writing numbers is a **base-ten** system. This should come as no surprise. People probably counted on their fingers when they first started using numbers.

Our base-ten system was invented in India and later improved in Arabia. It uses only 10 symbols, which are called **digits:** 0, 1, 2, 3, 4, 5, 6, 7, 8, and 9. In this system, you can write any number using only these 10 digits.

For a number written in the base-ten system, each digit has a value that depends on its **place** in the number. That is why it is called a **place-value** system.

1,000s thousands	100s hundreds	10s tens	1s ones
6	0	7	5

In the number 6,075,

6 is in the **thousands** place; its value is 6 thousands, or 6,000.

0 is in the **hundreds** place; its value is 0.

7 is in the **tens** place; its value is 7 tens, or 70.

5 is in the **ones** place; its value is 5.

The 0 in 6,075 serves a very important purpose. It "holds" the hundreds place so that the 6 can be in the thousands place. When used in this way, 0 is called a **placeholder.**

As you move from right to left in the place-value chart, the value of each place is **ten times** the value of the place to its right.

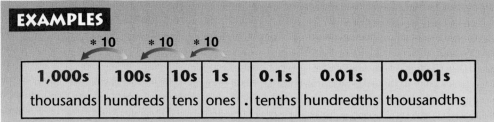

1,000s	100s	10s	1s	.	0.1s	0.01s	0.001s
thousands	hundreds	tens	ones	.	tenths	hundredths	thousandths

- The value of the tens place is $10 * 1 = 10$.
- The value of the hundreds place is $10 * 10 = 100$.
- The value of the thousands place is $10 * 100 = 1,000$.

As you move from left to right in the place-value chart, the value of each place is **one-tenth** of the value of the place to its left.

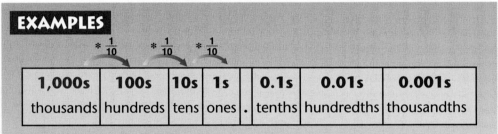

1,000s	100s	10s	1s	.	0.1s	0.01s	0.001s
thousands	hundreds	tens	ones	.	tenths	hundredths	thousandths

- The value of the hundreds place is $\frac{1}{10}$ of $1,000 = 100$.
- The value of the tens place is $\frac{1}{10}$ of $100 = 10$.
- The value of the ones place is $\frac{1}{10}$ of $10 = 1$.

- The value of the place to the right of the ones place is one tenth of the value of the ones place: $\frac{1}{10}$ of $1 = \frac{1}{10}$. This place is called the **tenths** place and is written as 0.1.

- The value of the place to the right of the tenths place is $\frac{1}{10}$ of $\frac{1}{10} = \frac{1}{100}$. This place is called the **hundredths** place and is written as 0.01.

- The value of the place to the right of the hundredths place is $\frac{1}{10}$ of $\frac{1}{100} = \frac{1}{1,000}$. This place is called the **thousandths** place and is written as 0.001.

The base-ten system works the same way for decimals as it does for whole numbers.

EXAMPLES

1,000s	100s	10s	1s	.	0.1s	0.01s	0.001s
thousands	hundreds	tens	ones	.	tenths	hundredths	thousandths
		3	6	.	7	0	4
			3	.	2	5	6

In the number 36.704,

7 is in the **tenths** place; its value is 7 tenths, or $\frac{7}{10}$, or 0.7.

0 is in the **hundredths** place; its value is 0.

4 is in the **thousandths** place; its value is 4 thousandths, or $\frac{4}{1,000}$, or 0.004.

In the number 3.256,

2 is in the **tenths** place; its value is 2 tenths, or $\frac{2}{10}$, or 0.2.

5 is in the **hundredths** place; its value is 5 hundredths, or $\frac{5}{100}$, or 0.05.

6 is in the **thousandths** place; its value is 6 thousandths, or $\frac{6}{1,000}$, or 0.006.

CHECK YOUR UNDERSTANDING

1. What is the value of the digit 2 in each of these numbers?

   a. 25.3   **b.** 0.27   **c.** 15.72   **d.** 5.328

2. Tell how much each digit in 98.765 is worth.

3. What is the smallest decimal you can write using the digits 8, 2, and 4?

Check your answers on page 278.

Comparing Decimals

One way to compare decimals is to model them with base-10 blocks.

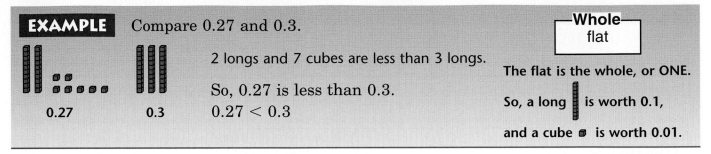

EXAMPLE   Compare 0.27 and 0.3.

2 longs and 7 cubes are less than 3 longs.

So, 0.27 is less than 0.3.

0.27 < 0.3

0.27   0.3

Whole

flat

The flat is the whole, or ONE.

So, a long ▌ is worth 0.1,

and a cube ▫ is worth 0.01.

Another way to compare decimals is to draw pictures of base-10 blocks.

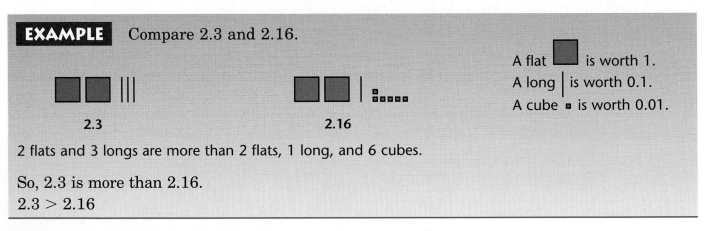

EXAMPLE   Compare 2.3 and 2.16.

2.3   2.16

A flat ▢ is worth 1.
A long │ is worth 0.1.
A cube ▫ is worth 0.01.

2 flats and 3 longs are more than 2 flats, 1 long, and 6 cubes.

So, 2.3 is more than 2.16.

2.3 > 2.16

A place-value chart can also be used to compare decimals.

EXAMPLE   Compare 3.915 and 3.972.

1s ones	.	0.1s tenths	0.01s hundredths	0.001s thousandths
3	.	9	1	5
3	.	9	7	2

The ones digits *are the same.* They are both worth 3.

The tenths digits *are the same.* They are both worth 9 tenths, or 0.9.

The hundredths digits are *not* the same. The 1 is worth 1 hundredth, or 0.01. The 7 is worth 7 hundredths, or 0.07.

So, 3.915 is less than 3.972.

3.915 < 3.972

You can write a 0 at the end of a decimal without changing the value of the decimal: 0.7 = 0.70. Adding 0s is sometimes called "padding with 0s." Think of it as trading for smaller pieces.

EXAMPLE 0.3 = 0.30

0.3   0.30

Whole
flat

The flat ▪ is worth 1 for the examples on this page.

Padding with 0s makes comparing decimals easier.

EXAMPLE Compare 0.2 and 0.05.

0.2 = 0.20 (Think about trading 2 longs for 20 cubes.)
20 cubes is more than 5 cubes.
20 hundredths is more than 5 hundredths.

0.20 > 0.05, so 0.2 > 0.05.

EXAMPLE Compare 0.99 and 1.

1 = 1.00 (Think about trading 1 flat for 100 cubes.)
99 cubes is less than 100 cubes.
99 hundredths is less than 100 hundredths.

0.99 < 1.00, so 0.99 < 1.

CHECK YOUR UNDERSTANDING

Compare the numbers in each pair.

1. 0.79, 0.3   **2.** 4.49, 4.6   **3.** $\frac{1}{2}$, 0.55   **4.** 0.999, 1.1

Check your answers on page 278.

Adding and Subtracting Decimals

There are many ways to add and subtract decimals.

One way to add and subtract decimals is to use base-10 blocks. The flat is usually the whole, or ONE.

EXAMPLE   2.34 + 1.27 = ?

First, use blocks to show 2.34 and 1.27.

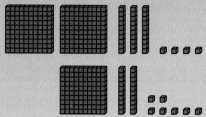

Second, trade 10 cubes for 1 long.

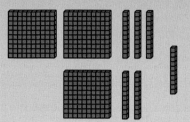

By counting all the blocks, you can see that you have 3 flats, 6 longs, and 1 cube.

This means that 2.34 + 1.27 = 3.61.

Finally, it's a good idea to make a quick estimate. Since 2.34 is more than 2 and 1.27 is more than 1, the answer should be more than 3, which it is.

To subtract with base-10 blocks, count out blocks for the larger number, take away blocks for the smaller number, then count the remaining blocks.

EXAMPLE   1.5 − 0.25 = ?

First, show 1.5 with blocks.

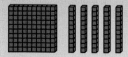

Second, since you need to take away 0.25, you need to trade a long for 10 cubes.

Finally, remove 2 longs and 5 cubes (0.25).

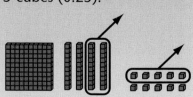

One flat, 2 longs, and 5 cubes are left.

So, 1.5 − 0.25 = 1.25.

It is often easier to use **base-10 shorthand** instead of real base-10 blocks.

> | For the examples on this page:
> |
> | A flat 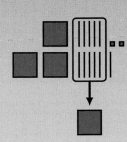 is worth 1.
> | A long │ is worth 0.1.
> | A block ▪ is worth 0.01.

EXAMPLE   1.52 + 2.6 = ?

First, draw pictures for each number.

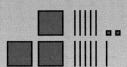

Next, draw a ring around 10 longs to show that they can be traded for a flat.

After the trade, there are 4 flats, 1 long, and 2 cubes.

This means that 1.52 + 2.6 = 4.12. This makes sense because 1.52 is near $1\frac{1}{2}$ and 2.6 is near $2\frac{1}{2}$, so the answer should be around 4, which it is.

Pictures of blocks are also useful for subtraction.

EXAMPLE   4.07 − 2.5 = ?

The picture shows 4 flats and 7 cubes for 4.07. One of the flats was traded for 10 longs. Then, 2 flats and 5 longs were taken away to show subtracting 2.5.

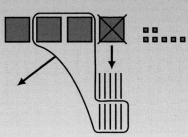

Since 1 flat, 5 longs, and 7 cubes are left, 4.07 − 2.5 = 1.57.

Most paper-and-pencil strategies for adding and subtracting whole numbers also work for decimals. The main difference is that you have to line up the places correctly, either by adding 0s to the end of the numbers or by lining up the ones place.

EXAMPLES   3.45 + 6.8 = ?

Partial-Sums Method:

	1s	0.1s	0.01s
	3 .	4	5
+	6 .	8	0

Add the ones.	$3 + 6 \rightarrow$	9 . 0 0
Add the tenths.	$0.4 + 0.8 \rightarrow$	1 . 2 0
Add the hundredths.	$0.05 + 0.00 \rightarrow$	0 . 0 5
Add the partial sums.	$9.00 + 1.20 + 0.05 \rightarrow$	**10** . **2** **5**

Column-Addition Method:

	1s	0.1s	0.01s
	3 .	4	5
+	6 .	8	0
	9 .	12	5
	10 .	2	5

Move 10 tenths to the ones column:
    12 tenths = 1 one and 2 tenths
    Trade the 1 one into the ones column.

3.45 + 6.8 = 10.25, using either method.

EXAMPLE   8.3 − 3.75 = ?

Trade-First Method:

First, write the problem in vertical format, being sure to line up the places correctly. Also, since 3.75 has two decimal places, write 8.3 as 8.30.

1s	0.1s	0.01s
8 .	3	0
− 3 .	7	5

Look at the 0.01s place. You cannot remove 5 hundredths from 0 hundredths.

1s	0.1s	0.01s
	2	10
8 .	~~3~~	~~0~~
− 3 .	7	5

So trade 1 tenth for 10 hundredths. Look at the 0.1s place. You cannot remove 7 tenths from 2 tenths.

1s	0.1s	0.01s
	12	
7	~~2~~	10
~~8~~ .	~~3~~	~~0~~
− 3 .	7	5
4 .	5	5

So trade 1 one for 10 tenths. Now subtract in each column.

8.3 − 3.75 = 4.55

EXAMPLE   8.3 − 3.75 = ?

Left-to-Right Subtraction Method:

Again, since 3.75 has two decimal places, write 8.3 as 8.30.

$$
\begin{array}{rr}
 & 8.30 \\
\text{Subtract the ones.} & -\ 3.00 \\
\hline
 & 5.30 \\
\text{Subtract the tenths.} & -\ 0.70 \\
\hline
 & 4.60 \\
\text{Subtract the hundredths.} & -\ 0.05 \\
\hline
 & 4.55 \\
\end{array}
$$

8.3 − 3.75 = 4.55

EXAMPLE   8.3 − 3.75 = ?

Counting-Up Method:

There are many ways to count up from 3.75 to 8.3. Here is one.

$$
\begin{array}{r}
3.75 \\
+\ (0.25) \\
\hline
4.00 \\
+\ (4.00) \\
\hline
8.00 \\
+\ (0.30) \\
\hline
8.30 \\
\end{array}
$$

Add the amounts you circled and counted up by:

$$
\begin{array}{r}
0.25 \\
4.00 \\
+\ 0.30 \\
\hline
4.55 \\
\end{array}
$$

You counted up by 4.55, so 8.3 − 3.75 = 4.55.

CHECK YOUR UNDERSTANDING

Add or subtract.

1. 2.03 + 1.8   **2.** 1.09 − 0.39   **3.** 2.3 − 1.28   **4.** 4.2 + 5.57

Check your answers on page 278.

Percents

A percent is another way to name a fraction or a decimal.
Percent means *per hundred*, or *out of a hundred*. So 1% has
the same meaning as the fraction $\frac{1}{100}$ and the decimal 0.01. The
statement, "48% of the students in the school are boys," means
that out of every 100 students in the school, 48 are boys.

$$\frac{\text{number of boys}}{\text{number of all students}} = \frac{48}{100}$$

EXAMPLES

$$35\% = \frac{35}{100} = 0.35 \qquad 50\% = \frac{50}{100} = 0.5 \qquad 12.5\% = \frac{12.5}{100} = 0.125 \qquad 500\% = \frac{500}{100} = 5.00$$

The word *percent* comes from the Latin *per centum*: *per* means
for and *centum* means *one hundred*.

Percents can be used in many different ways. Page 38 contains
illustrations of a few of the many ways percents are used.

Percent of a Number

Finding a percent of a number is the same as multiplying
the number by the percent. This kind of problem can be solved
in different ways. You can change the percent to a fraction,
work with a unit percent, or change the percent to a decimal.

Many common percents are equivalent to "easy" fractions. For
example, 25% is the same as $\frac{1}{4}$. Sometimes it's easier to work
with the fraction than with the percent.

EXAMPLE   What is 25% of 36?

Think:
$25\% = \frac{25}{100} = \frac{1}{4}$, so 25% of 36 is the same as $\frac{1}{4}$ of 36.
If you divide 36 into 4 equal groups, there are 9 in each group.

So, 25% of 36 is 9.

EXAMPLE What is 20% of 50?

$20\% = \frac{20}{100} = \frac{1}{5}$, so 20% of 50 is the same as $\frac{1}{5}$ of 50.
If you divide 50 into 5 groups, there are 10 in each group.

So, 20% of 50 is 10.

Not every percent is equal to an "easy" fraction like $\frac{1}{4}$ or $\frac{1}{5}$.
Sometimes it's easier to work with 1% instead.

EXAMPLE What is 5% of 300?

$1\% = \frac{1}{100}$, so 1% of 300 is the same as $\frac{1}{100}$ of 300.
If you divide 300 into 100 equal groups, there are 3 in each group.
So, 1% of 300 is 3. Then 5% of 300 is 5 * 3, or 15.

So, 5% of 300 is 15.

EXAMPLE What is 8% of 50?

1% of 50 is $\frac{1}{100}$ of 50. If you divide 50 into 100 equal groups, there is $\frac{1}{2}$ in each group. So, 1% of 50 is $\frac{1}{2}$.

Then 8% of 50 is $8 * \frac{1}{2}$, or 4.

Another way is to change the percent to a decimal and multiply.

EXAMPLE What is 35% of 45?

$35\% = \frac{35}{100} = 0.35$
35% of 45 is the same as 0.35 * 45.

The multiplication can be done using a calculator.
Key in: 0.35 ⊗ 45 (Enter)
Answer: 15.75

Some calculators have a ⌷%⌷ key, so you don't need to rename the percent as a decimal. To find 35% of 45 on such a calculator, key in 45 ⊗ 35 ⌷%⌷ (Enter) .

35% of 45 is 15.75.

CHECK YOUR UNDERSTANDING

Solve.

1. 25% of 16   **2.** 50% of 180   **3.** 75% of 80   **4.** 10% of 90   **5.** 1% of 500

Check your answers on page 278.

World of Percent

Percents are used in many places every day to give us information about our world.

Nutrition Facts

Serving Size 1 Cookie (26g/0.9 oz)
Servings Per Container 10

Amount Per Serving

Calories 130   Calories from Fat 50

	% Daily Value*
Total Fat 6g	
Saturated Fat 2.5g	9%
Polyunsaturated Fat 0g	13%
Monounsaturated Fat 2.5g	
Cholesterol 10mg	
Sodium 35mg	3%
Total Carbohydrate 16g	1%
Dietary Fiber 2g	5%
Sugars 9g	8%
Protein 1g	

Airline Set to Cut Service 21%

Sale—50% Off Everything Must Go

For Wednesday, there is a 30% chance of showers.

You can get a furnace filter that captures 94 percent of the dust, dander, pollen, and other particles that float through your house.

Voter Turnout Pegged at 55% of Registered Voters

Raisin-Lite Cookies

50% Less Fat
than our regular cookies

At present, computers are a leading cause of increased demand for electrical power, accounting for an estimated 5 percent of commercial demand.

Total attendance was 8% higher than in the previous year.

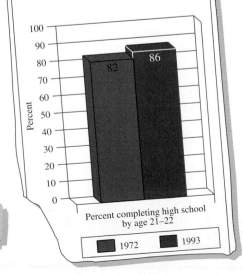

Staying in School

Education Department figures show that high school completion rates have grown over the last two decades.

Percent completing high school by age 21–22

82   86

■ 1972   ■ 1993

Fractions & Rational Numbers

Fractions and Rational Numbers

Uses of Fractions

The numbers $\frac{1}{2}$, $\frac{2}{3}$, $\frac{5}{4}$, $\frac{7}{1}$, and $\frac{25}{100}$ are all **fractions.** A fraction is written with two numbers. The top number is called the **numerator.** The bottom number is called the **denominator.** The numerator of a fraction can be any number; the denominator can be any number except 0. In this book most numerators are whole numbers, and most denominators are nonzero whole numbers.

When reading fractions, read the numerator first, then read the denominator.

$$\text{three-fourths} \quad \frac{3 \leftarrow \text{numerator} \rightarrow 25}{4 \leftarrow \text{denominator} \rightarrow 100} \quad \text{twenty-five hundredths}$$

One common use of fractions is in sharing. For example, when two people share something equally, each person gets half of it. When three people share equally, each person gets a third. Another common use of fractions is in measuring (half a cup, a quarter of an hour, and so on).

In *Everyday Mathematics,* fractions are used in ways that may be new to you. Fractions are used in the following ways:

- to show rates (such as cost per ounce)
- to compare (such as comparing the circumference of a circle to its diameter)
- to name percents ($\frac{1}{2}$ is 50%)
- to show divisions ($15 \div 3$ can be written $\frac{15}{3}$)
- to show the scale of a map or a picture

Here are some other examples of uses of fractions:

- **Ingredients in a recipe** for jambalaya: $\frac{3}{4}$ cup rice, 4 ounces each of chicken and sausage, 4 cups peppers, $1\frac{2}{3}$ cups chopped onions, $1\frac{1}{2}$ tablespoons chopped thyme, $\frac{1}{8}$ teaspoon salt.

$\frac{1}{2}$ teaspoon

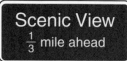
$\frac{3}{4}$ yard

Scenic View
$\frac{1}{3}$ mile ahead

$\frac{1}{3}$ mile

$\frac{5}{8}$ of a pizza

half past 8

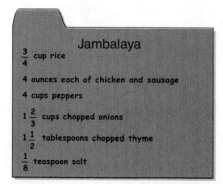

Jambalaya
$\frac{3}{4}$ cup rice

4 ounces each of chicken and sausage

4 cups peppers

$1\frac{2}{3}$ cups chopped onions

$1\frac{1}{2}$ tablespoons chopped thyme

$\frac{1}{8}$ teaspoon salt

- The **scale on a map** is given as 1:10,000 (another way of expressing $\frac{1}{10,000}$). This means, for example, that for every centimeter on the map, the real-world distance is 10,000 centimeters or 100 meters.

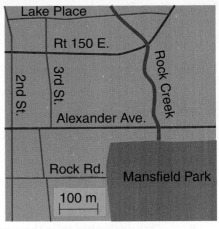

$$\frac{\text{map distance}}{\text{real distance}} = \frac{1 \text{ cm}}{100 \text{ m}}$$

- Over many throws of a fair, 6-sided die, you will get each number about 1 out of 6 times, or $\frac{1}{6}$ of the time. The probability of getting each number on the die is $\frac{1}{6}$. If you throw two dice, the probability of getting 12 is $\frac{1}{36}$.

- A movie critic gave the film *Little Kids* a rating of $3\frac{1}{2}$ stars (on a scale of 0 to 4 stars).

Little Kids

★ ★ ★ ⁀

- A toy company's stock listing: close $49\frac{1}{4}$, change $-1\frac{3}{4}$. This means that at the end of the day, shares sold for $49.25 each. This price is $1.75 dollars less than at the end of the previous day.

- One-fifth of the length of a telephone pole should be in the ground.

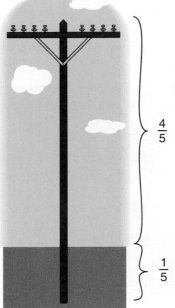

$\frac{4}{5}$

$\frac{1}{5}$

Understanding the many ways people use fractions will help you solve problems more easily.

Fractions for Parts of a Whole

Fractions are used to name a part of a whole thing that is divided into equal parts. For example, the circle at the right has been divided into 8 equal parts. Each part is $\frac{1}{8}$ of the circle.

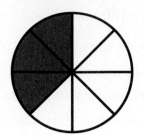

Three of the parts are green, so $\frac{3}{8}$ (three-eighths) of the circle is green.

$\underline{3}$ ← **Numerator tells the number of green parts**
8 ← **Denominator tells the number of equal parts in the whole circle**

In *Everyday Mathematics,* the whole thing that is divided into equal parts is called the ONE. To understand a fraction used to name part of a whole, you need to know what the ONE is.

EXAMPLE Sally ate half a pizza. Is that a lot?

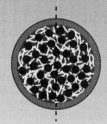

The answer depends on how big the pizza was. If the pizza was small, then $\frac{1}{2}$ *is not* a lot. If the pizza was large, then $\frac{1}{2}$ *is* a lot.

Fractions for Parts of a Collection

A fraction may be used to name part of a collection of things that is divided into equal parts.

EXAMPLE Look at the collection of counters.

What fraction of the counters is red?

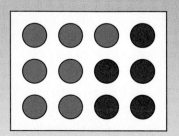

There are 12 counters in all.
Five of the counters are red.
Five out of 12 counters are red.

This fraction shows what part of the collection is red.

$\underline{5}$ ← the number of red counters
12 ← the number of counters in all

To understand the fraction for a part of a collection, you need to know how big the whole collection is.

> **EXAMPLE**   Only half of Sam's cousins can come to his party. Is that many people?
>
> It depends on how many cousins Sam has. If Sam has only 4 cousins, then 2 cousins are coming; that's not many people. But if Sam has 24 cousins, then 12 cousins are coming. That's many people.

Fractions in Measuring

Fractions are used to make more careful measurements.

Think about the inch scale on a ruler. Suppose the spaces between the whole-inch marks are left unmarked. With a ruler like this, you can measure only to the nearest inch.

Ruler has inch marks only. You can measure to the nearest inch.

Many rulers divide the inch space into eighths or sixteenths. With those rulers, you can measure to the nearest $\frac{1}{8}$- or $\frac{1}{16}$-inch.

Ruler has $\frac{1}{2}$- and $\frac{1}{4}$-inch marks. You can measure to the nearest $\frac{1}{4}$-inch.

To understand a fraction used in a measurement, you need to know what the unit is. To say, "Susan lives $\frac{1}{2}$ from here" makes no sense. Susan might live half a block away or half a mile. The unit in measurement is like the ONE when fractions are used to name a part of a whole.

Fractions in Probability

Sometimes a fraction is used to tell the chance of something happening. This chance, or probability, of an event happening is always a number from 0 to 1. An impossible event has a probability of 0; it has no chance of happening. An event with a probability of 1 is sure to happen. An event with a probability of $\frac{1}{2}$ has an equal chance of happening or not happening.

> **EXAMPLE**   When you pick a ball out of this jar without looking, the chance of getting a white ball is $\frac{5}{8}$. The chance of getting a blue ball is $\frac{3}{8}$.
>
> probability of picking a white ball $= \frac{\text{number of white balls}}{\text{total number of balls}} = \frac{5}{8}$
>
> probability of picking a blue ball $= \frac{\text{number of blue balls}}{\text{total number of balls}} = \frac{3}{8}$

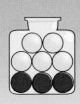

Fractions and Division

Division problems can be written using a slash / instead of the division symbol ÷. For example, $21 \div 3$ can also be written $21 / 3$. Division problems can also be written as fractions. For example, $21 \div 3$ can be written $\frac{21}{3}$. One of the many uses of fractions is to show divisions.

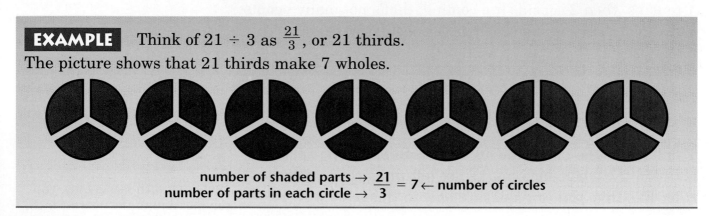

EXAMPLE Think of $21 \div 3$ as $\frac{21}{3}$, or 21 thirds.
The picture shows that 21 thirds make 7 wholes.

$$\text{number of shaded parts} \rightarrow \frac{21}{3} = 7 \leftarrow \text{number of circles}$$
$$\text{number of parts in each circle} \rightarrow$$

Even fractions that are less than 1 can be thought of as divisions.

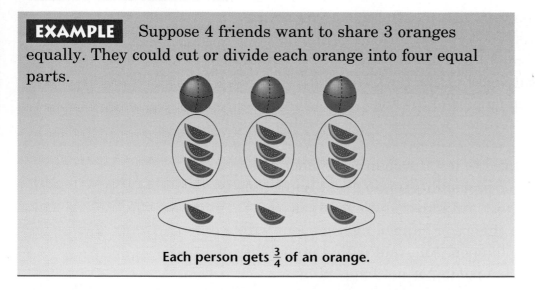

EXAMPLE Suppose 4 friends want to share 3 oranges equally. They could cut or divide each orange into four equal parts.

Each person gets $\frac{3}{4}$ of an orange.

The connection between fractions and division is built into your calculator. To show that $\frac{21}{3} = 21 \div 3$, press 21 ⊙ 3 (Enter). The answer in the display will show 7, which is a name for the fraction $\frac{21}{3}$.

Fractions in Rates and Ratios

Fractions are often used to name rates and ratios. A **rate** compares two numbers with different units. For example, 30 miles per hour is a rate that compares distance with time. It can be written as $\frac{30 \text{ miles}}{1 \text{ hour}}$.

A ratio is like a rate, but it compares two quantities that have the same unit.

Rate	Example
speed (jogging)	$\frac{\text{distance}}{\text{time}} = \frac{8 \text{ blocks}}{5 \text{ minutes}}$
price	$\frac{\text{cost}}{\text{quantity}} = \frac{99¢}{3 \text{ cartons of yogurt}}$
conversion of units	$\frac{\text{distance in yards}}{\text{distance in feet}} = \frac{1 \text{ yard}}{3 \text{ feet}}$

Ratio	Example
won/lost record	$\frac{\text{games won}}{\text{games lost}} = \frac{5}{7}$
students in a class	$\frac{\text{number of girls}}{\text{number of boys}} = \frac{8}{12}$

Other Uses of Fractions

Fractions are used to compare distances on maps to distances in the real world and to describe size changes.

EXAMPLE Two places 5 centimeters apart on the map would be 500 meters apart in the real world.

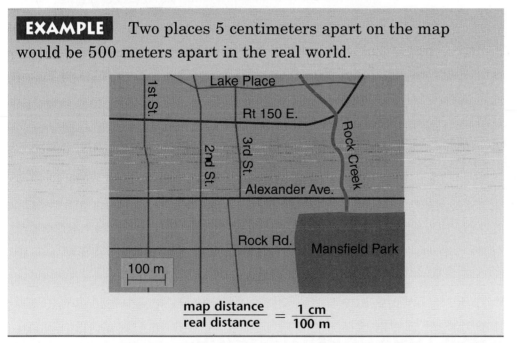

$$\frac{\text{map distance}}{\text{real distance}} = \frac{1 \text{ cm}}{100 \text{ m}}$$

EXAMPLE A length of 3 centimeters on the original will be 6 centimeters on the copy.

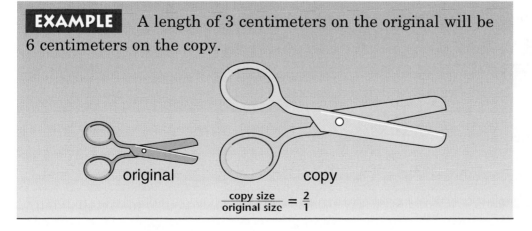

original   copy

$$\frac{\text{copy size}}{\text{original size}} = \frac{2}{1}$$

Mixed Numbers

Numbers like $1\frac{1}{2}$, $2\frac{3}{5}$, and $4\frac{3}{8}$ are called **mixed numbers.** A mixed number has a whole-number part and a fraction part. In the mixed number $2\frac{3}{5}$, the whole-number part is 2 and the fraction part is $\frac{3}{5}$. The value of the mixed number is the sum of the whole-number part and the fraction part: $2\frac{3}{5} = 2 + \frac{3}{5}$. Mixed numbers are used in many of the same ways that fractions are used.

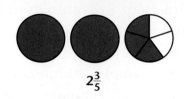

$2\frac{3}{5}$

Mixed numbers can be renamed as fractions. For example, if a circle is ONE, then $2\frac{3}{5}$ names two whole circles and $\frac{3}{5}$ of another circle.

If you divide the 2 whole circles into fifths, then you can see that $2\frac{3}{5} = \frac{13}{5}$.

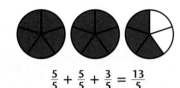

$\frac{5}{5} + \frac{5}{5} + \frac{3}{5} = \frac{13}{5}$

To rename a mixed number as a fraction, first rename the whole-number part as a fraction with the same denominator as the fraction part. Then add all of the fractions. For example, $4\frac{3}{8} = \frac{8}{8} + \frac{8}{8} + \frac{8}{8} + \frac{8}{8} + \frac{3}{8} = \frac{35}{8}$.

Fractions like $\frac{13}{5}$ are called **improper fractions.** An improper fraction is a fraction that is greater than or equal to 1: $\frac{4}{3}$, $\frac{5}{5}$, $\frac{125}{10}$, and so on. In a **proper fraction,** the numerator is smaller than the denominator; in an improper fraction, the numerator is greater than or equal to the denominator.

> **N O T E**
>
> Even though they are called *improper,* there is nothing wrong or inappropriate about improper fractions. You shouldn't feel that they should be avoided.

CHECK YOUR UNDERSTANDING

Write a mixed number for each picture.

1.

2.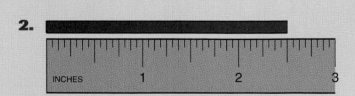

Write an improper fraction for each mixed number.

3. $2\frac{1}{4}$

4. $1\frac{2}{3}$

5. $3\frac{1}{8}$

Check your answers on page 278.

Equivalent Fractions

Fractions that name the same amount are called **equivalent fractions.**

EXAMPLE   The four circles below are the same size, but they are divided into different numbers of parts. The green areas are the same in each circle. These circles show different fractions that are equivalent to $\frac{1}{2}$.

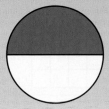 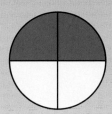 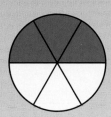 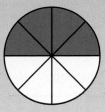

2 equal parts	4 equal parts	6 equal parts	8 equal parts
1 part green	2 parts green	3 parts green	4 parts green
$\frac{1}{2}$ of the circle	$\frac{2}{4}$ of the circle	$\frac{3}{6}$ of the circle	$\frac{4}{8}$ of the circle
is green.	is green.	is green.	is green.

The fractions $\frac{1}{2}$, $\frac{2}{4}$, $\frac{3}{6}$, and $\frac{4}{8}$ are all equivalent.

You can write $\frac{1}{2} = \frac{2}{4}$ $\frac{1}{2} = \frac{4}{8}$ $\frac{2}{4} = \frac{4}{8}$

$\frac{1}{2} = \frac{3}{6}$ $\frac{2}{4} = \frac{3}{6}$ $\frac{3}{6} = \frac{4}{8}$

EXAMPLE   On Ms. Klein's bus route, she picks up 24 students, 18 boys and 6 girls.

G	G	G	G	G	G
B	B	B	B	B	B
B	B	B	B	B	B
B	B	B	B	B	B

G	G	G	G	G	G
B	B	B	B	B	B
B	B	B	B	B	B
B	B	B	B	B	B

G	G	G	G	G	G
B	B	B	B	B	B
B	B	B	B	B	B
B	B	B	B	B	B

1 girl is $\frac{1}{24}$ of the total number of students.
$\frac{6}{24}$ of the students are girls.

2 girls are $\frac{2}{24}$, or $\frac{1}{12}$ of the total number of students.
$\frac{3}{12}$ of the students are girls.

$\frac{1}{4}$ of the students are girls.

Rules for Finding Equivalent Fractions

Here are two shortcuts for finding equivalent fractions.

Using Multiplication

If the numerator and the denominator of a fraction are both multiplied by the same number (not 0), the result is a fraction that is equivalent to the original fraction.

EXAMPLE Change $\frac{2}{5}$ to an equivalent fraction.

Multiply the numerator and the denominator of $\frac{2}{5}$ by 3. In symbols, you can write $\frac{2 * 3}{5 * 3} = \frac{6}{15}$.

So, $\frac{2}{5}$ is equivalent to $\frac{6}{15}$.

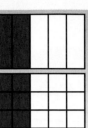

Using Division

If the numerator and the denominator of a fraction are both divided by the same number (not 0), the result is a fraction that is equivalent to the original fraction.

To understand why division works, think about "undoing" the multiplication. Since division "undoes" multiplication, you can divide the numerator and the denominator by the same number to find an equivalent fraction.

EXAMPLE Find fractions that are equivalent to $\frac{18}{24}$.

$$\frac{18 \div 2}{24 \div 2} = \frac{9}{12} \qquad \frac{18 \div 3}{24 \div 3} = \frac{6}{8} \qquad \frac{18 \div 6}{24 \div 6} = \frac{3}{4}$$

CHECK YOUR UNDERSTANDING

1. **a.** What fraction of this rectangle is shaded?
   b. Give two other fractions for the shaded part.
2. Name 3 fractions that are equivalent to $\frac{1}{2}$.
3. Name 3 fractions that are equivalent to $\frac{60}{360}$.

Check your answers on page 278.

Table of Equivalent Fractions

The table below lists equivalent fractions. All the fractions in a row name the same number. For example, all the fractions in the last row are names for the number $\frac{7}{8}$.

Simplest Name	Equivalent Fraction Name								
0 (zero)	$\frac{0}{1}$	$\frac{0}{2}$	$\frac{0}{3}$	$\frac{0}{4}$	$\frac{0}{5}$	$\frac{0}{6}$	$\frac{0}{7}$	$\frac{0}{8}$	$\frac{0}{9}$
1 (one)	$\frac{1}{1}$	$\frac{2}{2}$	$\frac{3}{3}$	$\frac{4}{4}$	$\frac{5}{5}$	$\frac{6}{6}$	$\frac{7}{7}$	$\frac{8}{8}$	$\frac{9}{9}$
$\frac{1}{2}$	$\frac{2}{4}$	$\frac{3}{6}$	$\frac{4}{8}$	$\frac{5}{10}$	$\frac{6}{12}$	$\frac{7}{14}$	$\frac{8}{16}$	$\frac{9}{18}$	$\frac{10}{20}$
$\frac{1}{3}$	$\frac{2}{6}$	$\frac{3}{9}$	$\frac{4}{12}$	$\frac{5}{15}$	$\frac{6}{18}$	$\frac{7}{21}$	$\frac{8}{24}$	$\frac{9}{27}$	$\frac{10}{30}$
$\frac{2}{3}$	$\frac{4}{6}$	$\frac{6}{9}$	$\frac{8}{12}$	$\frac{10}{15}$	$\frac{12}{18}$	$\frac{14}{21}$	$\frac{16}{24}$	$\frac{18}{27}$	$\frac{20}{30}$
$\frac{1}{4}$	$\frac{2}{8}$	$\frac{3}{12}$	$\frac{4}{16}$	$\frac{5}{20}$	$\frac{6}{24}$	$\frac{7}{28}$	$\frac{8}{32}$	$\frac{9}{36}$	$\frac{10}{40}$
$\frac{3}{4}$	$\frac{6}{8}$	$\frac{9}{12}$	$\frac{12}{16}$	$\frac{15}{20}$	$\frac{18}{24}$	$\frac{21}{28}$	$\frac{24}{32}$	$\frac{27}{36}$	$\frac{30}{40}$
$\frac{1}{5}$	$\frac{2}{10}$	$\frac{3}{15}$	$\frac{4}{20}$	$\frac{5}{25}$	$\frac{6}{30}$	$\frac{7}{35}$	$\frac{8}{40}$	$\frac{9}{45}$	$\frac{10}{50}$
$\frac{2}{5}$	$\frac{4}{10}$	$\frac{6}{15}$	$\frac{8}{20}$	$\frac{10}{25}$	$\frac{12}{30}$	$\frac{14}{35}$	$\frac{16}{40}$	$\frac{18}{45}$	$\frac{20}{50}$
$\frac{3}{5}$	$\frac{6}{10}$	$\frac{9}{15}$	$\frac{12}{20}$	$\frac{15}{25}$	$\frac{18}{30}$	$\frac{21}{35}$	$\frac{24}{40}$	$\frac{27}{45}$	$\frac{30}{50}$
$\frac{4}{5}$	$\frac{8}{10}$	$\frac{12}{15}$	$\frac{16}{20}$	$\frac{20}{25}$	$\frac{24}{30}$	$\frac{28}{35}$	$\frac{32}{40}$	$\frac{36}{45}$	$\frac{40}{50}$
$\frac{1}{6}$	$\frac{2}{12}$	$\frac{3}{18}$	$\frac{4}{24}$	$\frac{5}{30}$	$\frac{6}{36}$	$\frac{7}{42}$	$\frac{8}{48}$	$\frac{9}{54}$	$\frac{10}{60}$
$\frac{5}{6}$	$\frac{10}{12}$	$\frac{15}{18}$	$\frac{20}{24}$	$\frac{25}{30}$	$\frac{30}{36}$	$\frac{35}{42}$	$\frac{40}{48}$	$\frac{45}{54}$	$\frac{50}{60}$
$\frac{1}{8}$	$\frac{2}{16}$	$\frac{3}{24}$	$\frac{4}{32}$	$\frac{5}{40}$	$\frac{6}{48}$	$\frac{7}{56}$	$\frac{8}{64}$	$\frac{9}{72}$	$\frac{10}{80}$
$\frac{3}{8}$	$\frac{6}{16}$	$\frac{9}{24}$	$\frac{12}{32}$	$\frac{15}{40}$	$\frac{18}{48}$	$\frac{21}{56}$	$\frac{24}{64}$	$\frac{27}{72}$	$\frac{30}{80}$
$\frac{5}{8}$	$\frac{10}{16}$	$\frac{15}{24}$	$\frac{20}{32}$	$\frac{25}{40}$	$\frac{30}{48}$	$\frac{35}{56}$	$\frac{40}{64}$	$\frac{45}{72}$	$\frac{50}{80}$
$\frac{7}{8}$	$\frac{14}{16}$	$\frac{21}{24}$	$\frac{28}{32}$	$\frac{35}{40}$	$\frac{42}{48}$	$\frac{49}{56}$	$\frac{56}{64}$	$\frac{63}{72}$	$\frac{70}{80}$

> **NOTE**
>
> Each fraction in the first column is in simplest form. A fraction is in simplest form if no equivalent fraction can be obtained by dividing the numerator and the denominator by a whole number. Every fraction is either in simplest form or is equivalent to a fraction in simplest form.

Lowest terms means the same as *simplest form*.

CHECK YOUR UNDERSTANDING

1. True or false?

   a. $\frac{1}{2} = \frac{7}{14}$
   b. $\frac{5}{8} = \frac{30}{48}$
   c. $\frac{3}{5} = \frac{18}{45}$
   d. $\frac{0}{3} = \frac{0}{128}$

2. **a.** Use the table to find 3 other fractions that are equivalent to $\frac{3}{4}$.

   b. Add 2 more equivalent fractions that are not in the table.

Check your answers on page 278.

Equivalent Fractions on a Ruler

Rulers marked in inches usually have tick marks of different lengths. The longest tick marks on the ruler below show the whole inches. The next longest show the half inches, then the quarter inches, and the eighths of an inch. The shortest show the sixteenths of an inch.

Every tick mark on this ruler can be named by a number of sixteenths. Some tick marks can also be named by halves, fourths, and eighths. The picture below shows the pattern of fraction names for a part of the ruler.

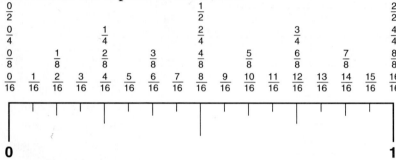

This pattern continues past 1 inch, with mixed numbers naming the tick marks.

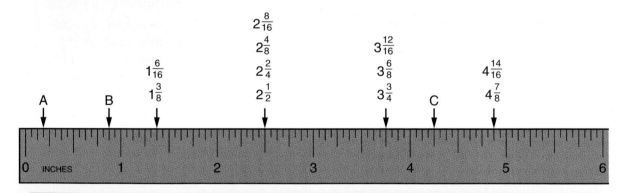

CHECK YOUR UNDERSTANDING

1. Name a fraction or mixed number for each mark labeled A, B, and C on the ruler above.

2. What is the length of this nail?

   a. in quarter inches
   b. in eighths of an inch
   c. in sixteenths of an inch

Check your answers on page 278.

Comparing Fractions

When you compare fractions, you have to pay attention to both the numerator and the denominator.

Like Denominators

Fractions are easy to compare when they have the same denominator. For example, to decide which is larger, $\frac{7}{8}$ or $\frac{5}{8}$, think of them as 7 eighths and 5 eighths. Just as 7 bananas is more than 5 bananas, and 7 dollars is more than 5 dollars, 7 eighths is more than 5 eighths.

<	is less than
>	is greater than
=	is equal to

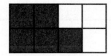 

$$\frac{5}{8} < \frac{7}{8} \text{ or } \frac{7}{8} > \frac{5}{8}$$

To compare fractions that have the same denominators, just look at the numerators. The fraction with the larger numerator is larger.

NOTE

Fractions with **like denominators** have the same denominator. $\frac{1}{4}$ and $\frac{3}{4}$ have like denominators. Fractions with **like numerators** have the same numerator. $\frac{2}{3}$ and $\frac{2}{5}$ have like numerators.

EXAMPLES $\frac{4}{5} > \frac{3}{5}$ because 4 > 3. $\frac{2}{9} < \frac{7}{9}$ because 2 < 7.

Like Numerators

If the numerators of two fractions are the same, then the fraction with the smaller denominator is larger. Remember, a smaller denominator means the ONE has fewer parts and each part is bigger. For example, $\frac{3}{5} > \frac{3}{8}$ because fifths are bigger than eighths, so 3 fifths is more than 3 eighths.

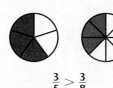

$$\frac{3}{5} > \frac{3}{8}$$

EXAMPLES $\frac{1}{2} > \frac{1}{3}$ because halves are bigger than thirds.
$\frac{3}{8} < \frac{3}{4}$ because eighths are smaller than fourths.

Unlike Numerators and Unlike Denominators

Several strategies can help you compare fractions when both
the numerators and the denominators are different.

Comparing to $\frac{1}{2}$

Compare $\frac{3}{7}$ and $\frac{5}{8}$. One way to tell which is
bigger is to notice that $\frac{5}{8}$ is
more than $\frac{1}{2}$ and $\frac{3}{7}$ is less than
$\frac{1}{2}$. So $\frac{3}{7} < \frac{5}{8}$.

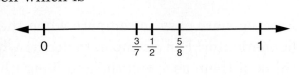

Comparing to 0 and 1

Comparing fractions to 0 and 1 can also
be helpful. For example, $\frac{7}{8} > \frac{3}{4}$ because $\frac{7}{8}$ is
closer to 1. ($\frac{7}{8}$ is $\frac{1}{8}$ away from 1
but $\frac{3}{4}$ is $\frac{1}{4}$ away from 1. Since
eighths are smaller than
fourths, $\frac{7}{8}$ is closer to 1.)

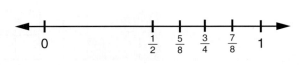

Using Equivalent Fractions

One way to compare fractions that *always*
works is to find equivalent fractions that
have the same denominator. For example, to
compare $\frac{5}{8}$ and $\frac{3}{5}$, look at the *Table of
Equivalent Fractions* on page 49. The table
shows that both fifths and eighths can be
written as 40ths: $\frac{5}{8} = \frac{25}{40}$ and $\frac{3}{5} = \frac{24}{40}$. Since
$\frac{25}{40} > \frac{24}{40}$, you know that $\frac{5}{8} > \frac{3}{5}$.

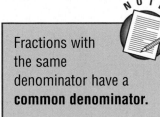

NOTE

Fractions with
the same
denominator have a
common denominator.

Using Decimal Equivalents

Using decimal equivalents is another way to
compare fractions. For example, to compare
$\frac{2}{5}$ and $\frac{3}{8}$, use a calculator to change both
fractions to decimals:

$\frac{2}{5}$: Key in: 2 ⊕ 5 ⟨Enter⟩   Answer: 0.4

$\frac{3}{8}$: Key in: 3 ⊕ 8 ⟨Enter⟩   Answer: 0.375

Since $0.4 > 0.375$, you know that $\frac{2}{5} > \frac{3}{8}$.

CHECK YOUR UNDERSTANDING

Compare. Write <, >, or =.

1. $\frac{1}{8} \,\square\, \frac{3}{8}$ **2.** $\frac{2}{3} \,\square\, \frac{2}{5}$ **3.** $\frac{3}{4} \,\square\, \frac{3}{5}$ **4.** $\frac{4}{9} \,\square\, \frac{2}{3}$

Check your answers on page 278.

Adding and Subtracting Fractions

Like Denominators

Adding or subtracting fractions that have the same denominator is easy—just add or subtract the numerators.

You can use division to put the answer in simplest form.

$$\frac{2}{7} + \frac{3}{7} = \frac{5}{7}$$

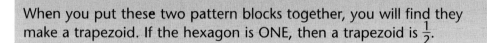

EXAMPLES $\dfrac{3}{8} + \dfrac{1}{8} = \dfrac{4}{8} = \dfrac{4 \div 4}{8 \div 4} = \dfrac{1}{2}$ $\dfrac{7}{10} - \dfrac{3}{10} = \dfrac{4}{10} = \dfrac{4 \div 2}{10 \div 2} = \dfrac{2}{5}$

Unlike Denominators

When you are adding and subtracting fractions that have unlike denominators, you must be especially careful. One way is to model the problem with pattern blocks. Remember that different denominators mean the ONE is divided into different numbers (and so, different sizes) of parts.

EXAMPLE $\dfrac{1}{3} + \dfrac{1}{6} = ?$

If the hexagon is ONE, then the rhombus is $\frac{1}{3}$ and the triangle is $\frac{1}{6}$.

When you put these two pattern blocks together, you will find they make a trapezoid. If the hexagon is ONE, then a trapezoid is $\frac{1}{2}$.

So, $\dfrac{1}{3} + \dfrac{1}{6} = \dfrac{1}{2}$.

$$\frac{1}{3} + \frac{1}{6} = \frac{1}{2}$$

EXAMPLE $\dfrac{5}{6} - \dfrac{2}{3} = ?$

If the hexagon is ONE, then $\frac{5}{6}$ is 5 triangles and $\frac{2}{3}$ is 2 rhombuses.

To take away $\frac{2}{3}$ (2 rhombuses) from $\frac{5}{6}$ (5 triangles), you would need to take away 4 triangles.

Then there would be 1 triangle or $\frac{1}{6}$ left.

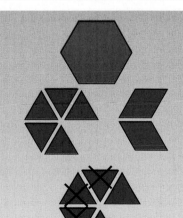

So, $\dfrac{5}{6} - \dfrac{2}{3} = \dfrac{1}{6}$.

$$\frac{5}{6} - \frac{2}{3} = \frac{1}{6}$$

Fractions and Rational Numbers

Clock Fractions

A clock face can be used to model fractions with 2, 3, 4, 5, 6, 10, 12, 15, 20, 30, and 60 in the denominator.

NOTE

Thousands of years ago, the ancient Babylonians divided the day into 24 hours, the hour into 60 minutes, and the minute into 60 seconds. This system for time keeping is a good model for working with many fractions.

EXAMPLES

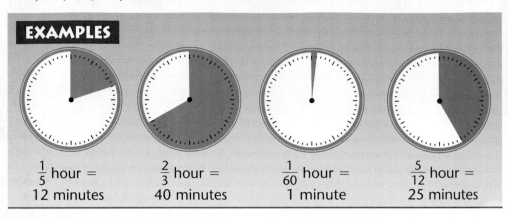

$\frac{1}{5}$ hour = 12 minutes

$\frac{2}{3}$ hour = 40 minutes

$\frac{1}{60}$ hour = 1 minute

$\frac{5}{12}$ hour = 25 minutes

A clock face can help in solving simple fraction addition and subtraction problems.

EXAMPLES $\frac{1}{3} + \frac{1}{6} = ?$ $\frac{3}{4} - \frac{1}{3} = ?$

$\frac{1}{3}$ hour = 20 minutes
$\frac{1}{6}$ hour = 10 minutes

$$\frac{1}{3} + \frac{1}{6} = \frac{1}{2}$$

$\frac{3}{4}$ hour = 45 minutes
$\frac{1}{3}$ hour = 20 minutes

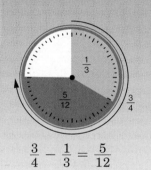

$$\frac{3}{4} - \frac{1}{3} = \frac{5}{12}$$

Using a Calculator

Some calculators can add and subtract fractions.

EXAMPLE $\frac{3}{8} + \frac{1}{4} = ?$

Key in: 3 ⓝ 8 ⓓ ⊕ 1 ⓝ 4 ⓓ ⓔⁿᵗᵉʳ Answer: $\frac{5}{8}$

CHECK YOUR UNDERSTANDING

Solve. Use pattern blocks or clock faces to help you.

1. $\frac{2}{3} + \frac{1}{6}$ **2.** $\frac{5}{6} - \frac{1}{2}$ **3.** $\frac{5}{12} - \frac{1}{4}$ **4.** $\frac{1}{2} + \frac{2}{3}$

Check your answers on page 278.

Sometimes tools like pattern blocks or clock faces are not helpful for solving a fraction addition or subtraction problem. Here is a method that always works.

Using a Common Denominator

To add or subtract fractions that have different denominators, first rename them as fractions with a common denominator. A quick common denominator to use is the product of the denominators.

EXAMPLE $\frac{1}{4} + \frac{2}{3} = ?$

A quick way to find a common denominator for these fractions is to multiply the denominators: $4 * 3 = 12$.
Rename $\frac{1}{4}$ and $\frac{2}{3}$ as 12ths:

$$\frac{1}{4} = \frac{1 * 3}{4 * 3} = \frac{3}{12}$$

$$\frac{2}{3} = \frac{2 * 4}{3 * 4} = \frac{8}{12}$$

So, $\frac{1}{4} + \frac{2}{3} = \frac{3}{12} + \frac{8}{12} = \frac{11}{12}$.

EXAMPLE $\frac{3}{4} - \frac{2}{5} = ?$

A common denominator for these fractions is $4 * 5 = 20$.
Rename $\frac{3}{4}$ and $\frac{2}{5}$ as 20ths:

$$\frac{3}{4} = \frac{3 * 5}{4 * 5} = \frac{15}{20}$$

$$\frac{2}{5} = \frac{2 * 4}{5 * 4} = \frac{8}{20}$$

So, $\frac{3}{4} - \frac{2}{5} = \frac{15}{20} - \frac{8}{20} = \frac{7}{20}$.

CHECK YOUR UNDERSTANDING

Add or subtract.

1. $\frac{3}{4} + \frac{2}{5}$ 2. $\frac{7}{8} - \frac{1}{2}$ 3. $\frac{5}{12} - \frac{1}{4}$ 4. $\frac{1}{2} + \frac{1}{3} + \frac{1}{4}$

Check your answers on page 278.

Multiplying Fractions and Whole Numbers

There are several ways to think about multiplying a whole number and a fraction.

Using a Number Line

One way to multiply a whole number and a fraction is to think about "hops" on a number line: The whole number tells how many hops to make, and the fraction tells how long each hop should be. For example, to solve $4 * \frac{2}{3}$, imagine taking 4 hops on a number line, each $\frac{2}{3}$ unit long.

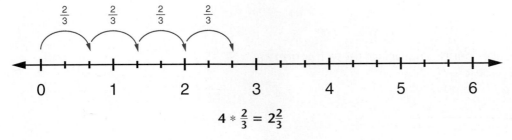

$$4 * \frac{2}{3} = 2\frac{2}{3}$$

Addition

Another way is to use addition.
For example, to find $4 * \frac{2}{3}$, draw 4 models of $\frac{2}{3}$.

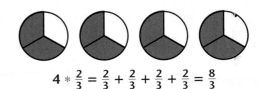

$$4 * \frac{2}{3} = \frac{2}{3} + \frac{2}{3} + \frac{2}{3} + \frac{2}{3} = \frac{8}{3}$$

Using Area

Another strategy for fraction multiplication is to use area.
For example, to solve $4 * \frac{2}{3}$, first draw four squares.
Next, shade $\frac{2}{3}$ of each square.

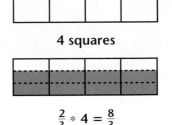

4 squares

$$\frac{2}{3} * 4 = \frac{8}{3}$$

CHECK YOUR UNDERSTANDING

Use addition or a number line to solve these problems.

1. $5 * \frac{2}{3}$ **2.** $6 * \frac{3}{4}$ **3.** $3 * \frac{4}{5}$

4. $4 * \frac{3}{4}$ **5.** $5 * \frac{4}{5}$ **6.** $3 * \frac{2}{3}$

Check your answers on page 278.

Finding a Fraction of a Set

You can think of multiplication with fractions as finding a fraction of a set. For example, think of the problem $\frac{2}{5} * 30$ as "What is $\frac{2}{5}$ of 30¢?" One way to solve this problem is first to find $\frac{1}{5}$ of 30, and then to use that answer to find $\frac{2}{5}$ of 30.

EXAMPLE $\frac{2}{5} * 30 = ?$

Step 1: Find $\frac{1}{5}$ of 30.
To do this, arrange 30 pennies into 5 groups, then count the number of pennies in one group.
$30 \div 5 = 6$, so $\frac{1}{5}$ of 30 is 6.

Step 2: Next find $\frac{2}{5}$ of 30.
Since $\frac{1}{5}$ of 30 is 6, $\frac{2}{5}$ of 30 is $2 * 6$.

$\frac{2}{5} * 30 = 12$

EXAMPLE $\frac{2}{3} * 15 = ?$

Step 1: Find $\frac{1}{3}$ of 15.
$15 \div 3 = 5$, so $\frac{1}{3}$ of 15 is 5.

Step 2: Next find $\frac{2}{3}$ of 15.
Since $\frac{1}{3}$ of 15 is 5, $\frac{2}{3}$ of 15 is $2 * 5$.

$\frac{2}{3} * 15 = 10$

CHECK YOUR UNDERSTANDING

Find each answer.

1. $\frac{1}{4} * 36 = ?$ 2. $\frac{4}{5} * 20 = ?$

3. Rita and Hunter earned \$12 raking lawns. Since Rita did most of the work, they decided that Rita should get $\frac{2}{3}$ of the money. How much does each person get?

Check your answers on page 278.

Positive and Negative Rational Numbers

People have used **counting numbers** (1, 2, 3, and so on) for thousands of years. Long ago people found that the counting numbers did not meet all of their needs. They needed numbers for in-between measures such as $2\frac{1}{2}$ inches and $6\frac{5}{6}$ hours.

Positive rational numbers were invented to meet these needs. Positive rational numbers can be expressed as fractions, decimals, and percents. Positive numbers include most of the numbers that are familiar to you, such as $\frac{1}{2}$, $\frac{5}{6}$, 15.3, 3.75, 25%, and 90%.

However, even positive rational numbers did not meet every need. For example, problems such as $5 - 7$ and $2\frac{3}{4} - 5\frac{1}{4}$ did not have positive number answers. This led to the invention of **negative rational numbers.** Negative numbers are numbers that are less than 0. The numbers $-\frac{1}{2}$, -2.75, and -100 are negative numbers. The number -2 is read "negative 2."

Negative rational numbers serve several purposes:

• To express locations such as temperatures below zero on a thermometer and depths below sea level.
• To show changes such as yards lost in a football game.
• To extend the number line to the left of zero.
• To calculate answers to many subtraction problems.

The **opposite** of every positive number is a negative number, and the opposite of every negative number is a positive number. The diagram below shows this relationship.

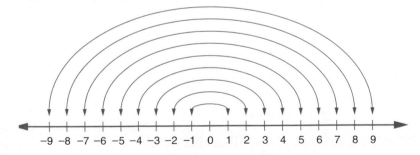

The number 0 is neither positive nor negative; 0 is also its own opposite. The **rational numbers** include the positive rational numbers, the negative rational numbers, and 0.

Fractions, Decimals, and Percents

Fractions, decimals, and percents are different ways to write numbers. Sometimes it's easier to work with a fraction instead of a decimal or with a percent instead of a fraction.

Renaming a Fraction as a Decimal

You can rename a fraction as a decimal by first finding an equivalent fraction with a denominator of 10, 100, or 1,000, and then writing a decimal.

EXAMPLES $\frac{1}{2} = \frac{1 * 50}{2 * 50} = \frac{50}{100} = 0.50$ $\frac{4}{5} = \frac{4 * 2}{5 * 2} = \frac{8}{10} = 0.8$

This only works for certain fractions. Another way to rename a fraction as a decimal is to divide the numerator by the denominator. You can use a calculator for this division.

EXAMPLES

$\frac{3}{4}$: Key in: 3 ÷ 4 (Enter) Answer: 0.75 $\frac{5}{8}$: Key in: 5 ÷ 8 (Enter) Answer: 0.625

$\frac{4}{9}$: Key in: 4 ÷ 9 (Enter) Answer: 0.4444... $\frac{3}{11}$: Key in: 3 ÷ 11 (Enter) Answer: 0.2727...

Renaming a Decimal as a Fraction

To change a decimal to a fraction, write the decimal as a fraction with a denominator of 10, 100, or 1,000. You can rename the fraction in simplest form.

EXAMPLES Write each decimal as a fraction.

For 0.5, the rightmost digit is 5, which is in the 10ths place.
So, $0.5 = \frac{5}{10}$, or $\frac{1}{2}$.

For 0.307, the rightmost digit is 7, which is in the 1,000ths place.
So, $0.307 = \frac{307}{1,000}$.

For 4.75, the rightmost digit is 5, which is in the 100ths place.
So, $4.75 = \frac{475}{100}$, $4\frac{75}{100}$, or $4\frac{3}{4}$.

Renaming a Decimal as a Percent

To rename a decimal as a percent, first write the decimal as a fraction with a denominator of 100. Then use the meaning of percent ("over 100") to rename the fraction as a percent.

EXAMPLES Rename each decimal as a percent.

$$0.5 = 0.50 = \frac{50}{100} = 50\% \qquad 0.01 = \frac{1}{100} = 1\% \qquad 1.2 = 1.20 = \frac{120}{100} = 120\%$$

Renaming a Percent as a Fraction

To rename a percent as a fraction, write it as a fraction with a denominator of 100.

EXAMPLES Rename each percent as a fraction in simplest form.

$$50\% = \frac{50}{100} = \frac{1}{2} \qquad 75\% = \frac{75}{100} = \frac{3}{4} \qquad 1\% = \frac{1}{100}$$

Renaming a Percent as a Decimal

To rename a percent as a decimal, first rename it as a fraction over 100. Then rename the fraction as a decimal.

EXAMPLES Rename each percent as a decimal.

$$45\% = \frac{45}{100} = 0.45 \qquad 120\% = \frac{120}{100} = 1.2 \qquad 1\% = \frac{1}{100} = 0.01$$

Renaming a Fraction as a Percent

To rename a fraction as a percent, first rename it as a decimal. Then rename the decimal as a percent.

EXAMPLES Rename each fraction as a percent.

$$\frac{1}{2} = 0.50 = \frac{50}{100} = 50\% \qquad \frac{3}{5} = 0.60 = \frac{60}{100} = 60\% \qquad \frac{3}{8} = 0.375 = \frac{375}{1,000} = \frac{37.5}{100} = 37.5\%$$

CHECK YOUR UNDERSTANDING

Write each number as a fraction, a decimal, and a percent.

1. $\frac{1}{2}$ 2. 0.75   3. 10%   4. $\frac{4}{5}$

Check your answers on page 279.

Data & Probability

Collecting Data

There are different ways to collect information about something. You can count, measure, ask questions, or observe and describe what you see.

The information you collect is called **data.**

Surveys

Much of the information used to make decisions comes from **surveys.** Many surveys collect data about people. Stores survey customers to find out what products they should carry. Television stations survey viewers to learn what programs are popular. The survey data are collected in several ways, including face-to-face interviews, telephone interviews, and written questions that are answered and returned by mail.

Not all surveys gather information about people. For example, there are surveys about cars, buildings, and animal groups.

EXAMPLE		
A bird survey is conducted each year in the Chicago area during December and January. Bird watchers list the different bird species they see, and they count the number of each species seen. The lists are combined to create a final data set.	From the 1999–2000 Chicago bird survey:	
	Species	**Number of birds seen**
	blue heron	10
	canada goose	3,768
	house sparrow	2,446
	robin	213

Samples

A **sample** is a small part of a group chosen to represent the whole group. Data are collected only from this small group.

EXAMPLE		
A survey of teenagers collects data on people aged 13 to 19. There are about 27 million teenagers in the United States. It is not possible to collect data from every one of them. Data are collected from a sample of teenagers instead.	From a recent survey of American teens:	
	Average Time Spent Each Day (in hours:minutes)	
	Watching TV	3:16
	Listening to CDs/tapes	1:05
	Listening to radio	0:48
	Reading	0:44
	Using a computer	0:31
	Playing video games	0:27
	Using the Internet	0:13

Organizing Data

Once the data have been collected, it helps to organize them to make them easier to understand. **Line plots** and **tally charts** are two methods of organizing data.

EXAMPLE   Mr. Jackson's class got the following scores on a five-word spelling test. Make a line plot and a tally chart to show the data below.

5 3 5 0 4 4 5 4 4 4 2 3 4 5 3 5 4 3 4 4

Scores on a 5-Word Spelling Test

```
                              x
                              x
                              x
                              x
                              x   x
Number                    x   x   x
of                        x   x   x
Students                  x   x   x
               x      x   x   x   x
             _____
               0   1   2   3   4   5
                   Number Correct
```

In this line plot, there are 4 Xs above the number 3. Four students got a score of 3 on the test.

Scores on a 5-Word Spelling Test

Number Correct	Number of Students
0	/
1	
2	/
3	////
4	//// ////
5	////

In this tally chart, there are 4 tallies to the right of 3. Four students got a score of 3 on the test.

Both the line plot and the tally chart help to organize the data. They make it easier to describe the data. For example,

- Five students had 5 words correct.
- 4 correct is the score that came up most often.
- 0 correct and 2 correct are scores that came up least often.
- No student got exactly 1 correct.

CHECK YOUR UNDERSTANDING

Here are the number of hits made by 12 players in a baseball game.

0 2 4 1 0 2 1 3 2 1 0 2

Organize the data.   **1.** Make a tally chart.   **2.** Make a line plot.

Check your answers on page 279.

Sometimes the data are spread out over a wide range of numbers. This makes a tally chart and a line plot difficult to draw. In such cases, you can make a tally chart in which the results are grouped.

EXAMPLE Ms. Beck asked her students to make a count of the number of books they read over the summer. These were the results:

9 13 3 10 16 0 12 5 16 4 10 11 13 5 20

5 15 1 12 24 7 13 0 38 2 11 14 18 6 12

The table below sorts the data into **intervals** of 5. This is called a tally chart of **grouped data.**

- If a student read from 0 to 4 books, one tally mark is recorded for the "0–4" interval.

- If a student read from 5 to 9 books, one tally mark is recorded for the "5–9" interval, and so on.

The chart shows that most students read fewer than 20 books. The most frequent number of books read was from 10 to 14.

Books Read by Students

Number of Books	Number of Students
0–4	ＨＨ /
5–9	ＨＨ /
10–14	ＨＨ ＨＨ /
15–19	////
20–24	//
25 or more	/

CHECK YOUR UNDERSTANDING

Michael Jordan played in 12 games of the 1996 NBA Playoffs. He scored the following number of points:

35 29 26 44 28 46 27 35 21 35 17 45

Copy and complete the tally chart of grouped data.

Number of Points	Number of Games
10–19	
20–29	
30–39	
40–49	

Check your answers on page 279.

Statistical Landmarks

The **landmarks** for a set of data are used to describe the data.

- The **minimum** is the smallest value.
- The **maximum** is the largest value.
- The **range** is the difference between the minimum and the maximum.
- The **mode** is the value or values that occur most often.
- The **median** is the middle value.

EXAMPLE Here is a record of children's absences for one week at Medgar Evers School.

Monday	Tuesday	Wednesday	Thursday	Friday
27	19	12	16	16

Find the landmarks for the data.

Minimum (lowest) number: 12   Maximum (highest) number: 27
Range of numbers: $27 - 12 = 15$ Mode (most frequent number): 16

To find the median (middle value):

- List the numbers in order from smallest to largest or largest to smallest.

  12   16   16   19   27

- Cross out one number from each end of the list.

  ~~12~~   16   16   19   ~~27~~

- Continue and cross out one more number from each end of the list.

- The median is the number that remains after all others have been crossed out.

  ~~12~~   ~~16~~   [16]   ~~19~~   ~~27~~

  ↑
  median

CHECK YOUR UNDERSTANDING

Here are math quiz scores (number correct) for 11 students: 0 2 4 1 2 1 3 2 1 0 2

Find the landmarks for the data.

1. Find the minimum.   **2.** Find the maximum.   **3.** Find the range.
4. Find the mode.   **5.** Find the median.

Check your answers on page 279.

EXAMPLE The **line plot** shows students' scores on a 20-word spelling test. Find the landmarks for the data.

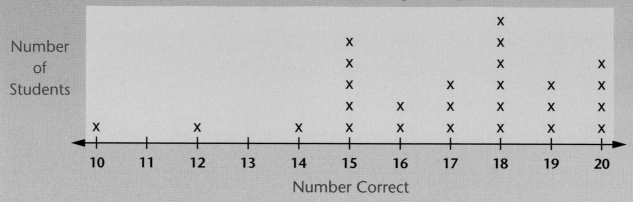

Scores on a 20-Word Spelling Test

Minimum: 10   Maximum: 20   Range: 20 − 10 = 10   Mode: 18

To find the median (middle value), first list the numbers in order:

10 12 14 15 15 15 15 15 16 16 17 17 17 18 18 18 18 18 18 19 19 19 20 20 20 20

Cross out one number from each end of this list. Continue to cross out one number from each end until there are only two numbers left. The two numbers remaining are the middle scores.

1̶0̶ 1̶2̶ 1̶4̶ 1̶5̶ 1̶5̶ 1̶5̶ 1̶5̶ 1̶5̶ 1̶6̶ 1̶6̶ 1̶7̶ 1̶7̶ [17 18] 1̶8̶ 1̶8̶ 1̶8̶ 1̶8̶ 1̶8̶ 1̶9̶ 1̶9̶ 1̶9̶ 2̶0̶ 2̶0̶ 2̶0̶ 2̶0̶

middle scores

There are two middle scores, 17 and 18.
The median is 17.5, which is the number halfway between 17 and 18.

CHECK YOUR UNDERSTANDING

1. Here are math quiz scores (number correct) for 12 students:
4 2 0 3 4 2 3 1 1 3 4 2.
Find the minimum, maximum, range, mode, and median for this set of data.

2. Find the median for this set of numbers: 23 12 7 31 16 23 18 9 7 12

Check your answers on page 279.

The Mean (or Average)

The **mean** of a set of numbers is often called the *average*.

To find the mean:

Step 1: Add the numbers.

Step 2: Divide the sum by the number of addends.

EXAMPLE   Find the mean of this set of numbers: 2, 6, 7.

The bars at the right represent these three numbers.

Step 1: Add the numbers. 2 + 6 + 7 = 15

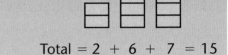

Total = 2 + 6 + 7 = 15

Step 2: Divide by the number of addends. 15 ÷ 3 = 5

The mean (average) of 2, 6, and 7 is 5.

Replace the original bar picture by one that has three bars of length 5. If you have a set of numbers, the mean can be used to divide the total into equal shares.

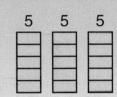

Total of 15 has been divided into 3 equal shares

EXAMPLE   On a four-day trip, Jay's family drove 200, 100, 140, and 260 miles. What is the mean number of miles they drove per day?

Step 1: Add the numbers. 200 + 100 + 140 + 260 = 700

Step 2: Divide by the number of addends. 700/4 = 175

The mean is 175 miles. They drove an average of 175 miles per day.

> **NOTE**
>
> If you are using a calculator, key in: 200 ⊕ 100 ⊕ 140 ⊕ 260 ⏎ .
> Divide the sum by 4: 700 ÷ 4 ⏎
> Answer: 175

CHECK YOUR UNDERSTANDING

Foster went on a seven-day bike trip. He recorded the miles covered each day:

Mon: 25   Tue: 21   Wed: 19   Thurs: 26   Fri: 22   Sat: 17   Sun: 24

1. Find the total distance.   **2.** Find the mean (average) distance covered per day.

Check your answers on page 279.

Bar Graphs

A **bar graph** is a drawing that uses bars to represent numbers. Bar graphs display information in a way that makes it easy to show comparisons. A bar graph has a title that describes the information in the graph. Each bar has a label. Units are given to show how something was counted or measured. When possible, the graph gives the source of the information.

EXAMPLE This is a **vertical bar graph**.

- Each bar represents the mean (average) number of pounds of fruit that a person eats in one year.
- It is easy to compare amounts by comparing the bars. People eat more pounds of bananas than any other kind of fruit.

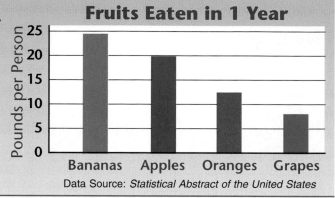

Fruits Eaten in 1 Year

Data Source: *Statistical Abstract of the United States*

EXAMPLE This is a **horizontal bar graph**.

- Each bar represents the length of a river.
- It is easy to compare lengths by comparing the bars. The Mississippi and Missouri Rivers are both more than 2,000 miles long. The Rio Grande River is about twice as long as the Ohio River.

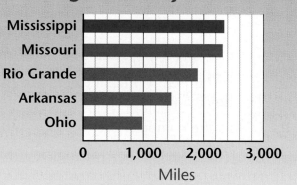

Lengths of Major U.S. Rivers

Data Source: *The World Almanac*

CHECK YOUR UNDERSTANDING

Read the bar graph.

1. Find the average number of vacation days in each country.

2. Compare the number of vacation days in Canada and the United States.

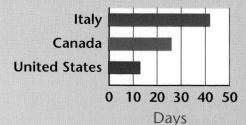

Average Number of Vacation Days Per Year

Data Source: World Tourism Organization

Check your answers on page 279.

Line Graphs

Line graphs are used to display information that shows trends. They sometimes show how something has changed over a period of time.

Line graphs are sometimes called **broken-line graphs.** Line segments connect the points on the graph. Joined end-to-end, the segments look like a broken line.

Line graphs have both a horizontal and a vertical scale. Each of these scales is called an **axis** (plural: **axes**). Each axis is labeled to show what is being measured and what the unit of measure is.

Broken-Line Graph

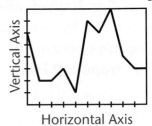

The segments joined end-to-end look like a broken line.

EXAMPLE   The broken-line graph to the right shows the number of farms in the United States from 1950 to 2000.

The horizontal axis is divided into 10-year intervals. The vertical axis shows the number of farms in the United States, in millions.

By studying the graph, you can see the trend or direction in the number of farms over the last 50 years.

• The number has decreased in each 10-year interval from 1950 to 1990.

• From 1990 to 2000, the number of farms stayed about the same.

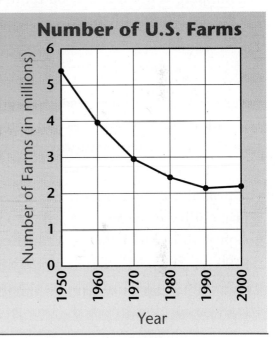

Number of U.S. Farms

CHECK YOUR UNDERSTANDING

The table at the right shows the number of cars in a school parking lot at different times. Make a line graph to show this information.

Cars in a Parking Lot

Time	Number of Cars
6 A.M.	5
7 A.M.	12
8 A.M.	40
9 A.M.	50
10 A.M.	46

Check your answers on page 279.

Chance and Probability

Chance

Things that happen are called **events.** There are many events that you can be sure about:

- You are **certain** that the sun will rise tomorrow.
- It is **impossible** for you to grow to be 10 feet tall.

There are also many events that you *cannot* be sure about.

- You cannot be sure that you will get a letter tomorrow.
- You cannot be sure whether it will be sunny next Tuesday.

Sometimes you might talk about the **chance** that something will happen. If Joan is a good tennis player, you may say, "Joan has a *good chance* of winning the match." If Joan is a poor player, you may say, "It is *very unlikely* that Joan will win."

Probability

Sometimes a number is used to tell the chance of something happening. This number is called a **probability.** It is a number from 0 to 1. The closer a probability is to 1, the more likely it is that an event will happen.

- A probability of 0 means the event is *impossible*. The probability is 0 that you will live to the age of 200.
- A probability of 1 means that the event is *certain*. The probability is 1 that the sun will rise tomorrow.

A probability can be written as a fraction, a decimal, or a percent.

> **EXAMPLE** The weather bureau predicts that there is an 80% chance of rain today and a 3 in 4 chance of rain tomorrow. On which day is it more likely to rain?
>
> A probability of 80% can also be written as 0.8, or $\frac{80}{100}$.
> A 3 in 4 chance means that the probability is $\frac{3}{4}$, 0.75, or 75%.
> Since 0.8 is greater than 0.75, it is more likely to rain today.

CHECK YOUR UNDERSTANDING

The weather bureau predicts a 15% chance of snow on Sunday and a 1 in 6 chance of snow on Monday. On which day is it more likely to snow?

Check your answer on page 279.

Calculating a Probability

The examples below show four common ways for finding probabilities.

Make a Guess	John guesses that he has an 80% chance (an 8 in 10 chance) of returning home by 9 o'clock.

Conduct an Experiment	Kathleen dropped 100 tacks: 60 landed point up and 40 landed point down. The chance of a tack landing point up is $\frac{60}{100}$, or 60%.

Use a Data Table   Art got 48 hits in his last 100 times at bat.

Hits	48
Walks	11
Outs	41
Total	100

He estimates the probability that he will get a hit the next time at bat is $\frac{48}{100}$, or 48%.

Assume that All Possible Results Have the Same Chance

A die has 6 faces. Each face has the same chance of coming up.

The probability of rolling a 5 is $\frac{1}{6}$.
The probability of rolling either 4 or a 5 is double this—$\frac{2}{6}$, or $\frac{1}{3}$.
The probability of rolling an even number (2, 4, or 6) is $\frac{3}{6}$, or $\frac{1}{2}$.

EXAMPLES What is the probability that the spinner shown will land on an even number? On a prime number?

The spinner will land on an even number if it lands on 2, 4, 6, 8, or 10. Each of these numbers is likely to come up $\frac{1}{10}$ of the time.
So the total probability that one of these numbers will come up is
$\frac{1}{10} + \frac{1}{10} + \frac{1}{10} + \frac{1}{10} + \frac{1}{10}$, or $\frac{5}{10}$.

The probability of landing on an even number is $\frac{5}{10}$, $\frac{1}{2}$, or 50%.

The spinner will land on a prime number if it lands on 2, 3, 5, or 7. Each of these numbers has a probability of $\frac{1}{10}$ of coming up.

The total probability that one of these prime numbers will come up is
$\frac{1}{10} + \frac{1}{10} + \frac{1}{10} + \frac{1}{10}$, or $\frac{4}{10}$.

The probability of landing on a prime number is $\frac{4}{10}$, $\frac{2}{5}$, or 40%.

EXAMPLE What is the probability that the spinner shown above will land on a blue or yellow section that is an even number?

The blue and yellow sections are numbered 1, 3, 4, 6, 8, and 9. Three of these sections show an even number: 4, 6, and 8. Each of these numbers is likely to come up $\frac{1}{10}$ of the time. The total probability that one of the numbers 4, 6, or 8 will come up is $\frac{1}{10} + \frac{1}{10} + \frac{1}{10} = \frac{3}{10}$.

The probability of landing on a blue or yellow section that is an even number is $\frac{3}{10}$, or 0.3, or 30%.

CHECK YOUR UNDERSTANDING

Use the spinner above. Find each probability below.

1. Land on a number less than 7.

2. Land on an odd number.

3. Land on a number that is not prime.

4. Land on an orange or red section.

5. Land on a section that is yellow and not a prime number.

6. Land on a prime number in a red or yellow section.

Check your answers on page 279.

Geometry & Constructions

Geometry in Our World

The world is filled with geometry. There are angles, segments, lines, and curves everywhere you look. There are 2-dimensional and 3-dimensional shapes of every type.

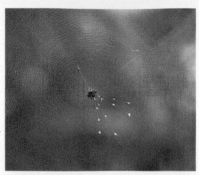

Many wonderful geometric patterns can be seen in nature. You can find patterns in flowers, spider webs, leaves, seashells, even your own face and body.

The ideas of geometry are also found in the things people create. Think of the games you play. Checkers is played with round pieces. The gameboard is covered with squares. Basketball and tennis are played with spheres. They are played on rectangular courts that are painted with straight and curved lines. The next time you play or watch a game, notice how geometry is important to the way the game is played.

The places we live in are built from plans that use geometry. Buildings almost always have rectangular rooms. They often have triangular roofs. Archways are sometimes curved. Staircases may be straight or spiral. Buildings and rooms are often decorated with beautiful patterns. You see these decorations on doors and windows; on walls, floors, and ceilings; and on railings of staircases.

The clothes people wear are often decorated with geometric shapes. So are the things they use every day. Everywhere in the world, people create things using geometric patterns. Examples include quilts, pottery, baskets, and tiles. Some patterns are shown here. Which are your favorites?

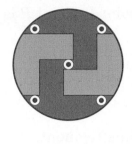

Make a practice of noticing geometric shapes around you. Pay attention to bridges, buildings, and other structures. Look at the ways in which simple shapes such as triangles, rectangles, and circles are combined. Notice interesting designs. Share these with your classmates and your teacher.

In this section, you will study geometric shapes and learn how to construct them. As you learn, try to create your own beautiful designs.

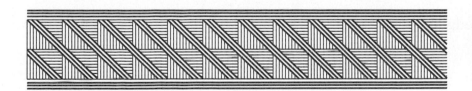

Points and Line Segments

A **point** is a location in space. You often make a dot with a pencil to show where a point is.

Letters are used to name points. The letter names make it easy to talk about the points. For example, in the illustration at the right, point *A* is closer to point *B* than it is to point *P*. Point *P* is closer to point *B* than it is to point *A*.

A **line segment** is made up of 2 points and the straight path between them. You can use any tool with a straight edge to draw the path between two points.

- The two points are called **endpoints** of the line segment.

- The line segment is the shortest path between the endpoints.

The line segment below is called *line segment* AB or *line segment* BA.

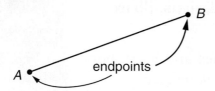

The symbol for a line segment is a raised bar. The bar is written above the letters that name the endpoints for the segment. The name of the line segment above can be written $\overline{AB}$ or $\overline{BA}$.

Straightedge and Ruler

A **straightedge** is a strip of wood, plastic, or metal that may be used to draw a straight path. A **ruler** is a straightedge that is marked so that it may be used to measure lengths.

- Every ruler is a straightedge.

- However, every straightedge is not a ruler.

ruler   straightedge

Rays and Lines

A **ray** is a straight path that has a starting point and goes on forever in *one* direction.

To draw a ray, draw a line segment and extend the path beyond one endpoint. Then add an arrowhead to show that the path goes on forever.

The ray at the right is called *ray* RA.

Point *R* is the endpoint of ray *RA*. The endpoint is always the first letter in the name of a ray. The second letter can be any other point on the ray.

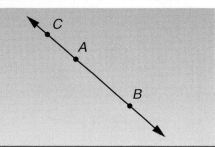

The symbol for a ray is a raised arrow, pointing to the right. For example, ray *RA* can be written $\overrightarrow{RA}$.

A **line** is a straight path that goes on forever in *both* directions.

To draw a line, draw a line segment and extend the path beyond each endpoint. Then add an arrowhead at each end.

line *FE*, or line *EF*, or $\overleftrightarrow{FE}$, or $\overleftrightarrow{EF}$

The symbol for a line is a raised bar with two arrowheads $\overleftrightarrow{}$. The name of the line above can be written either as $\overleftrightarrow{FE}$ or as $\overleftrightarrow{EF}$. You can name a line by listing any two points on the line, in any order.

EXAMPLE   Write all the names for this line.

Points C, A, and B are all on the line.
Use any 2 points to write the name of the line:

$\overleftrightarrow{CA}$ or $\overleftrightarrow{AC}$ or $\overleftrightarrow{CB}$ or $\overleftrightarrow{BC}$ or $\overleftrightarrow{AB}$ or $\overleftrightarrow{BA}$

CHECK YOUR UNDERSTANDING

1. Draw and label $\overleftrightarrow{CD}$.

2. Draw and label a point *R* that is not on $\overleftrightarrow{CD}$.

3. Draw and label $\overrightarrow{RC}$ and $\overrightarrow{RD}$.

Check your answers on pages 279.

Angles

An **angle** is formed by 2 rays or 2 line segments that share the same endpoint.

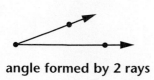

angle formed by 2 rays

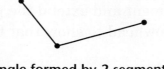

angle formed by 2 segments

The endpoint where the rays or segments meet is called the **vertex** of the angle. The rays or segments are called the **sides** of the angle.

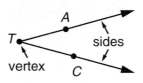

Naming Angles

The symbol for an angle is ∠. An angle can be named in two ways:

1. Name the vertex. The angle shown above is angle *T*. Write this as ∠*T*.

2. Name 3 points: the vertex and one point on each side of the angle. The angle above can be named angle *ATC* (∠*ATC*) or angle *CTA* (∠*CTA*). The vertex must always be listed in the middle, between the points on the sides.

Measuring Angles

The **protractor** is a tool used to measure angles. Angles are measured in **degrees.** A degree is the unit of measure for the size of an angle.

The **degree symbol** ° is often used in place of the word *degrees.* The measure of ∠*T* (shown above) is 30 degrees, or 30°.

Sometimes there is confusion about which angle should be measured. The small curved arrow in each picture shows which angle opening should be measured.

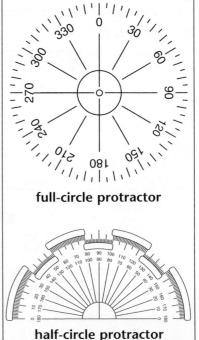

full-circle protractor

Measure of ∠A is 60°.

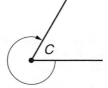

Measure of ∠B is 225°.

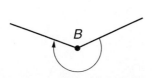

Measure of ∠C is 300°.

half-circle protractor

Classifying Angles

Angles may be classified according to size.

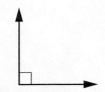

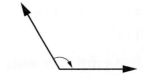

A **right angle**
measures 90°.

An **acute angle**
measures between
0° and 90°.

An **obtuse angle**
measures between
90° and 180°.

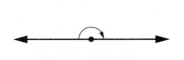

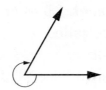

A **straight angle**
measures 180°.

A **reflex angle**
measures between
180° and 360°.

A **right angle** is an angle whose sides form a square corner.
You may draw a small corner symbol inside an angle to show
that it is a right angle.

A **straight angle** is an angle whose sides form one straight
path.

CHECK YOUR UNDERSTANDING

1. Draw a right angle.

2. Draw an obtuse angle.

3. Refer to the figure shown at the right.
   a. Which angles are right angles?
   b. Which angles are acute angles?
   c. Which angles are obtuse angles?
   d. Which angles are reflex angles?
   e. Which angles are straight angles?
   f. Give another name for ∠E.

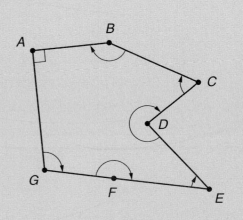

Check your answers on page 280.

Parallel Lines and Segments

Parallel lines are lines on a flat surface that never meet.
Think of a railroad track that goes on forever. The two rails are
parallel lines. The rails never meet or cross and they are always
the same distance apart.

Parallel line segments are segments that are always the same
distance apart. The top and bottom edges of this page are parallel
segments because they are always about 11 inches apart. The
symbol for *parallel* is a pair of vertical lines ∥. If $\overline{BF}$ and $\overline{TG}$ are
parallel, write $\overline{BF} \parallel \overline{TG}$.

If lines or segments cross each other, they **intersect.** Lines or
segments that intersect and form right angles are called
perpendicular lines or segments. The symbol for
perpendicular is ⊥, which looks like an upside-down letter T. If
$\overleftrightarrow{RS}$ and $\overleftrightarrow{XY}$ are perpendicular, write $\overleftrightarrow{RS} \perp \overleftrightarrow{XY}$.

EXAMPLES

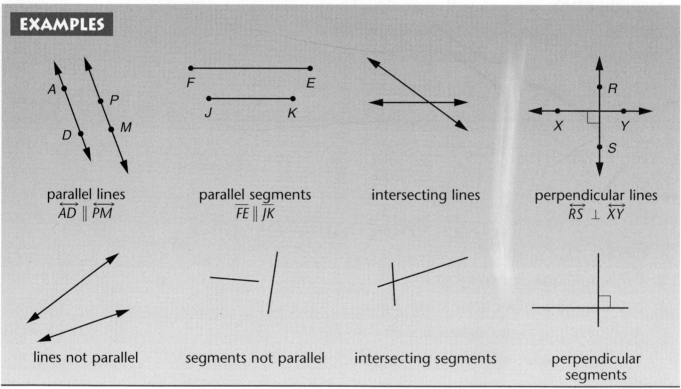

parallel lines
$\overleftrightarrow{AD} \parallel \overleftrightarrow{PM}$

parallel segments
$\overline{FE} \parallel \overline{JK}$

intersecting lines

perpendicular lines
$\overleftrightarrow{RS} \perp \overleftrightarrow{XY}$

lines not parallel

segments not parallel

intersecting segments

perpendicular
segments

CHECK YOUR UNDERSTANDING

Draw and label the following.

1. Parallel line segments AB and CD

2. A line segment that is perpendicular to
   both $\overline{AB}$ and $\overline{CD}$

Check your answers on page 280.

Line Segments, Rays, Lines, and Angles

Figure	Name or Symbol	Description
•A	A	**point:** A location in space.
F E endpoints	$\overline{EF}$ or $\overline{FE}$	**line segment:** A straight path between 2 points, called its endpoints.
N M endpoint	$\overrightarrow{MN}$	**ray:** A straight path that goes on forever in one direction from an endpoint.
R P	$\overleftrightarrow{PR}$ or $\overleftrightarrow{RP}$	**line:** A straight path that goes on forever in both directions.
vertex S T P	$\angle T$ or $\angle STP$ or $\angle PTS$	**angle:** Two rays or line segments with a common endpoint called the vertex.
B A S R	$\overleftrightarrow{AB} \parallel \overleftrightarrow{RS}$	**parallel lines:** Lines that never meet and are everywhere the same distance apart.
	$\overline{AB} \parallel \overline{RS}$	**parallel line segments:** Segments that are everywhere the same distance apart.
R E D S	none	**intersecting lines:** Lines that meet.
	none	**intersecting line segments:** Segments that meet.
B R S C	$\overleftrightarrow{BC} \perp \overleftrightarrow{RS}$	**perpendicular lines:** Lines that intersect at right angles.
	$\overline{BC} \perp \overline{RS}$	**perpendicular line segments:** Segments that intersect at right angles.

CHECK YOUR UNDERSTANDING

Draw and label each of the following.

1. point D **2.** $\overleftrightarrow{GH}$ **3.** $\angle BEN$ **4.** $\overline{QR}$ **5.** $\overleftrightarrow{XY} \parallel \overleftrightarrow{JK}$ **6.** $\overrightarrow{NO}$

Check your answers on page 280.

Polygons

A **polygon** is a flat, 2-dimensional figure made up of line segments called **sides.** A polygon can have any number of sides, as long as it has at least three.

- The sides of a polygon are connected end-to-end and make a closed path.
- The sides of a polygon do not cross (intersect).

Each endpoint where two sides meet is called a **vertex.** The plural of the word *vertex* is **vertices.**

Figures that Are Polygons

4 sides, 4 vertices   3 sides, 3 vertices   7 sides, 7 vertices

Figures that Are NOT Polygons

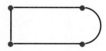 

All sides of a polygon must be line segments. Curved lines are not line segments.

The sides of a polygon must form a closed path.

A polygon must have at least 3 sides.

The sides of a polygon must not cross.

Polygons are named after their number of sides. The prefix for a polygon's name tells the number of sides it has.

Prefixes

tri-	3
quad-	4
penta-	5
hexa-	6
hepta-	7
octa-	8
nona-	9
deca-	10
dodeca-	12

Convex Polygons

A **convex** polygon is a polygon in which all the sides are pushed outward. The polygons below are convex.

triangle

quadrangle
(or quadrilateral)

pentagon

hexagon

heptagon

octagon

nonagon

decagon

Nonconvex (Concave) Polygons

A **nonconvex**, or **concave**, polygon is a polygon in which at least two sides are pushed in. The four polygons at the right are nonconvex.

quadrangle (or   hexagon
quadrilateral)

Regular Polygons

A polygon is a **regular polygon** if
- the sides all have the same length, and
- the angles are all the same size.

pentagon   octagon

equilateral triangle

square

pentagon

hexagon

octagon

nonagon

These are regular polygons. Regular polygons are always convex.

CHECK YOUR UNDERSTANDING

1. What is the name of a polygon having
   a. 4 sides?   **b.** 6 sides?   **c.** 8 sides?

2. a. Draw a convex hexagon.   **b.** Draw a concave octagon.

3. Explain why the cover of this book is not a regular polygon.

Check your answers on page 280.

Triangles

Triangles are the simplest type of polygon. The prefix *tri-* means *three*. All triangles have 3 vertices, 3 sides, and 3 angles.

For the triangle shown here:

B

side

vertex

Angle *A* is formed by sides that meet at vertex *A*.

A

C

• The vertices are the points *B*, *C*, and *A*.

• The sides are $\overline{BC}$, $\overline{BA}$, and $\overline{CA}$.

• The angles are ∠*B*, ∠*C*, and ∠*A*.

Triangles have 3-letter names. You name a triangle by listing the letter names for the vertices, in order. The triangle above has 6 possible names: triangle *BCA*, *BAC*, *CAB*, *CBA*, *ABC*, or *ACB*.

Triangles have many different sizes and shapes. You will work with two types of triangles that have been given special names.

An **equilateral triangle** is a triangle whose three sides all have the same length. Equilateral triangles have many different sizes, but all equilateral triangles have the same shape.

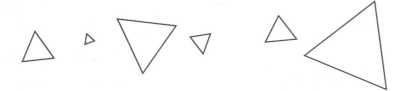

A **right triangle** is a triangle with one right angle (square corner). Right triangles have many different shapes and sizes.

A right triangle cannot be an equilateral triangle because the side opposite the right angle is always longer than each of the other sides.

CHECK YOUR UNDERSTANDING

1. a. Draw and label an equilateral triangle named *SAC*.

  b. Write the five other possible names for this triangle.

2. Draw a right triangle with two sides that are the same length.

Check your answers on page 280.

Quadrangles

A **quadrangle** is a polygon that has 4 sides. Another name for quadrangle is **quadrilateral.** The prefix *quad-* means *four*. All quadrangles have 4 vertices, 4 sides, and 4 angles.

For the quadrangle shown here:

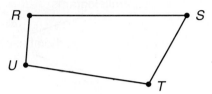

- The sides are $\overline{RS}$, $\overline{ST}$, $\overline{TU}$, and $\overline{UR}$.

- The vertices are *R*, *S*, *T*, and *U*.

- The angles are $\angle R$, $\angle S$, $\angle T$, and $\angle U$.

A quadrangle is named by listing in order the letter names for the vertices. The quadrangle above has 8 possible names:

RSTU, RUTS, STUR, SRUT, TURS, TSRU, URST, UTSR

Some quadrangles have two pairs of parallel sides. These quadrangles are called **parallelograms.**

Reminder: Two sides are parallel if they are everywhere the same distance apart.

Figures that Are Parallelograms

    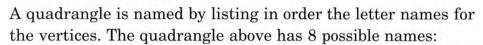

Opposite sides are parallel in each figure.

Figures that Are NOT Parallelograms

 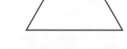 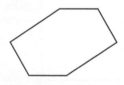

No parallel sides.

Only 1 pair of parallel sides.

3 pairs of parallel sides. A parallelogram must have exactly 2 pairs of parallel sides.

Many special types of quadrangles have been given names. Some of these are parallelograms; others are not parallelograms. See the table on the next page for examples of each type.

The tree diagram below shows how the types of quadrangles are related. For example, quadrangles are divided into two major groups—"parallelograms" and "not parallelograms."

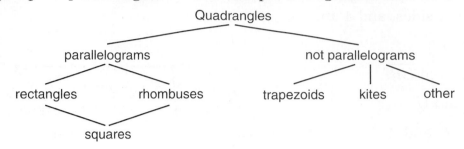

Quadrangles that Are Parallelograms

rectangle		**Rectangles** are parallelograms. A rectangle has 4 right angles (square corners). The sides do not all have to be the same length.
rhombus		**Rhombuses** are parallelograms. A rhombus has 4 sides that are all the same length. The angles of a rhombus are usually not right angles, but they may be.
square		**Squares** are parallelograms. A square has 4 right angles (square corners). Its 4 sides are all the same length. All squares are rectangles. All squares are also rhombuses.

Quadrangles that Are NOT Parallelograms

trapezoid		**Trapezoids** have exactly 1 pair of parallel sides. The 4 sides of a trapezoid can all have different lengths.
kite		A **kite** is a quadrangle with 2 pairs of equal sides. The equal sides are next to each other. The 4 sides cannot all have the same length. (A rhombus is not a kite.)
other		Any closed figure with 4 sides that is not a parallelogram, a trapezoid, or a kite.

CHECK YOUR UNDERSTANDING

What is the difference between the quadrangles in each pair below?

1. a square and a rectangle **2.** a kite and a rhombus **3.** a trapezoid and a parallelogram

Check your answers on pages 280 and 281.

Geometric Solids

Polygons and circles are flat, **2-dimensional** figures. The surfaces they enclose take up a certain amount of area, but they do not have any thickness and do not take up any volume. **Three-dimensional** shapes have length, width, *and* thickness. They take up volume. Boxes, pails, books, and balls are all examples of 3-dimensional shapes.

A **geometric solid** is the surface or surfaces that surround a 3-dimensional shape. The surfaces of a geometric solid may be flat or curved or both. A **flat surface** of a solid is called a **face**. A **curved surface** of a solid does not have any special name.

A **cube** has 6 square faces that are the same size. Three of the cube's faces cannot be seen in the figure at the right.

A **cylinder** has 3 surfaces. The flat top and flat bottom are faces and are formed by circles. A curved surface connects the top and bottom faces. A food can is a good model of a cylinder.

A **cone** has 2 surfaces. The flat bottom is a face that is formed by a circle. A curved surface is connected to the bottom face and comes to a point. An ice cream cone is a good model of a cone. However, keep in mind that a cone is closed; it has a "lid."

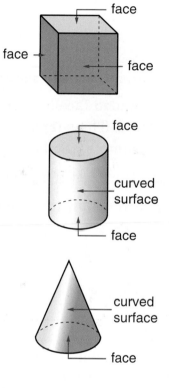

The **edges** of a geometric solid are the line segments or curves where surfaces meet. A corner of a geometric solid is called a **vertex** (plural *vertices*). A vertex is usually a point at which edges meet, but the vertex of a cone is an isolated corner. It is completely separated from the edge of the cone.

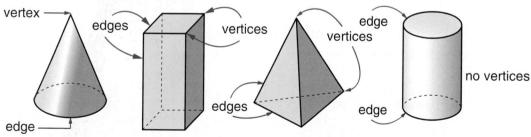

A **sphere** has one curved surface but no edges and no vertices. A basketball or globe is a good model of a sphere.

no edges, no vertices

CHECK YOUR UNDERSTANDING

1. a. How are cylinders and cones alike?   **b.** How do they differ?

2. a. How are spheres and cones alike?   **b.** How do they differ?

Check your answers on page 281.

Polyhedrons

A **polyhedron** is a geometric solid whose surfaces are all formed by polygons. These surfaces are the faces of the polyhedron. A polyhedron does not have any curved surfaces.

Pyramids and **prisms** are two important kinds of polyhedrons.

All of the following polyhedrons are pyramids.

   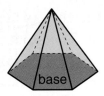

triangular pyramid   square pyramid   pentagonal pyramid   hexagonal pyramid

The shaded face of each of these pyramids is called the **base** of the pyramid. The shape of the base is used to name the pyramid. For example, the base of a triangular pyramid has a triangular shape.

All of the faces of a pyramid that are not a base meet at the same vertex.

All of the following polyhedrons are prisms.

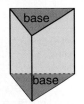 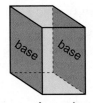 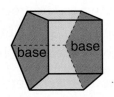 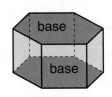

triangular prism   rectangular prism   pentagonal prism   hexagonal prism

The two shaded faces of each prism are called the **bases** of the prism. The bases of a prism are the same size and shape. They are parallel.

The shape of the bases of a prism are used to name the prism. For example, the bases of a pentagonal prism have the shape of a pentagon.

Many polyhedrons are not pyramids or prisms. Some are illustrated below.

Polyhedrons that Are NOT Pyramids or Prisms

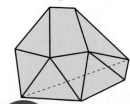 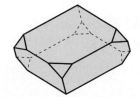 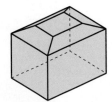

Regular Polyhedrons

A polyhedron is **regular** if:

• Each face is formed by a regular polygon.
• The faces all have the same size and shape.
• Every vertex looks exactly the same as every other vertex.

There are only five kinds of regular polyhedrons.

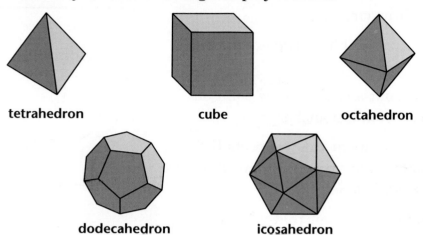

tetrahedron   cube   octahedron

dodecahedron   icosahedron

Name	Shape of face	Number of faces
tetrahedron	equilateral triangle	4
cube	square	6
octahedron	equilateral triangle	8
dodecahedron	regular pentagon	12
icosahedron	equilateral triangle	20

CHECK YOUR UNDERSTANDING

1. **a.** How many faces does a rectangular pyramid have?

   b. How many faces have a rectangular shape?

2. **a.** How many faces does a rectangular prism have?

   b. How many faces have a rectangular shape?

3. Which solid has more faces, a triangular pyramid or a triangular prism?

4. Which regular polyhedrons have faces that are formed by equilateral triangles?

5. **a.** How many edges does an octahedron have?

   b. How many vertices?

6. **a.** How are tetrahedrons and octahedrons alike?

   b. How are they different?

Check your answers on page 281.

Circles and Spheres

A **circle** is a curved line that forms a closed path on a flat surface. All of the points on a circle are the same distance from the **center of the circle.**

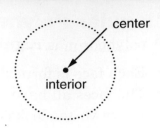

The center is not part of the circle. The interior is not part of the circle.

The **compass** is a tool used to draw circles.

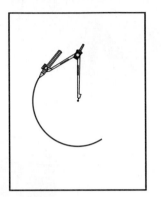

- The point of a compass, called the **anchor,** is placed at the center of the circle.

- The pencil in a compass traces out a circle. Every point on the circle is the same distance from the anchor.

The **radius** of a circle is any line segment that connects the center of the circle with any point on the circle. The word *radius* can also refer to the length of this segment.

The **diameter** of a circle is any line segment that passes through the center of the circle and has both of its endpoints on the circle. The word *diameter* can also refer to the length of this segment.

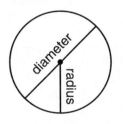

A **sphere** is a geometric solid that has a single curved surface. Spheres are shaped like basketballs or globes. All of the points on the surface of the sphere are the same distance from the **center of the sphere.**

All spheres have the same shape, but all spheres do not have the same size. The size of a sphere is the distance across its center.

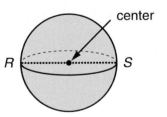

- The line segment *RS* passes through the center of the sphere. This line segment is called the **diameter of the sphere.**

- The length of the line segment *RS* is also called the diameter of the sphere.

Globes and basketballs are examples of spheres that are hollow. Their interiors are empty. The hollow interior is not part of the sphere. The sphere includes only the points on its curved surface.

Marbles and baseballs are examples of spheres that have solid interiors. In cases like these, think of the solid interior as part of the sphere.

Congruent Figures

Sometimes figures have the same shape and size. These figures are **congruent.** Figures are congruent if they match exactly when one figure is placed on top of the other.

EXAMPLE   Line segments are congruent if they have the same length.

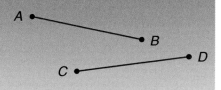

$\overline{AB}$ and $\overline{CD}$ are both 3 centimeters long. They have the same shape and the same length. These line segments are congruent.

EXAMPLE   Angles are congruent if they have the same degree measure.

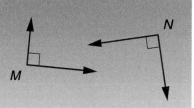

$\angle M$ and $\angle N$ are both right angles. They have the same shape, and they each measure 90°. The angle openings match exactly when one angle is placed on top of the other.

EXAMPLE   Circles are congruent if their diameters are the same length.

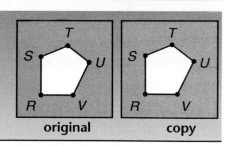

The circles here have $\frac{1}{2}$-inch diameters. They have the same shape and the same size. The three circles are congruent.

EXAMPLE   A copy machine was used to copy the pentagon *RSTUV*.

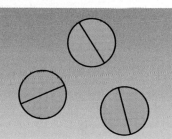

original   copy

If you cut out the copy, it will match exactly when placed on top of the original. The sides will match exactly. All the angles will match exactly. The original figure and the copy are congruent.

CHECK YOUR UNDERSTANDING

Which of these methods could you use to make a congruent copy of the square below?

a. Use a copy machine to copy the square.

b. Use tracing paper and trace over the square.

c. Cut out the square and trace around it.

d. Measure the sides with a ruler, then draw the sides at right angles to each other using a protractor.

Check your answers on page 281.

Reflections, Translations, and Rotations

In geometry, a figure can be moved from one place to another.
Three different ways to move a figure are shown below.

- A **reflection** moves a figure by "flipping" it over a line.
- A **translation** moves a figure by "sliding" it to a new
  location.
- A **rotation** moves a figure by "turning" it around a point.

reflection	translation	rotation
Flip the **F.**	Slide the **F.**	Turn the **F.**

The original figure, before it has been moved, is called the
preimage. The new figure produced by the move is called the
image.

Each point of the original figure is moved to a new point called
its **matching point.**

For each of the moves shown above, the original figure and the
final figure have the same size and shape.

Reflections

A reflection is a "flipping" motion of a figure. The line that
the figure is flipped over is called the **line of reflection.**
The figure and its reflection are on opposite sides of the
line of reflection.

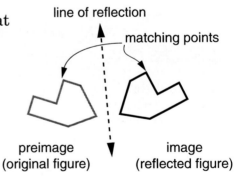

line of reflection

matching points

preimage
(original figure)

image
(reflected figure)

For any reflection:

- The figure and its reflection have the same size
  and shape.

- The figure and its reflection are reversed.

- Each point and the point it moves to (its matching point) are
  the same distance from the line of reflection.

Translations

A translation is a "sliding" motion of a figure. Each point of the figure slides the same distance in the same direction. Imagine a drawing of the letter T on grid paper.

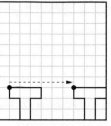

horizontal translation

- If each point of the letter T slides 6 grid squares to the right, the result is a *horizontal translation*.

- If each point of the letter T slides 8 grid squares upward, the result is a *vertical translation*.

- Suppose that each point of the letter T slides 6 grid squares to the right, then 8 grid squares upward. The result is the same as a *diagonal translation*.

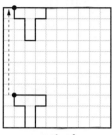

vertical translation

Rotations

When a figure is rotated, it is turned a certain number of degrees around a particular point.

A figure can be rotated *clockwise* (the direction that clock hands move). A figure can also be rotated *counterclockwise* (the opposite direction of the way clock hands move).

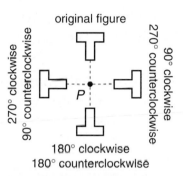

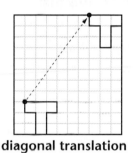

diagonal translation

CHECK YOUR UNDERSTANDING

1. Copy the figure and reflect it over $\overleftrightarrow{AB}$.

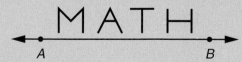

2. Which figure is a 90° clockwise rotation of 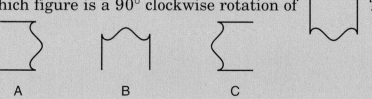 ?

Check your answers on page 281.

Frieze Patterns

A frieze pattern is a design made of shapes that are lined up. Frieze patterns are often found on the walls of buildings, on the borders of rugs and tiled floors, and on clothing.

In many frieze patterns, the same design is reflected over and over. For example, the following frieze pattern was used to decorate a sash worn by a Mazahua woman from San Felipe Santiago in the state of New Mexico. The strange-looking beasts in the frieze are probably meant to be horses.

Some frieze patterns are made by repeating (translating) the same design instead of reflecting it. These patterns look as if they were made by sliding the design along the strip. An example of such a frieze pattern is the elephant and horse design below that was found on a woman's sarong from Sumba, Indonesia. All the elephants and horses are facing in the same direction.

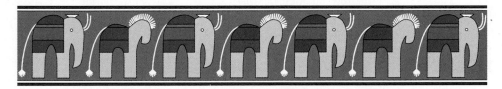

The following frieze pattern is similar to one painted on the front page of a Koran in Egypt about 600 years ago. (The Koran is the sacred book of Islam.) The pattern is more complicated than the two above. It was created with a combination of reflections, rotations, and translations.

Line Symmetry

A dashed line is drawn through the figure at the right. The line divides the figure into two parts. Both parts look exactly alike but are facing in opposite directions.

The figure is **symmetric about a line.** The dashed line is called a **line of symmetry** for the figure.

You can use a reflection to get the figure shown at the right.

• Think of the line of symmetry as a line of reflection.
• Reflect the left side of the figure over the line.
• Together, the left side and its reflection (the right side) form the figure.

An easy way to check whether a figure has *line symmetry* is to fold it in half. If the two halves match exactly, the figure is symmetric. The fold line is the line of symmetry.

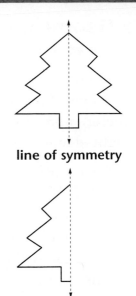

line of symmetry

Reflect the left side to get the figure above.

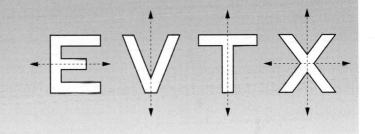

EXAMPLES The letters E, V, T, and X are symmetric. The lines of symmetry are drawn for each letter.

The letter X has two lines of symmetry. If you could fold along either line, the two halves would match exactly.

The figures below are all symmetric. The line of symmetry is drawn for each figure. If there is more than one line of symmetry, they are all drawn.

flag of Jamaica

butterfly

human body

ellipse

rectangle

square

CHECK YOUR UNDERSTANDING

1. Trace each pattern-block (PB) shape on your Geometry Template onto a sheet of paper. Draw the lines of symmetry for each shape.

2. How many lines of symmetry does a circle have?

Check your answers on page 281.

The Geometry Template

The **Geometry Template** has many uses.

The template has two rulers. The inch scale measures in inches and fractions of an inch. The centimeter scale measures in centimeters and millimeters. Use either side of the template as a straightedge for drawing line segments.

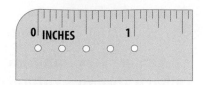

There are 17 different geometric figures on the template. The figures labeled "PB" are **pattern-block shapes.** These are half the size of actual pattern blocks. There is a hexagon, a trapezoid, two different rhombuses, an equilateral triangle, and a square. These will come in handy for some of the activities you do this year.

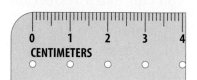

Each triangle on the template is labeled with the letter T and a number. Triangle "T1" is an equilateral triangle whose sides all have the same length. Triangles "T2" and "T5" are right triangles. Triangle "T3" is a triangle whose sides all have different lengths. Triangle "T4" is a triangle that has two sides of the same length.

The remaining shapes are circles, squares, a regular octagon, a regular pentagon, a kite, a rectangle, a parallelogram, and an ellipse.

The two circles near the inch scale can be used as ring-binder holes. Use these to store your template in your notebook.

Use the **half-circle** and **full-circle protractors** at the bottom of the template to measure and draw angles. You will construct and measure circle graphs in *Fifth Grade Everyday Mathematics* with the **Percent Circle** (at the top of the template).

Notice the tiny holes near the 0-, $\frac{1}{4}$-, $\frac{2}{4}$-, and $\frac{3}{4}$-inch marks of the inch scale and at each inch mark from 1 to 7. On the centimeter side, the holes are placed at each centimeter mark from 0 to 10. These holes can be used to draw circles.

EXAMPLE   Draw a circle with a 4-inch radius.

Place one pencil point in the hole at 0. Place another pencil point in the hole at 4 inches. Hold the pencil at 0 inches steady while rotating the pencil at 4 inches (along with the template) to draw the circle.

Hold this
pencil steady.

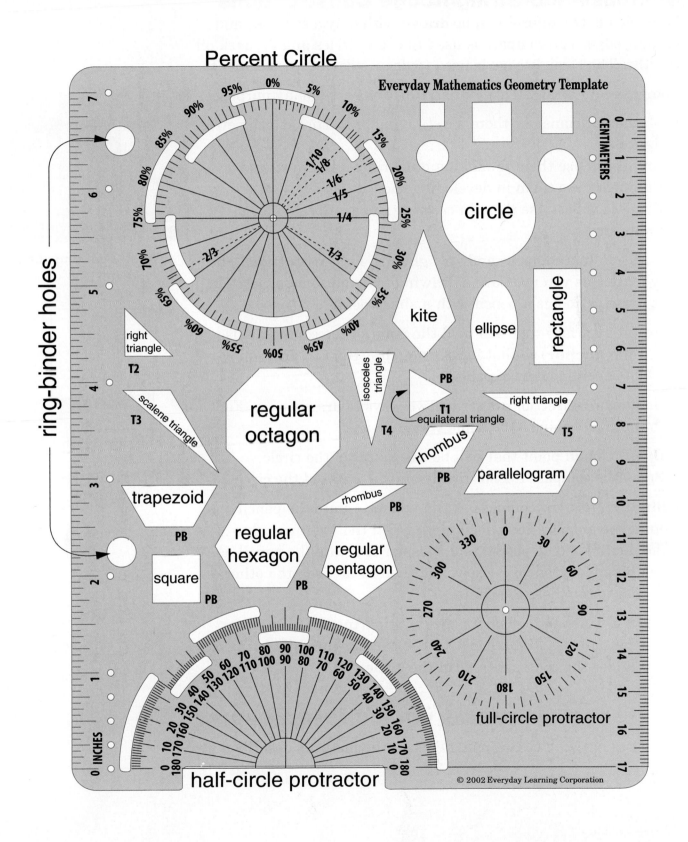

Percent Circle

Everyday Mathematics Geometry Template

ring-binder holes

circle

rectangle

kite

ellipse

right triangle
T2

scalene triangle
T3

isosceles triangle
T4

right triangle
T5

equilateral triangle
T1
PB

regular octagon

rhombus
PB

parallelogram

rhombus
PB

trapezoid
PB

regular hexagon
PB

regular pentagon
PB

square
PB

full-circle protractor

half-circle protractor

CENTIMETERS

INCHES

© 2002 Everyday Learning Corporation

Compass-and-Straightedge Constructions

Many geometric figures can be drawn with only a compass and straightedge. The compass is used to draw circles and to mark off lengths. The straightedge is used to draw straight line segments.

Compass-and-straightedge **constructions** serve many purposes.

- Mathematicians use them for studying properties of geometric figures.
- Architects use them in making blueprints and drawings.
- Engineers use them in developing their designs.
- Graphic artists use them in creating illustrations on a computer.

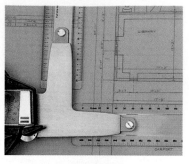

Architect's drawing of a house plan

In addition to a compass and straightedge for constructions, the only materials you need are a drawing tool and some paper. The best drawing tool is a pencil with a sharp point.

Draw on a surface that will hold the point of the compass (also called the **anchor**) so that it does not slip. You can draw on a stack of several sheets of paper.

The following directions describe two ways to draw circles. For each method, begin in the same way.

Method 1

- Draw a small point that will be the center of the circle.
- Press the compass anchor firmly on the center of the circle.

Method 1 Hold the compass at the top and rotate the pencil around the anchor. The pencil must go all the way around to make a circle. Some people find it easier to rotate the pencil as far as possible in one direction, and then rotate it in the other direction to complete the circle.

Method 2 This method works best with partners. One partner holds the compass in place. The other partner carefully turns the paper under the compass to form the circle.

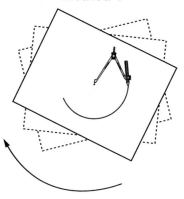

Method 2

CHECK YOUR UNDERSTANDING

Practice drawing circles using each of the methods described above.

Copying a Line Segment

Follow each step carefully. Use a clean sheet of paper.

Step 1: Draw line segment *AB*.

Step 2: Draw a second line segment. It should be longer than segment *AB*. Label one of its endpoints *C*.

Step 3: Place the compass anchor at *A* and the pencil point at *B*.

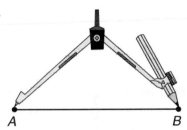

Step 4: Without changing your compass opening, place the compass anchor on *C* and draw a small arc that crosses the line segment. Label the point where the arc crosses the line segment point *D*.

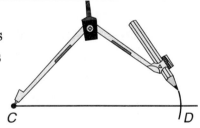

Line segment *CD* should be the same length as line segment *AB*.

Line segment CD is **congruent** to line segment *AB*.

CHECK YOUR UNDERSTANDING

1. Draw a line segment. Using a compass and straightedge only, copy the line segment.

2. After you have made your copy, measure the segments with a ruler to see how accurately you copied the original line segment.

Constructing a Parallelogram

Follow each step carefully. Use a clean sheet of paper.

Step 1: Draw an angle and label it *ABC*.

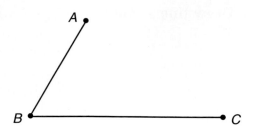

Step 2: Place the compass anchor at *B* and the pencil point at *C*. Without changing your compass opening, place the compass anchor on point *A* and draw an arc.

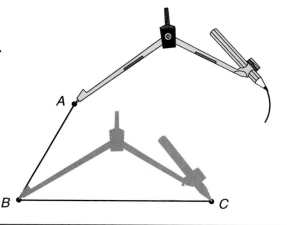

Step 3: Place the compass anchor at *B* and the pencil point at *A*. Without changing your compass opening, place the compass anchor on point *C* and draw another arc that crosses the first arc. Label the point where the two arcs cross point *D*.

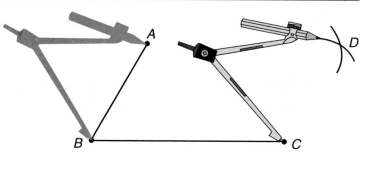

Step 4: Draw line segments *AD* and *CD*.

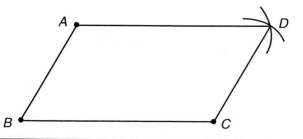

CHECK YOUR UNDERSTANDING

Use a compass and straightedge to construct a parallelogram.

Constructing a Regular Inscribed Hexagon

Follow each step carefully. Use a clean sheet of paper.

Step 1: Draw a circle and keep the same compass opening. Make a dot on the circle. Place the compass anchor on the dot and make a mark with the pencil point on the circle. Keep the same compass opening for Steps 2 and 3.

Step 2: Place the compass anchor on the mark you just made. Make another mark with the pencil point on the circle.

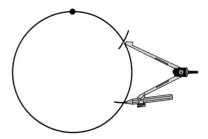

Step 3: Do this four more times to divide the circle into 6 equal parts. The 6th mark should be on the dot you started with or very close to it.

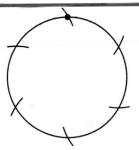

Step 4: With your straightedge, connect the 6 marks on the circle to form a regular hexagon.

Use your compass to check that the sides of the hexagon are all the same length.

The hexagon is **inscribed** in the circle because each vertex of the hexagon is on the circle.

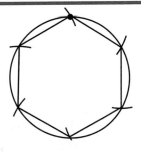

CHECK YOUR UNDERSTANDING

1. Draw a circle. Using a compass and straightedge, construct a regular hexagon that is inscribed in the circle.

2. Draw a line segment from the center of the circle to each vertex of the hexagon to form 6 triangles. Use your compass to check that the sides of each triangle are the same length

Constructing an Inscribed Square

Follow the directions below to make an inscribed square.

A square is **inscribed** in a circle if all the vertices of the square are *on* the circle.

Step 1: Use your compass to draw a circle on a sheet of paper. Cut it out.

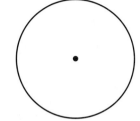

With your pencil, make a dot in the center of the circle where the hole from the compass is. Mark on both the front and the back of the circle.

Step 2: Fold the circle in half. Make sure the edges match and the fold line passes through the center.

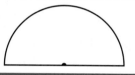

Step 3: Fold the circle in half again so that the edges match.

Step 4: Unfold your circle. The folds should pass through the center of the circle and form four right angles.

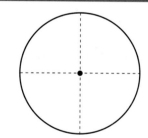

Step 5: Connect the endpoints of the folds with a straightedge to make a square that is inscribed in the circle.

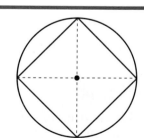

CHECK YOUR UNDERSTANDING

Construct a square inscribed in a circle.

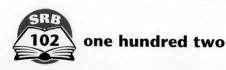

Constructing a Perpendicular Line Segment (Part 1)

You can construct a line segment that is perpendicular to another line segment through a point *on* the line segment.

Follow each step carefully. Use a clean sheet of paper.

Step 1: Draw line segment AB. Make a dot on $\overline{AB}$, and label it point P.

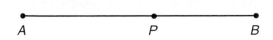

Step 2: Place the compass anchor on P, and draw an arc that crosses $\overline{AB}$ at point C.

Keeping the compass anchor on point P and the same compass opening, draw another arc that crosses $\overline{AB}$ at point D.

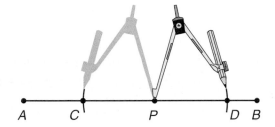

Step 3: Make sure the compass opening is greater than the length of $\overline{CP}$. Place the compass anchor on point C and draw an arc above $\overline{AB}$.

Keeping the same compass opening, place the compass anchor on point D and draw another arc above $\overline{AB}$ that crosses the first arc.

Label the point where the two arcs cross point Q.

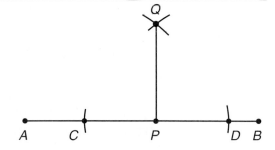

Step 4: Draw $\overline{QP}$.

$\overline{QP}$ is **perpendicular** to $\overline{AB}$.

CHECK YOUR UNDERSTANDING

Draw a line segment. Draw a point on the segment and label it point R.

Use a compass and straightedge. Construct a line segment through point R that is perpendicular to the segment you drew.

Use a protractor to check that the segments are perpendicular.

Constructing a Perpendicular Line Segment (Part 2)

You can construct a line segment perpendicular to another line segment from a point *not on* the line segment.

Follow each step carefully. Use a clean sheet of paper.

Step 1: Draw line segment *PQ*.

Draw a point *M* not on $\overline{PQ}$.

Step 2: Place the compass anchor on point *M* and draw an arc that crosses $\overline{PQ}$ at two points.

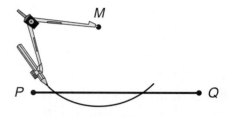

Step 3: Place the compass anchor on one of the points and draw an arc below $\overline{PQ}$.

Step 4: Keeping the same compass opening, place the compass anchor on the other point and draw another arc that crosses the first arc.

Label the point where the two arcs cross point *N*. Then draw the line segment *MN*.

$\overline{MN}$ is **perpendicular** to $\overline{PQ}$.

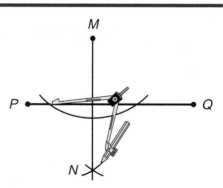

CHECK YOUR UNDERSTANDING

Draw a line segment *HI* and a point *G* above the line segment. Using a compass and straightedge, construct a line segment from point *G* that is perpendicular to $\overline{HI}$.

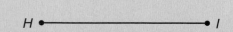

Measurement

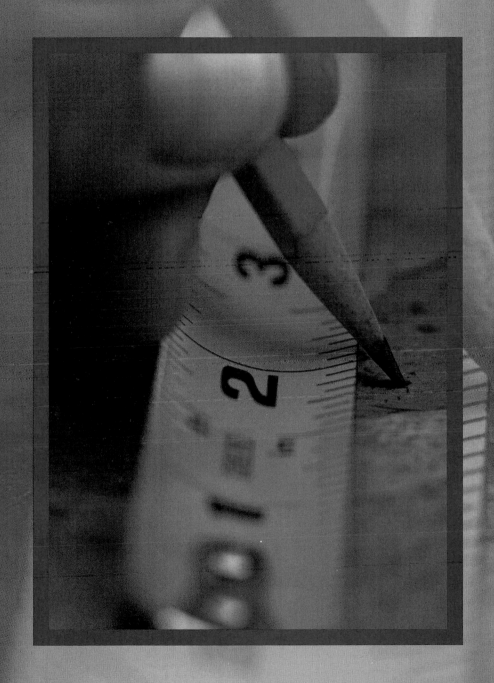

Natural Measures and Standard Units

Systems of weights and measures have been used in many parts of the world since ancient times. People measured lengths and weights long before they had rulers and scales.

Ancient Measures of Weight

Shells and grains, such as wheat or rice, were often used as units of weight. For example, a small item might be said to weigh 300 grains. Large weights were often compared to the load that could be carried by a man or a pack animal.

Ancient Measures of Length

People used **natural measures** based on the body to measure length and distance. Some of these units are shown below.

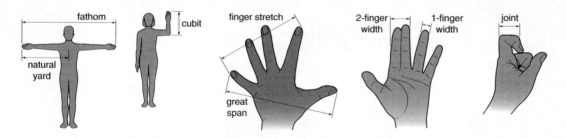

Standard Units of Length and Weight

Using shells and grains to measure weight is not exact. Even if the shells and grains are of the same type, they vary in size and weight.

Using body lengths to measure length is not exact. The body measures used depend upon the person who is doing the measuring. The problem is that different persons have hands and arms of different lengths.

One way to solve this problem is to make **standard units** of length and weight. Most rulers are marked off using inches and centimeters as standard units. Bath scales are marked off using pounds and kilograms as standard units. Standard units never change and are the same for everyone. If two people measure the same object using standard units, their measurements will be the same or almost the same.

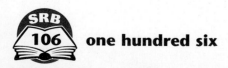

The Metric System and the U.S. Customary System

About 200 years ago, a system of weights and measures called the **metric system** was developed. The metric system uses standard units for length, weight, and temperature. In the metric system:

- The **meter** is the standard unit for length. The symbol for a meter is **m.** A meter is about the width of a front door.
- The **gram** is the standard unit for weight. The symbol for a gram is **g.** A paper clip weighs about $\frac{1}{2}$ gram.
- The **Celsius degree** or **°C** is the standard unit for temperature. Water freezes at 0°C and boils at 100°C. Room temperature is about 20°C.

Scientists almost always use the metric system to measure. It is easy to use because it is a base-ten system. Larger and smaller units are defined by multiplying or dividing the units given above by powers of ten—10, 100, 1000, and so on.

EXAMPLE All metric units of length are based on the meter. Each unit is defined by multiplying or dividing the meter by a power of 10.

Units of Length Based on the Meter

Units of Length Based on the Meter	Prefix	Meaning
1 decimeter (dm) = $\frac{1}{10}$ meter	deci-	$\frac{1}{10}$
1 centimeter (cm) = $\frac{1}{100}$ meter	centi-	$\frac{1}{100}$
1 millimeter (mm) = $\frac{1}{1,000}$ meter	milli-	$\frac{1}{1,000}$
1 kilometer (km) = 1,000 meters	kilo-	1,000

NOTE

The U.S. customary system is not based on powers of 10. This makes it more difficult to use than the metric system. For example, to change inches to yards, you must know that 36 inches equals 1 yard.

The metric system is used in most countries around the world. In the United States, the **U.S. customary system** is used for everyday purposes. The U.S. customary system uses standard units like the **inch, foot, yard, mile, ounce, pound,** and **ton.**

CHECK YOUR UNDERSTANDING

1. Which units in the list below are units in the metric system?

   foot   millimeter   pound   inch   gram   meter   centimeter   yard

2. What does the prefix "milli-" mean?   **3.** 5 meters = ? millimeters

Check your answers on page 281.

Length

Length is the measure of the distance between two points. Length is usually measured with a ruler. The edges of the Geometry Template are rulers. Tape measures, yardsticks, and meter sticks are rulers for measuring longer distances.

Part of a meter stick is shown here. The meter has been divided into smaller units—centimeters and millimeters.

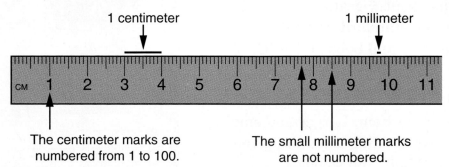

1 centimeter   1 millimeter

The centimeter marks are numbered from 1 to 100.

The small millimeter marks are not numbered.

On rulers, inches are usually divided into halves, quarters, eighths, and sixteenths. The marks to show different fractions of an inch are usually of different sizes.

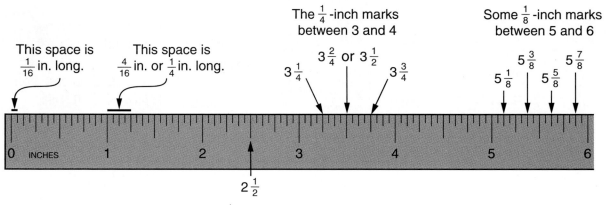

The $\frac{1}{4}$-inch marks between 3 and 4

Some $\frac{1}{8}$-inch marks between 5 and 6

This space is $\frac{1}{16}$ in. long.

This space is $\frac{4}{16}$ in. or $\frac{1}{4}$ in. long.

$3\frac{1}{4}$ $3\frac{2}{4}$ or $3\frac{1}{2}$ $3\frac{3}{4}$

$5\frac{1}{8}$ $5\frac{3}{8}$ $5\frac{5}{8}$ $5\frac{7}{8}$

$2\frac{1}{2}$

The $\frac{1}{2}$-inch mark between 2 and 3

CHECK YOUR UNDERSTANDING

Measure these line segments. Report each length in centimeters (cm) and in millimeters (mm).

1. —————————   2. ——————   3. ————————————

4. Measure each line segment above to the nearest quarter-inch.

Check your answers on page 281.

Converting Units of Length

The table below shows how different units of length in the metric system compare. You can use this table to rewrite a length using a different unit.

Comparing Metric Units of Length				Symbols for Units of Length	
1 cm = 10 mm	1 m = 1,000 mm	1 m = 100 cm	1 km = 1,000 m	mm = millimeter	cm = centimeter
1 mm = $\frac{1}{10}$ cm	1 mm = $\frac{1}{1,000}$ m	1 cm = $\frac{1}{100}$ m	1 m = $\frac{1}{1,000}$ km	m = meter	km = kilometer

EXAMPLES   Use the table above to rewrite each length using a different unit. Replace the unit given with an equal length that uses the new unit.

Problem	Solution
43 centimeters = ? millimeters	43 cm = 43 * 10 mm = 430 mm
43 centimeters = ? meters	43 cm = 43 * $\frac{1}{100}$ m = 0.43 m
6.4 kilometers = ? meters	6.4 km = 6.4 * 1,000 m = 6,400 m
7.3 meters = ? centimeters	7.3 m = 7.3 * 100 cm = 730 cm

The table below shows how different units of length in the U.S. customary system compare. You can use this table to rewrite a length using a different unit.

Comparing U.S. Customary Units of Length				Symbols for Units of Length	
1 ft = 12 in.	1 yd = 36 in.	1 yd. = 3 ft	1 ml. = 5,280 ft	in. = inch	ft = foot
1 in. = $\frac{1}{12}$ ft	1 in. = $\frac{1}{36}$ yd	1 ft = $\frac{1}{3}$ yd	1 ft = $\frac{1}{5,280}$ mi	yd = yard	mi = mile

EXAMPLES   Use the table to rewrite each length using a different unit. Replace the unit given with an equal length that uses the new unit.

Problem	Solution
6 feet = ? inches	6 ft = 6 * 12 in. = 72 in.
6 feet = ? yards	6 ft = 6 * $\frac{1}{3}$ yd = $\frac{6}{3}$ yd = 2 yd
3 miles = ? feet	3 mi = 3 * 5,280 ft = 15,840 ft
108 inches = ? yards	108 in. = 108 * $\frac{1}{36}$ yd = $\frac{108}{36}$ yd = 3 yd

Personal References for Units of Length

Sometimes it is hard to remember just how long a centimeter or a yard is, or how a kilometer and a mile compare. You may not have a ruler, yardstick, or tape measure handy. When this happens, you can estimate lengths by using the lengths of common objects and distances that you know.

Some examples of personal references for length are given below. A good personal reference is something that you see or use often, so you don't forget it. A good personal reference doesn't change size. For example, a wooden pencil is not a good personal reference for length, because it gets shorter as it is sharpened.

Personal References for Metric Units of Length

About 1 millimeter	**About 1 centimeter**
Thickness of a dime	Thickness of a crayon
Thickness of a thumbtack point	Width of the head of a thumbtack
Thickness of a paper match (the thin edge)	Thickness of a pattern block
About 1 meter	**About 1 kilometer**
One big step (for an adult)	1,000 big steps (for an adult)
Width of a front door	Length of 10 football fields
Tip of the nose to tip of the thumb, with arm extended (for an adult)	

Personal References for U.S. Customary Units of Length

About 1 inch	**About 1 foot**
Length of a paper clip	A man's shoe length
Width (diameter) of a quarter	Length of a license plate
Width of a man's thumb	Length of this book
About 1 yard	**About 1 mile**
One big step (for an adult)	2,000 average-size steps (for an adult)
Width of a front door	Length of 15 football fields (including the end zones)
Tip of the nose to tip of the thumb, with arm extended (for an adult)	

N O T E

The personal references for 1 meter can also be used for 1 yard.
1 yard = 36 inches;
1 meter is about 39.37 inches. One meter is often called a "fat yard," which means one yard plus one hand width.

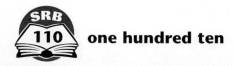

Perimeter

Sometimes we want to know the **distance around** a shape.
The distance around is called the **perimeter** of the shape. To
measure perimeter, we use units of length such as inches or
meters or miles.

> **EXAMPLE** Alex rode his bicycle once around the edge of a lake.
>
>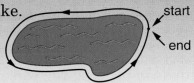
>
> The distance around the lake is 2.3 miles.
>
> The perimeter of the lake is 2.3 miles.

To find the perimeter of a polygon, add the lengths of its sides.
Remember to name the unit of length used to measure the shape.

> **EXAMPLE** Find the perimeter of polygon *ABCDE*.
>
> $3\text{ m} + 8\text{ m} + 5\text{ m} + 4\text{ m} + 10\text{ m} = 30\text{ m}$
>
>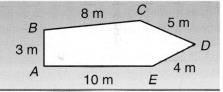
>
> The perimeter is 30 meters.

You can often use a shortcut to find a perimeter.

> **EXAMPLES** Find the perimeter of each polygon.
>
> **Rectangle**
>
> Add the length and width:
> $3\text{ cm} + 4\text{ cm} = 7\text{ cm}$
> Double this:
> $2 * 7\text{ cm} = 14\text{ cm}$
>
> The perimeter is 14 centimeters.
>
> **Square**
>
> All 4 sides have the same length.
> Multiply the length of one
> side by 4:
> $4 * 3\text{ ft} = 12\text{ ft}$
>
> The perimeter is 12 feet.

CHECK YOUR UNDERSTANDING

Find the perimeter.

1.

2.

3.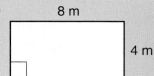

4. Measure the sides of this book to the nearest half-inch. What is the perimeter of the book?

Check your answers on page 281.

Circumference

The perimeter of a circle is the **distance around** the circle.

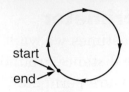

The perimeter of a circle has a special name. It is called the **circumference** of the circle.

The top of the can shown here is a circle. Its circumference can be measured with a tape measure. Wrap the tape measure once around the can. Then read the mark that touches the end of the tape. The circumference of the can's top is how far a can opener turns in opening the can.

The **diameter** of a circle is any line segment that passes through the center of the circle and has both endpoints on the circle. The length of a diameter segment is also called the diameter.

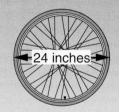

If you know the diameter, there is a simple rule for estimating the circumference:

Circumference Rule   The circumference of a circle is slightly more than three times the diameter of the circle.

EXAMPLE   The diameter of a bicycle wheel is 24 inches. Find the circumference of the wheel.

Use the Circumference Rule. The circumference is slightly more than 3 * 24 in., or 72 in. If the bicycle tire were cut and laid out flat, it would be slightly longer than 72 inches.

So, the circumference of the wheel is 72 inches.

CHECK YOUR UNDERSTANDING

1. Measure the diameter of the nickel, in millimeters.

2. Find the circumference of the nickel in millimeters.

3. What is the circumference of a pizza whose diameter is 12 inches?

Check your answers on page 281.

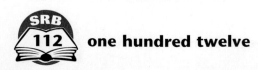

Area

Sometimes you want to know the amount of **surface inside** a shape. The amount of surface inside a shape is called its **area.**

You can find the area of a shape by counting the number of squares of a certain size that cover the shape. The squares must cover the entire shape and must not overlap, have any gaps, or cover any surface outside of the shape. Sometimes a shape cannot be covered by an exact number of squares. If this is so, count the number of whole squares and the fractions of squares that cover the shape.

EXAMPLE   What is the area of the rectangle?

The rectangle at the right is covered by squares that are 1 centimeter on each side. Each square is called a **square centimeter (cm²).**

Six of the squares cover the rectangle. The area of the rectangle is 6 square centimeters. This is written as 6 sq. cm, or 6 cm².

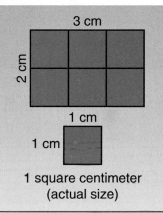

1 square centimeter (actual size)

There are many situations in which it is important to know the area.

- You may want to install carpeting in your living room. You need to find the area of the floor to figure out how much carpeting to buy. You would use **square yards (yd²)** in the United States and **square meters (m²)** in other parts of the world.
- Labels on cans of paint usually tell about how many **square feet (ft²)** of surface can be painted with the paint in that can. You may want to estimate how many gallons of paint to buy in order to paint the walls and ceilings of the rooms in your home. You need to find the total area of all the surfaces to be painted.
- In the "World Tour" section of this book, the size of each country you visit is given in **square miles.** This is useful when you want to compare the sizes of different countries.

Reminder: Be careful not to confuse the **area** of a shape with its **perimeter.** The **area** is the amount of surface *inside* the shape. The **perimeter** is the distance *around* the shape. Area is measured in units such as square inches, square feet, square centimeters, square meters, and square miles. Perimeter is measured in units such as inches, feet, centimeters, meters, and miles.

Area = 1 in.²
Perimeter = 4 in.

Area of Rectangles

When you cover a rectangular shape with unit squares, the squares can be arranged into rows. Each row contains the same number of squares and fractions of squares.

EXAMPLE Find the area of the rectangle.

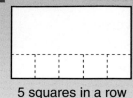

5 squares in a row   3 rows

3 rows with 5 squares in each row for a total of 15 squares.
Area = 15 square units

To find the area of a rectangle, use either formula below:

Area = (the number of squares in 1 row) * (the number of rows)
Area = length of a base * height

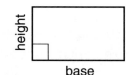

base

Either pair of parallel sides in a rectangle can be chosen as its **bases.** The **height** of a rectangle is the shortest distance between its bases.

Area Formulas

Rectangle	Square
$A = b * h$	$A = s^2$
A is the area, b is the length of a base, h is the height of the rectangle.	A is the area and s is the length of a side of the square.

EXAMPLES Find the area of the rectangle.

3 in.

4 in.

Use the formula $A = b * h$.
• length of base (b) = 4 in.
  height (h) = 3 in.
• area (A) = 4 in. * 3 in. = 12 in.^{2}

So, the area of the rectangle is 12 in.^{2}

Find the area of the square.

6 ft

Use the formula $A = s^2$.
• length of a side (s) = 6 ft
• area (A) = 6 ft * 6 ft = 36 ft^2

So, the area of the square is 36 ft.^{2}

CHECK YOUR UNDERSTANDING

Find the area of the following figures. Include the unit in your answers.

1. 3 units

2 units

2. 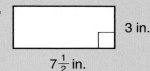 3 in.

$7\frac{1}{2}$ in.

3. 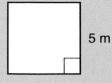 5 m

5 m

Check your answers on page 281.

Area of Parallelograms

In a parallelogram, either pair of opposite sides can be chosen as its **bases.** The **height** of the parallelogram is the shortest distance between the two bases.

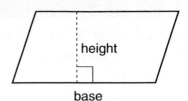

height

base

In the parallelograms at the right, the height is shown by a dashed line that is **perpendicular** (at a right angle) to the base. In the second parallelogram, the base has been extended and the dashed height falls outside the parallelogram.

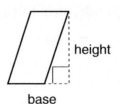

height

base

Any parallelogram can be cut into two pieces and the pieces rearranged to form a rectangle whose base and height are the same as the base and height of the parallelogram. The rectangle has the same area as the parallelogram. You can find the area of the parallelogram in the same way you find the area of the rectangle—by multiplying the length of the base by the height.

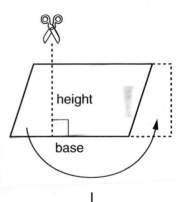

height

base

Formula for the Area of Parallelograms

$$A = b * h$$

A is the area, *b* is the length of the base, and *h* is the height of the parallelogram.

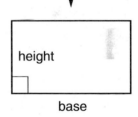

height

base

EXAMPLE Find the area of the parallelogram.

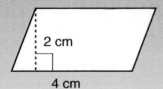

2 cm

4 cm

Use the formula $A = b * h$.
- length of base (*b*) = 4 cm
- height (*h*) = 2 cm
- area (*A*) = 4 cm * 2 cm
  $= 8 \text{ cm}^2$

So, the area of the parallelogram is 8 cm².

CHECK YOUR UNDERSTANDING

Find the area of each parallelogram. Include the unit in your answers.

1.
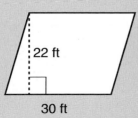
22 ft

30 ft

2.
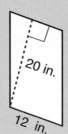
20 in.

12 in.

3.
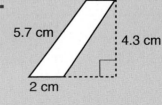
5.7 cm

4.3 cm

2 cm

Check your answers on page 281.

Area of Triangles

Any of the sides of a triangle can be chosen as its **base**. The **height** of the triangle (for that base) is the shortest distance between the base and the **vertex** opposite the base. The height is always perpendicular to the base.

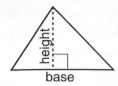 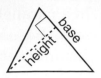

In the triangles at the right, the height is shown by a dashed line that is **perpendicular** (at a right angle) to the base. In one of the triangles, the base has been extended and the dashed height line falls outside the triangle.

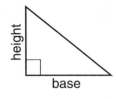 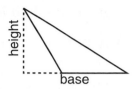

Any triangle can be combined with a second triangle of the same size and shape to form a parallelogram. Each triangle at the right has the same base and height as the parallelogram. The area of each triangle is half the area of the parallelogram. Therefore, the area of a triangle is half the product of the base multiplied by the height.

Area Formulas

Parallelograms	Triangles
$A = b * h$	$A = \frac{1}{2} * (b * h)$
A is the area, *b* is the length of a base, *h* is the height.	*A* is the area, *b* is the length of a base, *h* is the height.

EXAMPLE   Find the area of the triangle.

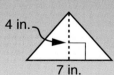

Use the formula $A = \frac{1}{2} * (b * h)$.
- length of base (b) = 7 in.
- height (h) = 4 in.
- area (A) $= \frac{1}{2} * (7 \text{ in.} * 4 \text{ in.})$
  $= \frac{1}{2} * 28 \text{ in.}^2 = 14 \text{ in.}^2$

So, the area of the triangle is 14 in.^{2}.

CHECK YOUR UNDERSTANDING

Find the area of each triangle. Include the unit in your answers.

1.
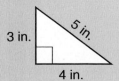

2.
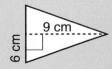

3.
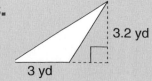

Check your answers on page 282.

Volume and Capacity
Volume

The **volume** of a solid object such as a brick or a ball is a measure of how much *space the object takes up*. The volume of a container such as a freezer is a measure of *how much the container will hold*.

Volume is measured in **cubic units.** A base-10 cube has sides that are 1 centimeter long; it is called a **cubic centimeter.**

A cube with 1-inch sides is called a **cubic inch.**

Other cubic units are used to measure large volumes. A **cubic foot** has 1-foot sides. A **cubic yard** has 1-yard sides and can hold 27 cubic feet. A **cubic meter** has 1-meter sides and can hold more than 35 cubic feet.

1 cubic centimeter
(actual size)

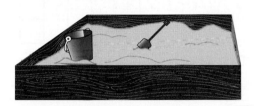

The volume of an object can be very useful to know. For example, suppose you wanted to buy sand to fill a sandbox. To estimate how much sand to buy, you would measure the length, width, and height of the empty sandbox. The length, width, and height are called the **dimensions** of the box. You would then use these dimensions to calculate how many cubic feet (or cubic yards) of sand to order. You could do similar calculations to determine how much concrete would be needed to build a patio, or how much gravel to buy for a path in the backyard.

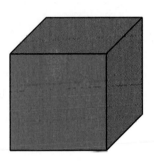

1 cubic inch
(actual size)

Capacity

We often measure things poured into or out of containers such as liquids, grains, salt, and so on. The volume of a container that is filled with a liquid or a solid that can be poured is often called its **capacity.**

Capacity is usually measured in units such as **gallons, quarts, pints, cups, fluid ounces, liters,** and **milliliters.** These are standard units, but they are not cubic units.

The tables at the right compare different units of capacity.

Metric Units

1 liter (L) = 1,000 milliliters (mL)
1 milliliter = $\frac{1}{1,000}$ liter

U.S. Customary Units

1 gallon (gal) = 4 quarts (qt)
1 gallon = 2 half-gallons
1 half-gallon = 2 quarts
1 quart = 2 pints (pt)
1 pint = 2 cups (c)
1 cup = 8 fluid ounces (fl oz)
1 pint = 16 fluid ounces
1 quart = 32 fluid ounces
1 half-gallon = 64 fluid ounces
1 gallon = 128 fluid ounces

Volume of Rectangular Prisms

A rectangular prism is a 3-dimensional shape that looks like a box. You can think of the volume of the prism as the total number of unit cubes needed to fill the interior of the prism. The size of the unit cube used will depend on the size of the prism for which you want to find the volume. For smaller prisms, you may use cubic centimeters or cubic inches; for larger prisms, you may use cubic feet, cubic yards, or cubic meters.

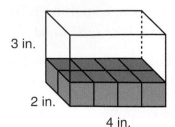

3 in.
2 in.
4 in.
8 cubes fill 1 layer

> **EXAMPLE** Find the volume of the prism at the right.
> length (l) = 4 in.; width (w) = 2 in.; height (h) = 3 in.
>
> Use cubic inches as the unit cubes. The cubes can be arranged in layers. There are 8 cubes in the bottom layer.
> There are 3 layers with 8 cubes in each layer for a total of 24 cubes.
> The volume is 24 cubic inches (24 in.^{3}).

You can find the volume of a prism without counting the number of unit cubes that fill it. If you know the dimensions of the prism, the formulas below can be used to calculate its volume.

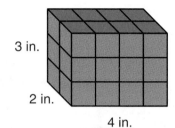

3 in.
2 in.
4 in.
3 layers filled

Volume of a Rectangular Prism

$$V = l * w * h \quad \text{or} \quad V = B * h$$

V is the volume of the prism.

l is the length of its base, w is the width of its base.

h is the height of the prism.

B is the area of its base.

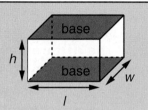

> **EXAMPLE** Use the formulas to find the volume of the prism.

| 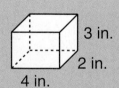 3 in. 2 in. 4 in. | Use the formula $V = l * w * h$
• length of base (l) = 4 in.
• width of base (w) = 2 in.
• height of prism (h) = 3 in.
• volume (V) =
 4 in. * 2 in. * 3 in. = 24 in.^{3} | Use the formula $V = B * h$
• area of base (B) = 8 in.^{2}
• height of prism (h) = 3 in.
• volume (V) =
 8 in.^{2} * 3 in. = 24 in.^{3} |

CHECK YOUR UNDERSTANDING

Find the volume.

1. A cube with sides 10 cm long.

2. A box whose bottom has an area of 180 in.^{2} The box's height is 11 in.

Check your answers on page 282.

Temperature

Temperature is a measure of the hotness or coldness of something. To read a temperature in degrees, you need a reference frame that begins with a zero point and has an interval for the scale. The two most commonly used temperature scales, Fahrenheit and Celsius, have different zero points.

Fahrenheit

This scale was invented in the early 1700s by the German physicist G.D. Fahrenheit. A salt-water solution freezes at 0°F (the zero point) at sea level. Pure water freezes at 32°F and boils at 212°F. The normal temperature for the human body is 98.6°F. The Fahrenheit scale is used primarily in the United States.

Celsius

This scale was developed in 1742 by the Swedish astronomer Anders Celsius. The zero point (0 degrees Celsius or 0°C) is the freezing point of pure water. Pure water boils at 100°C. The Celsius scale divides the interval between these two points into 100 equal parts. For this reason, it is sometimes called the *centigrade* scale. The normal temperature for the human body is 37°C. The Celsius scale is the standard for most people outside of the United States and for scientists everywhere.

A **thermometer** measures temperature. The common thermometer is a glass tube that contains a liquid. When the temperature goes up, the liquid expands and moves up the tube. When the temperature goes down, the liquid shrinks and moves down the tube.

Here are two formulas for converting from degrees Fahrenheit (°F) to degrees Celsius (°C) and vice versa:

$$C = \frac{5}{9} * (F - 32) \quad \text{and} \quad F = \frac{9}{5} * C + 32.$$

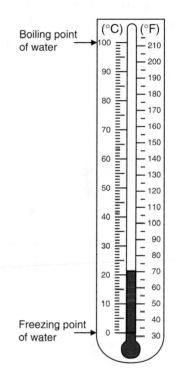

Boiling point of water → (°C) 100 (°F) 210

Freezing point of water → 0 / 30

The thermometer is marked to show both the Fahrenheit and Celsius scales. Key reference temperatures, such as the boiling and freezing points of water, are indicated. This thermometer shows a reading of 70°F (or about 21°C), which is normal room temperature.

EXAMPLE Find the Celsius equivalent of 82°F.

Use the formula $C = \frac{5}{9} * (F - 32)$ and replace F with 82°

$C = \frac{5}{9} * (82 - 32) = \frac{5}{9} * (50) = 27.77$

So, C is about 28°C.

Weight

Today, in the United States, two different sets of standard units are used to measure weight.

The suitcase weighs 14 pounds 6 ounces.

- The standard unit for weight in the metric system is the **gram.** A small, plastic base-10 cube weighs about 1 gram. Heavier weights are measured in **kilograms.** One kilogram equals 1,000 grams.

- Two standard units for weight in the U.S. customary system are the **ounce** and the **pound.** Heavier weights are measured in pounds. One pound equals 16 ounces. Some weights are reported in both pounds and ounces.

Metric Units	U.S. Customary Units
1 gram (g) = 1,000 milligrams (mg)	1 pound (lb) = 16 ounces (oz)
1 milligram = $\frac{1}{1,000}$ gram	1 ounce = $\frac{1}{16}$ pound
1 kilogram (kg) = 1,000 grams	1 ton (t) = 2,000 pounds
1 gram = $\frac{1}{1,000}$ kilogram	1 pound = $\frac{1}{2,000}$ ton
1 metric ton (t) = 1,000 kilograms	
1 kilogram = $\frac{1}{1,000}$ metric ton	

Rules of Thumb	Exact Equivalents
1 ounce equals about 30 grams	1 ounce = 28.35 grams
1 kilogram weighs about 2 pounds	1 kilogram = 2.205 pounds

EXAMPLE A bicycle weighs 14 kilograms. How many pounds is that?

Rough Solution: Use the Rule of Thumb. Since 1 kg equals about 2 lb, 14 kg weighs about 14 * 2 = 28 lb.

Exact Solution: Use the exact equivalent.
Since 1 kg = 2.205 lb, 14 kg = 14 * 2.205 = 30.87 lb.

> **NOTE**
>
> The "Rules of Thumb" table shows how units of weight in the metric system relate to units in the U.S. customary system. You can use this table to convert ounces to grams and kilograms to pounds. For most everyday purposes, you need only remember the simple Rules of Thumb.

CHECK YOUR UNDERSTANDING

Solve each problem.

1. A softball weighs 6 ounces. How many grams is that? Use a Rule of Thumb and an exact equivalent.

2. Andy's brother weighs 22 pounds 14 ounces. How many ounces is that?

Check your answers on page 282.

Measuring and Drawing Angles

Angles are measured in **degrees.** When writing the measure of an angle, a small raised circle (°) is used as a symbol for the word degree.

Angles are measured with a tool called a **protractor.** You will find both a full-circle and a half-circle protractor on your Geometry Template. Since there are 360 degrees in a circle, a 1° angle marks off $\frac{1}{360}$ of a circle.

The **full-circle protractor** on the Geometry Template is marked off in 5° intervals from 0° to 360°. It can be used to measure angles, but it *cannot* be used to draw angles of a given measure.

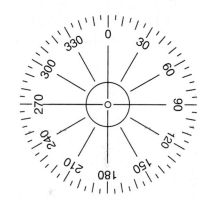

Sometimes you will use a full-circle protractor that is a paper cutout. This *can* be used to draw angles.

The **half-circle protractor** on the Geometry Template is marked off in 1° intervals from 0° to 180°.

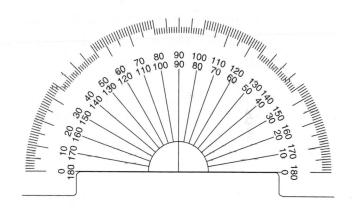

It has two scales, each of which starts at 0°. One scale is read clockwise, the other is read counterclockwise.

The half-circle protractor can be used both to measure and to draw angles of a given measure.

Two rays starting from the same endpoint form two angles. The smaller angle measures between 0° and 180°. The larger angle is called a **reflex angle**, and it measures between 180° and 360°. The sum of the measures of the smaller angle and the reflex angle is 360°.

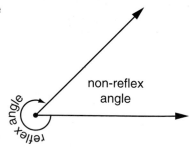

reflex angle

non-reflex angle

Measuring Angles with a Full-Circle Protractor

This is how to use the full-circle protractor to measure an angle.

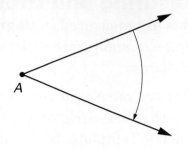

Step 1: Put the hole at the center of the protractor over the vertex of the angle.

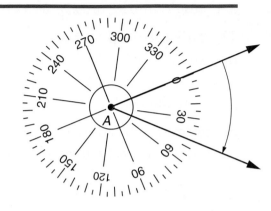

Step 2: Line up the 0° mark with the side of the angle so that you can measure the angle clockwise. Make sure that the hole stays over the vertex.

Step 3: Read the degree measure at the mark on the protractor that lines up with the second side of the angle. This is the measure of the angle.

The measure of ∠A is 45°.

CHECK YOUR UNDERSTANDING

Use your full-circle protractor to measure angles B and C.

1.

2.

∠B measures about _____°.   ∠C measures about _____°.

Check your answers on page 282.

Measuring Angles with a Half-Circle Protractor

EXAMPLE   To measure angle *PQR* with a half-circle protractor:

Step 1: Lay the baseline of the protractor on $\overrightarrow{QR}$.

Step 2: Slide the protractor so that the center of the baseline is over point *Q*, the vertex of the angle.

Step 3: Read the degree measure where $\overrightarrow{QP}$ crosses the edge of the protractor. There are two scales on the protractor. Use the scale that makes sense for the size of the angle you are measuring.

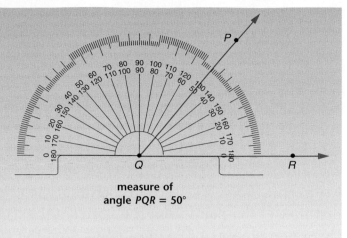

measure of
angle *PQR* = 50°

Drawing Angles with a Half-Circle Protractor

EXAMPLE   To draw a 40° angle:

Step 1: Draw a ray from point *A*.

Step 2: Lay the baseline of the protractor on the ray.

Step 3: Slide the protractor so that the center of the baseline is over point *A*.

Step 4: Make a mark at 40° on the protractor. There are two scales on the protractor. Use the scale that makes sense for the size of the angle you are drawing.

Step 5: Draw a ray from point *A* through the mark.

CHECK YOUR UNDERSTANDING

Measure each angle to the nearest degree.

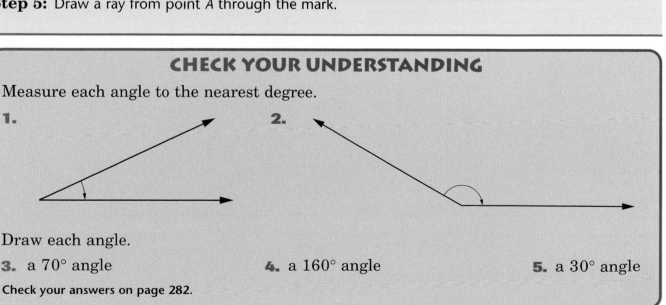

1.

2.

Draw each angle.

3. a 70° angle

4. a 160° angle

5. a 30° angle

Check your answers on page 282.

Plotting Ordered Number Pairs

A **rectangular coordinate grid** is used to name points in the plane. It is made up of two number lines, called **axes,** that meet at right angles at their zero points. The point where the two lines meet is called the **origin.**

Every point on a coordinate grid can be named by an **ordered number pair.** The two numbers that make up an ordered number pair are called the **coordinates** of the point. The first coordinate is always the *horizontal* distance of the point from the vertical axis. The second coordinate is always the *vertical* distance of the point from the horizontal axis. For example, the ordered pair (3,5) names point *A* on the grid at the right. The numbers 3 and 5 are the coordinates of point *A*.

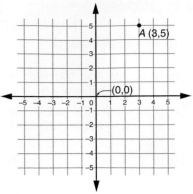

The ordered pair **(0,0)** names the origin.

EXAMPLE   Plot the ordered pair (5,3).

Step 1: Locate 5 on the horizontal axis.
Step 2: Locate 3 on the vertical axis.
Step 3: Draw a vertical line from point 5 on the horizontal
axis and a horizontal line from point 3 on the vertical axis.
The point (5,3) is located at the intersection of the two lines.
The order of the numbers in an ordered pair is important.
The ordered pair (5,3) does not name the same point as the
ordered pair (3,5).

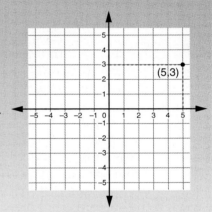

EXAMPLE   Locate $(-2,3)$, $(-4,-1)$, and $(3\frac{1}{2},0)$.

For each ordered pair, locate the first coordinate on the horizontal axis and the second coordinate on the vertical axis. Draw intersecting lines from these two points.

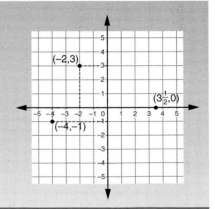

CHECK YOUR UNDERSTANDING

Draw a coordinate grid on graph paper and plot the following points.

1. (2,4)   **2.** $(-3,-3)$ **3.** $(0,-4)$ **4.** $(-2,1)$

Check your answers on page 282.

Map Scales and Distances

Map Scales

Mapmakers show large areas of land and water on small pieces of paper. Places that are actually thousands of miles apart may be only inches apart on a map. When you use a map, you can estimate real distances by using a **map scale.**

Different maps use different scales. On one map, 1 inch may represent 10 miles in the real world, while on another map, 1 inch may represent 100 miles.

On the map scale here, the bar is 2 inches long. Two inches on the map represent 2,000 real miles. One inch on the map represents 1,000 real miles.

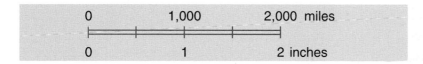

Sometimes you see a map scale written as "2 inches = 2,000 miles." This statement is not mathematically correct because 2 inches is not equal to 2,000 miles. What is meant is that a 2-inch distance on the map represents 2,000 miles in the real world.

Measuring Distances on a Map

Here are some ways to measure distances on a map.

Use a Ruler

Sometimes the distance you want to measure is along a straight line. Measure the straight-line distance with a ruler, then use the map scale to change the map distance to the real distance.

EXAMPLE Use the map and scale shown below to find the air distance from Denver to Chicago. The air distance is the straight-line distance between the two cities.

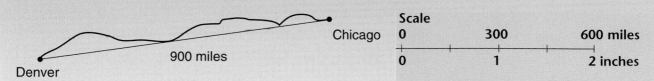

The line segment connecting Denver and Chicago is 3 inches long. The map scale shows that 1 inch represents 300 miles. So 3 inches must represent 3 * 300 miles, or 900 miles. The air distance is 900 miles.

Measurement

Use String and a Ruler

Sometimes you may need to find the length of a curved path such as a road or river. You can use a piece of string, a ruler, and the map scale to find the length.

- Lay a string along the path you want to measure. Mark the beginning and ending points on the string.
- Straighten out the string. Be careful not to stretch it. Use a ruler to measure between the beginning and ending points.
- Use the map scale to change the map distance into the real distance.

Use a Compass

Sometimes map scales are not given in inches or centimeters, so a ruler is not much help. In these cases you can use a compass to find distances. Using a compass can also be easier than using a ruler, especially if you are measuring a curved path and you do not have string.

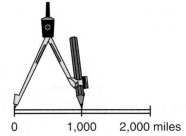

0   1,000   2,000 miles

Step 1: Adjust the compass so that the distance between the anchor point and the pencil point is the same as a distance on the map scale.

Step 2: Imagine a path connecting the starting point and ending point of the distance you want to measure. Put the anchor point of the compass at the starting point. Use the pencil point to make an arc on the path. Move the anchor point to the spot where the arc and the path meet. Continue walking the compass along the path until you reach or pass the ending point. Be careful not to change the size of the opening of the compass.

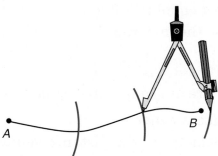

A

B

Step 3: Keep track of how many times you swing the compass. Each swing stands for the distance on the map scale. To estimate total distance, multiply the number of swings by the distance each swing stands for.

Algebra

Algebra

Algebra is a type of arithmetic that uses letters (or other symbols such as blanks or question marks) as well as numbers.

Number Sentences

Number sentences are like English sentences, except they use math symbols instead of words. Using symbols makes the sentences easier to write and work with.

So far, you have seen number sentences that contain **digits, operation symbols,** and **relation symbols.** A number sentence must contain a relation symbol. A number sentence made up only of these symbols is either **true** or **false.** For example, the number sentence $12 + 8 = 20$ is *true*; the number sentence $14 = 10$ is *false*.

Open Sentences

In some number sentences, one or more numbers may be missing. In place of the missing number there is a letter, a blank, a question mark, or some other symbol. Such sentences are called **open sentences.** The symbol that stands for the missing number is a **variable.** Open sentences are neither true nor false. For example, $9 + x = 15$ is an open sentence in which x stands for some number. If you replace the letter x with a number, you get a number sentence that is either true or false.

- If you replace x with 10 in the number sentence $9 + x = 15$, you get the number sentence $9 + 10 = 15$, which is false.
- If you replace x with 6 in the open sentence $9 + x = 15$, you get the number sentence $9 + 6 = 15$, which is true.

If a number used in place of the variable makes the number sentence true, the number is a **solution** of the open sentence. The number 6 is a solution of the open sentence $9 + x = 15$, because $9 + 6 = 15$ is a true number sentence.

Algebra is not a subject just for older students—you have been learning algebra ever since you first solved a problem like $8 + \_\_\_ = 13$ in first or second grade!

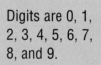

Digits are 0, 1, 2, 3, 4, 5, 6, 7, 8, and 9.

Operation symbols are $+$, $-$, $*$ or $\times$, and $\div$ or $/$.

Relation symbols are $<$, $=$, and $>$.

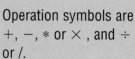

CHECK YOUR UNDERSTANDING

True or false?

1. $4 + 5 = 9$ **2.** $4 + 8 > 10$ **3.** $7 + 2 < 6 + 6$

Solve.

4. $5 + y = 12$ **5.** $48 = z * 6$ **6.** $10 - w = 4$

Check your answers on page 282.

Parentheses

The meaning of a number sentence is not always clear. Here is an example: $15 - 3 * 2 = n$. Should you subtract first? Or should you multiply first? Parentheses tell you which operation to do first.

EXAMPLE Solve. $(15 - 3) * 2 = n$

The parentheses tell you to subtract $15 - 3$ first. $(15 - 3) * 2 = n$
Then multiply by 2. $12 * 2 = n$

The answer is 24. $24 = n$

$(15 - 3) * 2 = 24$

EXAMPLE Solve. $15 - (3 * 2) = n$

The parentheses tell you to multiply $3 * 2$ first. $15 - (3 * 2) = n$
Then subtract the result. $15 - 6 = n$

The answer is 9. $9 = n$

$15 - (3 * 2) = 9$

EXAMPLES Make this number sentence true by inserting parentheses: $18 = 6 + 3 * 4$.

There are two ways to insert parentheses, but only one will result in a true sentence.

$18 = (6 + 3) * 4$ $18 = 6 + (3 * 4)$
$18 = 9 * 4$ $18 = 6 + 12$
$18 = 36$ $18 = 18$

18 is not equal to 36, so this statement is false. $18 = 18$, so this statement is true.

The correct way to insert parentheses is $18 = 6 + (3 * 4)$.

CHECK YOUR UNDERSTANDING

Solve.

1. $(2 * 2) + 10 = x$ **2.** $n = (3 - 3) / 6$ **3.** ___ $= (5 + 5) * (50 + 50)$

Insert parentheses to make these number sentences true.

4. $10 - 6 + 4 = 0$ **5.** $1 = 4 * 5 / 4 * 5$ **6.** $10 = 4 + 1 * 2$

Check your answers on page 282.

Order of Operations

In many situations, the order in which things are done is important. For example, you always put on your socks before your shoes.

In mathematics, too, certain things must be done in a certain order. For example, to solve $8 + 4 * 3 = \underline{\quad}$, you must know whether to add first or to multiply first. In arithmetic and algebra, there are rules that tell you what to do first and what to do next.

Rules for the Order of Operations

1. Do operations inside **parentheses** first. Follow rules 2–4.
2. Calculate all expressions with **exponents.**
3. **Multiply** and **divide** in order, from left to right.
4. **Add** and **subtract** in order, from left to right.

Some people find it's easier to remember the order of operations by memorizing this sentence:

Please **E**xcuse **M**y **D**ear **A**unt **S**ally.

Parentheses **E**xponents **M**ultiplication **D**ivision **A**ddition **S**ubtraction

---

EXAMPLE   Solve. $15 - 3 * 2 = ?$

Multiply first, then subtract.
$$15 - 3 * 2 = ?$$
$$15 - 6 = 9$$
$$15 - 3 * 2 = 9$$

The answer is 9.

EXAMPLE   Solve. $18 - (5 - 3 + 8) / 2 = ?$

$$18 - (5 - 3 + 8) / 2 = ?$$
Parentheses first. $18 - 10 / 2 = ?$
Then divide. $18 - 5 = 13$
Then subtract. $18 - (5 - 3 + 8) / 2 = 13$
The answer is 13.

CHECK YOUR UNDERSTANDING

Solve.

1. $15 - 6 / 2 + 2$ **2.** $5 * 8 / (2 + 2)$ **3.** $3 + 2 * 4 - 15 / 5$ **4.** $4 + 7 * 5$

Check your answers on page 282.

Relations

A **relation** tells how two things compare. The table at the right shows the most common relations that compare numbers and their symbols.

symbol	meaning
=	is equal to
≠	is not equal to
<	is less than
>	is greater than

Equations

Equality is the most important relation between numbers. Much of arithmetic is nothing more than finding equivalent names for numbers. For example, 75 is another name for 15 * 5.

Everyday Mathematics uses **name-collection boxes** as a simple way to show equality.

- The label shows a number.
- The names written inside the box are equivalent names for the number on the label.

Another way to state that two things are equal is to write a number sentence using the = symbol. Number sentences containing the = symbol are called **equations.**

12
1.2 * 10
12 − 0
3 * 4
$\frac{1}{2} * 24$
$6 ÷ \frac{1}{2}$

a name-collection box
for 12

EXAMPLES Here are some equations:

$$4 + 5 = 9 \qquad 12 - 6 = 8 \qquad 5 = 5$$

NOTE

An equation may be true or it may be false. Can you find the false equation in the examples at the left?

Inequalities

Number sentences that do not contain an = symbol are called **inequalities**. The most common relations in inequalities are > (is greater than), < (is less than), and ≠ (is not equal to).

EXAMPLES Here are some inequalities. The middle inequality is false.

$$5 + 6 < 15 \qquad 25 > 12 * 3 \qquad 36 ≠ 7 * 6$$

CHECK YOUR UNDERSTANDING

Compare. Use =, <, or > to make each number sentence true.

1. 100 ☐ 55 + 45
2. $\frac{1}{2}$ ☐ 0.5
3. $\frac{3}{4}$ ☐ $\frac{1}{4}$
4. 3 * 50 ☐ 100
5. $\frac{1}{2}$ * 100 ☐ 50
6. 3.2 ☐ 3.05

Check your answers on page 282.

Mathematical Models

A good way to learn about something is to work with a model of it. For example, a computer model of a city can help you understand how real cities grow and change. A scale model of the human body can help you understand how the different systems in your own body work together.

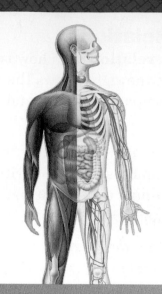

Models are important in mathematics too. A mathematical model can be as simple as acting out a problem with chips or blocks. Other mathematical models use drawings or symbols. Mathematical models can help you understand and solve problems.

Situation Diagrams

EXAMPLE Here are some examples of how you can use diagrams to model simple problems.

Problem	Diagram
Parts-and-Total Situation Samantha's class has 14 girls and 11 boys. How many students are there in all?	**Total** ? / **Part** 14 **Part** 11
Change Situation Toussaint had $20 and spent $11.49 on a CD. How much money did he have left?	**Start** $20 **Change** −$11.49 **End** ?
Comparison Situation In the summer the average high temperature in Cairo, Egypt, is 95°F. In the summer the average high temperature in Reykjavik, Iceland, is 56°F. How much warmer is it in Cairo?	**Quantity** 95°F / **Quantity** 56°F **Difference** ?

These diagrams work well for many simple problems, but for harder problems you need to use more powerful tools such as graphs, tables, and number models.

Number Models

Number sentences provide another way to model situations. In *Everyday Mathematics,* a number sentence that fits or describes some situation is called a **number model.** Often, two or more number models can fit a given situation.

Problem	Number Model
Samantha's class has 14 girls and 11 boys. How many students are there in all?	$14 + 11 = n$
Toussaint had $20 and spent $11.49 on a CD. How much money did he have left?	$r = \$20 - \$11.49$ or $\$20 = \$11.49 + r$
The average summer high temperature in Cairo, Egypt, is 95°F. The average summer high temperature in Reykjavik, Iceland, is 56°F. How much warmer is it in Cairo than in Reykjavik?	$d = 95°F - 56°F$ or $95°F = 56°F + d$

Number models also can help you show the answer after you have solved the problem: $\$20 = \$11.49 + \$8.51$.

Number models can help you solve problems. For example, the number sentence $\$20 = \$11.49 + r$ suggests counting up to find Toussaint's change from buying an $11.49 CD with a $20 bill.

CHECK YOUR UNDERSTANDING

Draw a diagram and write a number model for each problem. Then solve each problem.

1. Ella ran 5.5 miles on Monday, 6 miles on Tuesday, 3 miles on Wednesday, and 8 miles on Friday. How many miles did she run in all?

2. The Eagles scored 21 points in the first half. By the end of the game, they had scored 35 points. How many points did they score in the second half?

3. Maurice had $38 and Monica had $45. How much more money did Monica have?

Check your answers on page 282.

Variables and Unknowns

In mathematics, letters, blanks, question marks, or other symbols are often used in place of missing information. These symbols are called **variables.**

Variables are used in several different ways.

Variables Can Be Used to Stand for Unknown Numbers

For example, in the number sentence $5 + n = 8$, the variable n stands for an unknown number. To make the sentence true, the correct number has to be found for n. Finding the correct number is called "solving the number sentence."

> **EXAMPLES** Here are number sentences containing variables:
>
> $4 + \underline{} = 15$ $50 + 375 = ?$ $25 = 50 - x$ $y = 5 * 9$

128

Variables Can Be Used to State Properties of Number Systems

Properties of a number system are things that are true for all numbers. For example, any number multiplied by 1 is equal to itself. Variables are often used in statements that describe properties.

EXAMPLES

Property	Number Sentence
$a + b = b + a$	$5 + 8 = 8 + 5$ $60 + 30 = 30 + 60$
$a * b = b * a$	$5 * 2 = 2 * 5$ $20 * 4 = 4 * 20$
$1 * a = a$	$1 * 45 = 45$ $1 * 3.5 = 3.5$
$a = a$	$32 = 32$ $47.5 = 47.5$
$0 + a = a$	$0 + 5 = 5$ $0 + 1,000 = 1,000$

136

Variables Can Be Used in Formulas

Formulas are used in everyday life, in science, in business, and in many other situations as an easy way to describe relationships. The formula for the area of a rectangle, for example, is $A = b * h$, where A is the area, b is the length of the base, and h is the height.

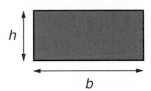

Variables Can Be Used to Express General Relations or Functions

Function machines and "What's My Rule?" tables have rules that tell you how to get the "out" numbers from the "in" numbers. For example, a doubling machine might have the rule, "Double the 'in' number." This rule can be written using variables: $y = 2 * x$.

> **NOTE**
>
> The formula $A = b * h$ can also be written without a multiplication symbol: $A = bh$. Putting variables next to each other means they are to be multiplied. In higher mathematics, in which there are many variables, multiplication symbols are normally left out. In *Everyday Mathematics*, however, the multiplication symbol is usually shown because this makes expressions easier to understand.

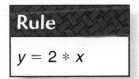

x	y
0	0
1	2
2	4
3	6
...	...

CHECK YOUR UNDERSTANDING

1. For each problem, write a number sentence using a letter for the unknown number.
   a. Some number plus 5 equals 8.   **b.** Some number times 3 equals 15.
2. Find the area of the parallelograms below. Use the formula $A = b * h$.

   a.
   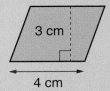
   3 cm
   4 cm

   b.
   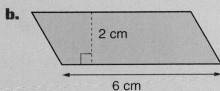
   2 cm
   6 cm

Check your answers on page 283.

Some Properties of Arithmetic

Certain facts are true of all numbers. Some of them are obvious—"every number equals itself," for example—but others are less obvious. Since you have been working with numbers for years, you probably already know most of these facts, or properties, although you probably don't know their mathematical names.

The Identity Properties

The sum of any number and 0 is that number. For example, $15 + 0 = 15$. The **identity** for addition is 0.

$$a + 0 = a \quad 0 + a = a$$

The product of any number and 1 is that number. For example, $75 * 1 = 75$. The **identity** for multiplication is 1.

$$a * 1 = a \quad 1 * a = a$$

The Commutative Properties

In addition, the order of the numbers makes no difference. For example, $8 + 5 = 5 + 8$. This is known as the **commutative property of addition.**

$$a + b = b + a$$

In multiplication, the order of the numbers makes no difference. For example, $7 * 2 = 2 * 7$. This is known as the **commutative property of multiplication.**

$$a * b = b * a$$

The Associative Properties

When three numbers are added, it makes no difference which two are added first. For example, $(3 + 4) + 5 = 3 + (4 + 5)$. This is known as the **associative property of addition.**

$$(a + b) + c = a + (b + c)$$

When three numbers are multiplied, it makes no difference which two are multiplied first. For example, $(3 * 4) * 5 = 3 * (4 * 5)$. This is known as the **associative property of multiplication.**

$$(a * b) * c = a * (b * c)$$

The Distributive Property

When you play *Multiplication Wrestling* or multiply with the partial-products method, you use the **distributive property.** $a * (b + c) = (a * b) + (a * c)$

For example, when you solve
$60 * 38$ with partial products,
you think of 38 as $30 + 8$ and
multiply each part by 60.

$$38$$
$$* \underline{60}$$
$$60 * 30 = 1800$$
$$60 * 8 = \underline{480}$$
$$60 * 38 = 2280$$

The distributive property says: $60 * (30 + 8) = (60 * 30) + (60 * 8)$.

EXAMPLE   Show how the distributive property works by finding the area of Rectangle A in two different ways.

Method 1: To find the area of Rectangle A, you could find the total width $(3 + 4)$ and multiply that by the height.

$$5 * (3 + 4) = 5 * 7$$
$$= 35$$

Method 2: Another way to find the area of Rectangle A would be to first find the area of the two smaller rectangles, then add them together.

$$(5 * 3) + (5 * 4) = 15 + 20$$
$$= 35$$

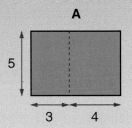

The area of Rectangle A is 35 square units.

This is an example of the distributive property.

$$5 * (3 + 4) = (5 * 3) + (5 * 4)$$

The distributive property works with subtraction too.

EXAMPLES   Find the area of the shaded rectangle in two different ways.

$$5 * (7 - 4) = 5 * 3 = 15 \text{ or}$$
$$(5 * 7) - (5 * 4) = 35 - 20 = 15$$

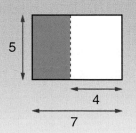

The area of the shaded rectangle is 15 square units.

CHECK YOUR UNDERSTANDING

Use the distributive property to fill in the blanks.

1. $8 * (12 + 9) = (8 * \underline{\quad}) + (8 * \underline{\quad})$

2. $(7 * 23) + (7 * 16) = 7 * (\underline{\quad} + \underline{\quad})$

3. $5 * (\underline{\quad} - \underline{\quad}) = (5 * 16) - (5 * 14)$

4. $(\underline{\quad} * 3) + (\underline{\quad} * 4) = 9 * (3 + 4)$

Check your answers on page 283.

Number Patterns

You can use dot pictures to explore number patterns.

Even Numbers

Even numbers are numbers that can be divided by 2 with a remainder of 0. One way to show even numbers with dots is shown below.

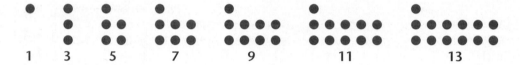

Odd Numbers

Odd numbers are numbers that have a remainder of 1 when they are divided by 2.

Triangular Numbers

Triangular numbers can be shown with dots arranged to form triangles. Each row has one more dot than the row above it.

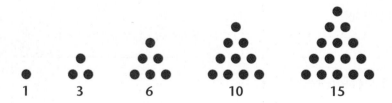

Square Numbers

Square numbers can be shown with dots arranged in a square having the same number of dots in each row and column. A square number is the product of a whole number multiplied by itself. For example, 16 is 4 * 4 or 4^2.

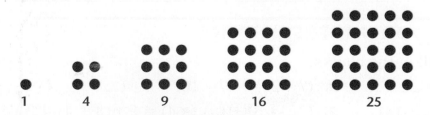

Rectangular Numbers

Rectangular numbers can be shown with dots arranged in a rectangle. The number of dots in each row is always 1 more than the number of rows.

Prime Numbers

A **prime number** is a whole number that is greater than 1 that cannot be divided by any whole number other than 1 and itself. This means that prime numbers cannot be fit into rectangular shapes. The prime numbers are 2, 3, 5, 7, 11, 13, 17, and so on.

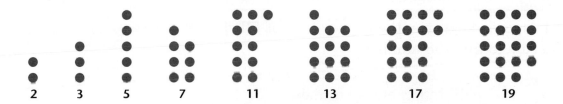

CHECK YOUR UNDERSTANDING

Draw a dot picture for each number and tell what kind of number it is. There may be more than one correct answer.

1. 14   **2.** 25   **3.** 13   **4.** 15

Is the number even or odd? Draw a dot picture to explain your reasoning.

5. 17   **6.** 18   **7.** 22   **8.** 27

9. List all the square numbers that are less than 100.

Check your answers on page 283.

Frames-and-Arrows Diagrams: Number Sequences

A **Frames-and-Arrows diagram** is one way to show a number pattern. There are three parts to a Frames-and-Arrows diagram:

• a set of **frames** that contains numbers

• **arrows** that show the path from one frame to the next

• a box with an arrow below it. The box has a **rule** inside. The rule tells how to get to the next frame.

EXAMPLE   Here is a Frames-and-Arrows diagram.

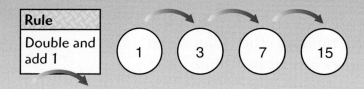

The rule in the box is "Double and add 1." If you double the number in any frame and add 1, you get the number in the next frame.

In some Frames-and-Arrows diagrams, the frames are not filled in. You must use the rule to find the numbers.

EXAMPLE   Use the rule to fill in the empty frames.

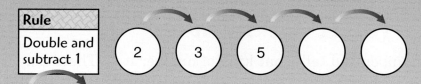

The rule is "Double and subtract 1."

First, check that this rule works for the frames that are filled in:

2 doubled is 4; 4 minus 1 is 3. 3 doubled is 6; 6 minus 1 is 5.

To fill in the first blank frame, double 5 and subtract 1:

5 doubled is 10; 10 minus 1 is 9. So 9 goes in the first blank frame.

To fill in the second blank frame, double 9 and subtract 1: 9 doubled is 18; 18 minus 1 is 17. So 17 goes in the last frame.

The filled-in diagram looks like this.

You can use the numbers in the frames to find the rule.

EXAMPLE Find the rule for this diagram.

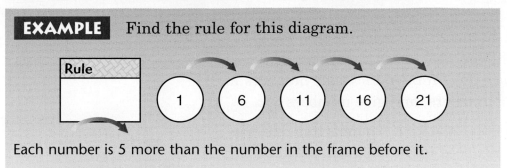

Each number is 5 more than the number in the frame before it.

So the rule is "Add 5."

Two-Rule Frames-and-Arrows Diagrams

A Frames-and-Arrows diagram can have two different rules. Each rule uses a different color arrow.

EXAMPLE Here is a two-rule Frames-and-Arrows diagram:

Double

Subtract 1

2   4   3   6   5   10

The black arrow goes with the rule "Double."
The blue arrow goes with the rule "Subtract 1."
You can check that the diagram is correct:
2 doubled is 4; 4 minus 1 is 3; and so on.

CHECK YOUR UNDERSTANDING

1. Find the missing numbers.

Rule

Subtract 11   99   88   ◯   ◯   ◯

2. Find the rule.

Rule

3   6   9   12   15

Check your answers on page 283.

Function Machines and "What's My Rule?" Problems

A **function machine** is an imaginary machine that takes something in, works on it, and then gives something out. Function machines in *Everyday Mathematics* take numbers in, use rules to change those numbers, and give numbers out.

Here is a picture of a function machine. The machine has the rule "∗ 7." Any number that goes into the machine will be multiplied by 7.

If you put 5 into this "∗ 7" machine, it will multiply 5 ∗ 7. The number 35 will come out.

If you put 60 into the machine, it will multiply 60 ∗ 7. The number 420 will come out.

You can use a table to keep track of what goes in and what comes out. The numbers that are put into the machine are written in the **in** column. The numbers that come out of the machine are written in the **out** column.

If you know the rule for a function machine, you can make a table of "in" and "out" numbers. If you have a table of "in" and "out" numbers, you may be able to find the rule. We call these **"What's My Rule?"** problems.

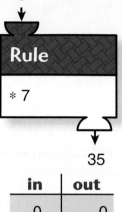

in	out
0	0
1	7
2	14
3	21
n	$n * 7$

EXAMPLE The rule is "∗ 20". Find the numbers that come out of the machine.

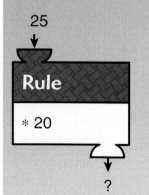

in	out
0	
7	
25	

This machine will multiply any number put into it by 20.

If 0 is put in, then 0 will come out. If 7 is put in, 140 will come out. If 25 is put in, 500 will come out.

If you know the rule and the "out" numbers, then you may be able to find the "in" numbers.

EXAMPLE The rule is "− 5." Find the numbers that were put into the machine.

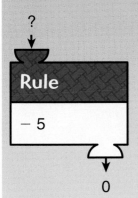

in	out
	0
	3
	15

This machine will subtract 5 from any number. The number that comes out is always 5 less than the number that was put in.

If 0 comes out, then 5 must be the number that was put in.
If 3 comes out, then 8 must be the number that was put in.
If 15 comes out, then 20 must be the number that was put in.

EXAMPLE Use the table to find the rule.

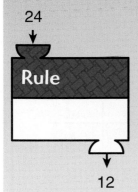

in	out
24	12
18	9
4	2
16	8

Each number in the out column is half of the number in the "in" column.

The rule is "÷ 2" or "take half."

Another way to show the workings of a function machine is to draw a graph. The "in" numbers are plotted on the horizontal axis; the "out" numbers are plotted on the vertical axis.

EXAMPLE Make a graph of this function machine.

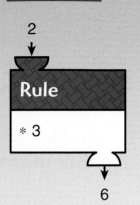

in	out
0	0
1	3
2	6
3	9

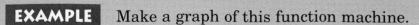

CHECK YOUR UNDERSTANDING

Use the rules to find the missing "in" and "out" numbers.

1.

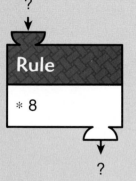

in	out
3	
5	
7	

2.

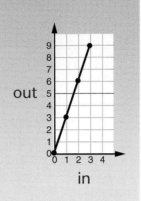

in	out
	75
	125
	50

Find the missing rules. Then find the missing "in" and "out" numbers.

3.

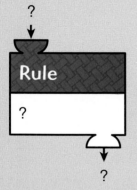

in	out
1	4
2	5
3	6
10	
	18

4.

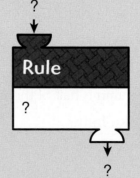

in	out
1	5
2	10
3	15
	35
9	

Check your answers on page 283.

"What's My Rule?" Problems

A "What's My Rule?" problem contains two of the following three kinds of information: "in" numbers, "out" numbers, and a rule. To solve the problem, you need to find the missing information.

> **NOTE**
>
> In the examples at the left, the solutions (the missing information) appear in color. When solving "What's My Rule?" problems, think of function machines.

EXAMPLE The rule and the "in" numbers are given. Find the "out" numbers.

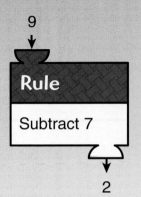

in	out	
9	2	[9 − 7 = 2]
27	20	[27 − 7 = 20]
0	−7	[0 − 7 = −7]
−5	−12	[−5 − 7 = −12]

EXAMPLE The rule and the "out" numbers are given. Find the "in" numbers.

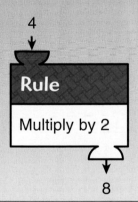

in	out	
4	8	[4 * 2 = 8]
24	48	[24 * 2 = 48]
$\frac{1}{2}$	1	[$\frac{1}{2}$ * 2 = 1]
0	0	[0 * 2 = 0]

EXAMPLE The "in" and "out" numbers are given. Find the rule.

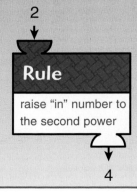

in	out	
2	4	[$2^2 = 4$]
5	25	[$5^2 = 25$]
1	1	[$1^2 = 1$]
10	100	[$10^2 = 100$]

EXAMPLE   The rule and some "in" and "out" numbers are given. Find the missing numbers.

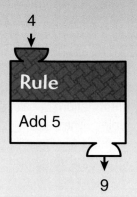

4

Rule

Add 5

9

in	out	
4	9	[4 + 5 = 9]
7	12	[7 + 5 = 12]
53	58	[53 + 5 = 58]
−6	−1	[−6 + (−1) = −5]

CHECK YOUR UNDERSTANDING

Solve these "What's My Rule?" problems.

1.   9

Rule

Divide by 3

?

in	out
9	?
36	?
1	?
1.5	?
123	?
390	?

2.   ?

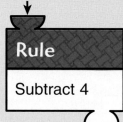

Rule

Subtract 4

7

in	out
?	7
?	24
?	−4
?	0
?	50
?	118

3.   4

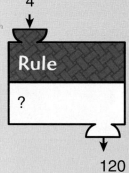

Rule

?

120

in	out
4	120
10	300
0	0
20	600
14	420
33	990

Check your answers on page 283.

Problem Solving

Mathematical Modeling

A **mathematical model** is something mathematical that fits something in the real world. A sphere, for example, is a model of a basketball. The number sentence $1.00 - 0.79 = 0.21$ is a model for buying a bottle of juice that costs 79¢ with a $1 bill and getting 21¢ change. The graph below is a model for the number of TV sets in several African countries.

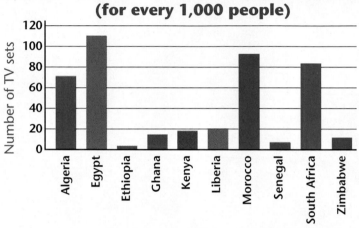

Number of TV Sets in Selected African Countries (for every 1,000 people)

You have used mathematical models to solve problems for many years. In Kindergarten, you probably used counters to solve simple problems. In first grade, you may have drawn pictures. In second and third grades, you learned to use other models such as situation diagrams and number models. As you continue studying mathematics, you will learn to make and use more complicated and powerful mathematical models.

Everyday Mathematics has many different kinds of problems. Some problems ask you to find something. Others ask you to make something. When you get older, you will prove things by giving convincing reasons why something is true or correct.

Problems to Find	**Problems to Make**
1. What is the total cost of 5 pounds of apples at $1.49 a pound and a gallon of milk at $2.89? **2.** What are the missing numbers? 1, 4, 9, 16, _____ , 36, _____ , 64	**3.** Use straws and connectors to make a square-based pyramid. **4.** Use a compass and straightedge to copy this triangle: 

A Guide for Solving Number Stories

Learning to solve problems is the main reason for studying mathematics. One way you learn to solve problems is by solving number stories. A **number story** is a story with a problem that can be solved with arithmetic.

A Guide for Number Stories
1. Understand the problem.
2. Plan what to do.
3. Carry out the plan.
4. Look back.

1. Understand the problem.

- Read the problem. Can you retell it in your own words?
- What do you know?
- What do you want to find out?
- Do you have all the information needed to solve the problem?

NOTE

Understanding the problem is the most important step. Good problem solvers spend most of their time making sure they really understand the problem.

2. Plan what to do.

- Is the problem like one you solved before?
- Is there a pattern you can use?
- Can you draw a picture or a diagram?
- Can you write a number model or make a table?
- Can you use counters, base-10 blocks, or some other tool?
- Can you estimate the answer and check if you're right?

NOTE

Sometimes it's easy to know what to do. Other times you need to be creative.

3. Carry out the plan.

- After you decide what to do, do it. Be careful.
- Make a written record of what you do.
- Answer the question.

4. Look back.

- Does your answer make sense?
- Does your answer agree with your estimate?
- Can you write a number model for the problem?
- Can you solve the problem in another way?

CHECK YOUR UNDERSTANDING

Use the "Guide for Number Stories" to help you solve the following problems. Explain your thinking at each step and your answer(s).

1. Mrs. Newhouse walked 2 miles per day for 2 days in a row, 3 miles per day for the next 3 days, and so on, until she walked 6 miles per day. On which day did she first walk 6 miles?

2. Wayne cut a rectangle with a perimeter of 24 inches into two squares. What were the length and width of the original rectangle?

Check your answers on page 284.

A Problem-Solving Diagram

Problems from everyday life, science, and business are often more complicated than number stories you solve in school. Sometimes the steps in the "Guide for Solving Number Stories" may not be helpful.

The diagram below shows another way to think about problem solving. This diagram is more complicated than a list, but it's more like what people do when they solve problems in science and business. The arrows connecting the boxes are meant to show that you don't always do things in the same order.

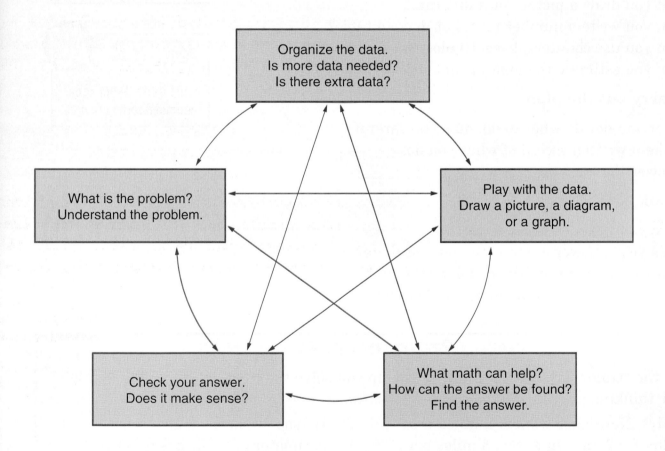

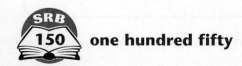

Thinking about the diagram on the previous page as you solve problems may help you be a better problem solver. Here are some things to try for each of the boxes in the diagram. Remember, these are not rules. They are only suggestions for things that might help.

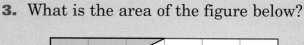

- What is the problem? Can you retell it in your own words? What do you know? What do you want to find out? Try to imagine what an answer might look like. Try to understand the problem.
- Study the data you have. Look for more data if you need it. Get rid of any data that you don't need. Organize the data in a list or in some other way.
- Play with the data. Try drawing a picture, a diagram, or a graph. Can you write a number model? Can you model the problem with counters or blocks?
- Do the math. Use arithmetic, geometry, or other mathematics to find an answer. Label the answer with units.
- Check your answer. Does it make sense? Compare your answer to a friend's answer. Try the answer in the problem. Can you solve the problem another way?

CHECK YOUR UNDERSTANDING

1. About how long would it take to count to one million?

2. On a piece of paper, draw the diagram below. Put the digits 1–6 in the circles so that the sum along each line is the same.

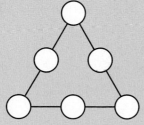

Can you find another way?

3. What is the area of the figure below?

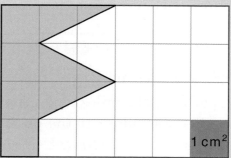

1 cm^2

Check your answers on page 284.

Situation Diagrams

There are three basic kinds of addition and subtraction situations: change situations, parts-and-total situations, and comparison situations.

Everyday Mathematics uses diagrams for each of these types of situations. The diagrams help you organize the information in a problem and can help you decide what to do. You can also use the diagrams to show the answer after you solve a problem.

Change Situations

In a change situation, there is a starting quantity, then a change, and finally an ending quantity. The change can be either change-to-more or change-to-less.

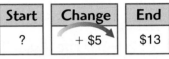

Start	Change	End
?	+ $5	$13

change diagram

> **EXAMPLE** Regina had some money. Then she earned $5. At the end, she had $13. How much did Regina have at first?

Parts-and-Total Situations

In a parts-and-total situation, there is a single quantity that can be separated into two or more parts.

Total	
24	
Part	Part
15	?

parts-and-total diagram

> **EXAMPLE** Ms. Whalen's class has 24 students, including 15 boys. How many girls are there in Ms. Whalen's class?

Comparison Situations

In a comparison situation, two quantities are compared.

Quantity
?

Quantity	Difference
$3.75	$2.25

comparison diagram

> **EXAMPLE** Zach has $3.75. Ben has $2.25 more than Zach. How much does Ben have?

CHECK YOUR UNDERSTANDING

Complete a diagram for each problem. Then solve the problems.

1. A path was 12 miles long. Another 9 miles was added to the path. How long is the path? (*Hint:* Use a change diagram.)

2. Bill is 137 cm tall. His sister Amy is 78 cm tall. How much taller is Bill than Amy? (*Hint:* Use a comparison diagram.)

3. Loren and Nick collect coins. Loren has 218 coins and Nick has 125 coins. How many coins do they have in all? (*Hint:* Use a parts-and-total diagram.)

Check your answers on page 284.

Interpreting a Remainder in Division

Some number stories are solved by dividing whole numbers. You may need to decide what to do when there is a non-zero remainder.

There are three possible choices:
- Ignore the remainder. Just the quotient is the answer.
- Round the quotient up to the next whole number.
- Write the remainder as a fraction or decimal. The remainder is part of the answer.

EXAMPLES

- Suppose 3 people share 14 counters equally. How many counters will each person get?

  $14 / 3 \rightarrow 4 \text{ R2}$

Ignore the remainder. The quotient is the answer.

Each person will have 4 counters, with 2 counters left over.

$14 / 3 \rightarrow 4 \text{ R2}$

- Suppose 14 photos are placed in a photo album. How many pages are needed if 3 photos can fit on a page?

You need to round the quotient up to the next whole number. The album will have 4 pages filled and another page only partially filled.

So, 5 pages are needed.

- Suppose three friends share a 14-inch-long string of licorice. How long is each piece if the friends receive equal shares?

  $14 / 3 \rightarrow 4 \text{ R2}$

The answer, 4 R2, shows that if each person receives 4 inches of licorice, 2 inches remain to be divided. Imagine that this 2-inch remainder is divided into thirds. It can be divided into three $\frac{2}{3}$-inch pieces.

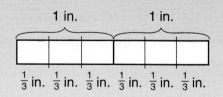

Write the remainder as a fraction. The remainder is part of the answer.

Each friend will get a $4\frac{2}{3}$-inch-long piece of licorice.

To rewrite a remainder as a fraction:

1. Make the remainder the *numerator* of the fraction.

2. Make the divisor the *denominator* of the fraction.

Problem	Answer	Remainder Rewritten As a Fraction	Answer Written As a Mixed Number	Answer Written As a Decimal
371 / 4	92 R3	$\frac{3}{4}$	$92\frac{3}{4}$	92.75

Estimation

An **estimate** is an answer that is close to an exact answer. You make estimates every day.

- You estimate how long it will take to walk to school.
- You estimate how much money you will need to buy some things at the store.
- You estimate how long it will take you to do your homework.

Sometimes you make an estimate because it is impossible to know the exact answer. When you predict the future, for example, you have to estimate since it's impossible to know exactly what will happen. A weather forecaster's prediction is an estimate of what will happen in the future.

Sometimes you will estimate because finding an exact answer is not practical. For example, the number of people in the United States is always an estimate. The count changes constantly because people are born and die every day.

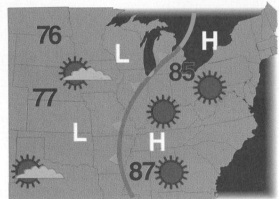

The weather will be sunny
and about 85 degrees tomorrow.

Sometimes you will estimate because finding an exact answer is not worth the trouble. You might estimate the cost of several items at the store, for example, to be sure you have enough money. There is no need to find an exact answer until you pay for the items.

Estimation in Problem Solving

Estimation can be useful even when you need to find an exact answer. Making an estimate when you first start working on a problem may help you understand the problem better. Estimating before you solve a problem is like making a rough draft of a writing assignment.

Estimation can also be useful after you have found an answer for a problem. You can use the estimate to check whether your answer makes sense. If your estimate is not close to the exact answer you found, then you need to check your work.

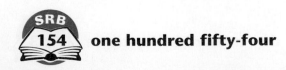

Leading-Digit Estimation

The best estimators are usually people who are experts. Someone who lays carpets for a living, for example, would probably be very good at estimating the size of rooms. A waiter would probably be very good at estimating the proper amount for a tip.

One way to estimate is to use only the first digit of a number. The other digits are replaced by zeros. This way of estimating is called **leading-digit** or **front-end estimation.**

Exact Number	Leading-Digit Estimate
349	300
6	6
78	70
8,765	8,000
128,871	100,000

EXAMPLE   Estimate the area of the rectangle.

Use leading-digit estimation.
The width is about 10 cm, and the length is about 60 cm.

13.2 cm

67.5 cm

So, the area of the rectangle is about 10 * 60 or 600 sq cm.

Leading-digit estimates are usually fairly rough. However, even a rough estimate can be useful for checking calculations. If the estimate and the exact answer are not close, you should look for a mistake in your work.

EXAMPLE   Erica added 526 + 348 and got 648. Was she correct?

Since the leading-digit estimate is 800, which is not close to 648, Erica is probably not correct. She should check her work.

Exact Number		Leading-Digit Estimate
526	→	500
+ 348	→	+ 300
		800

CHECK YOUR UNDERSTANDING

1. David multiplied 563 * 32 and got 1,792. Use leading-digit estimation to decide if he was correct.

2. Caroline said there are 168 hours in a week. Use leading-digit estimation to decide if she was correct.

Check your answers on page 284.

Rounding

Rounding is a way to make numbers simpler and easier to work with. The simpler numbers usually give better estimates than you would get with leading-digit estimation.

There are steps to follow to round a number to a given place.

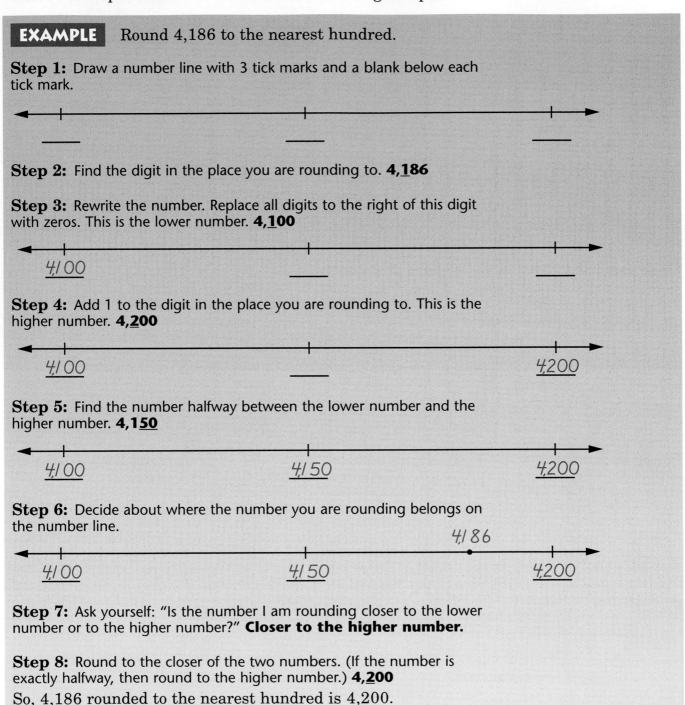

EXAMPLE   Round 4,186 to the nearest hundred.

Step 1: Draw a number line with 3 tick marks and a blank below each tick mark.

Step 2: Find the digit in the place you are rounding to. **4,1̲86**

Step 3: Rewrite the number. Replace all digits to the right of this digit with zeros. This is the lower number. **4,1̲00**

Step 4: Add 1 to the digit in the place you are rounding to. This is the higher number. **4,2̲00**

Step 5: Find the number halfway between the lower number and the higher number. **4,1̲50**

Step 6: Decide about where the number you are rounding belongs on the number line.

Step 7: Ask yourself: "Is the number I am rounding closer to the lower number or to the higher number?" **Closer to the higher number.**

Step 8: Round to the closer of the two numbers. (If the number is exactly halfway, then round to the higher number.) **4,2̲00**

So, 4,186 rounded to the nearest hundred is 4,200.

EXAMPLE   Round 7,385 to the nearest thousand.

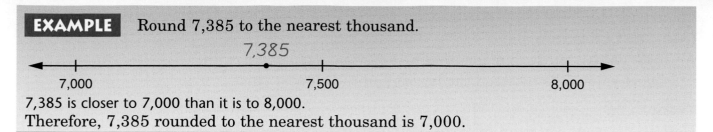

7,385 is closer to 7,000 than it is to 8,000.
Therefore, 7,385 rounded to the nearest thousand is 7,000.

EXAMPLE   Round 7,385 to the nearest hundred.

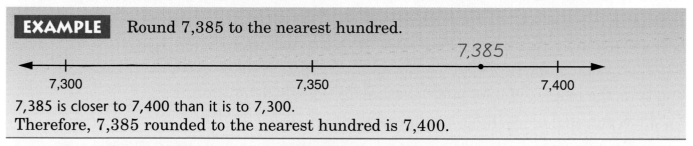

7,385 is closer to 7,400 than it is to 7,300.
Therefore, 7,385 rounded to the nearest hundred is 7,400.

EXAMPLE   Round 7,385 to the nearest ten.

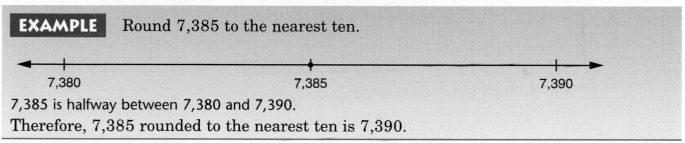

7,385 is halfway between 7,380 and 7,390.
Therefore, 7,385 rounded to the nearest ten is 7,390.

EXAMPLE   Round 5,293 to the nearest ten.

When you add 1 to the 9, the digit you are rounding to, you get 10.
Write 0 and add 1 to the digit to its left. The higher number is 5,300.

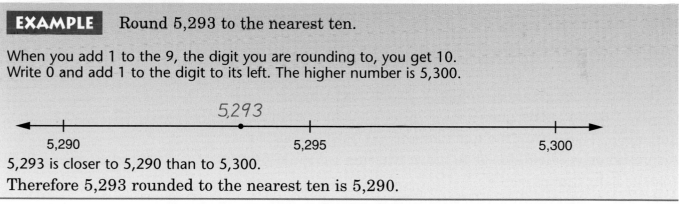

5,293 is closer to 5,290 than to 5,300.
Therefore 5,293 rounded to the nearest ten is 5,290.

CHECK YOUR UNDERSTANDING

Round to the nearest ten.

1. 87

2. 152

3. 7,910

Round to the nearest thousand.

4. 13,954

5. 4,792

6. 89,876

Check your answers on page 284.

Making Other Estimates

Interval Estimates

An **interval estimate** is made up of a range of possible values. The exact value falls between the lowest and the highest value in the range.

Here is one way to give an interval estimate:

- Name a number you are sure is *less than the exact value.*
- Name a number you are sure is *greater than the exact value.*

The smaller the difference between the upper and lower numbers, the more useful an interval estimate is likely to be.

An interval estimate can be stated in various ways.

> **EXAMPLES**   There are *at least* 30 [12s] in 400, but *not more than* 40 [12s].
>
> The number of books in the school library is *greater than* 2,000 but *less than* 2,500.
>
> *Between* 125 and 200 people live in my apartment building.

Magnitude Estimates

One kind of very rough estimate is called a **magnitude estimate.** When making a magnitude estimate, ask yourself: "Is the answer in the tens? In the hundreds? In the thousands?" and so on. These are good questions to ask to check answers displayed on a calculator or to judge whether information you read or hear makes sense.

> **EXAMPLE**   Make a magnitude estimate. 783.29 * 3.9
>
> 783.29 * 3.9 is about 800 * 4 or 3,200.
>
> So, the answer to 783.29 * 3.9 is in the thousands.

CHECK YOUR UNDERSTANDING

Make a magnitude estimate. Is the answer in the tens, hundreds, or thousands?

1. 2.89 * 35.7   **2.** 8,398 / 3   **3.** 7,293 − 6,514

Check yours answers on page 284.

Calculators

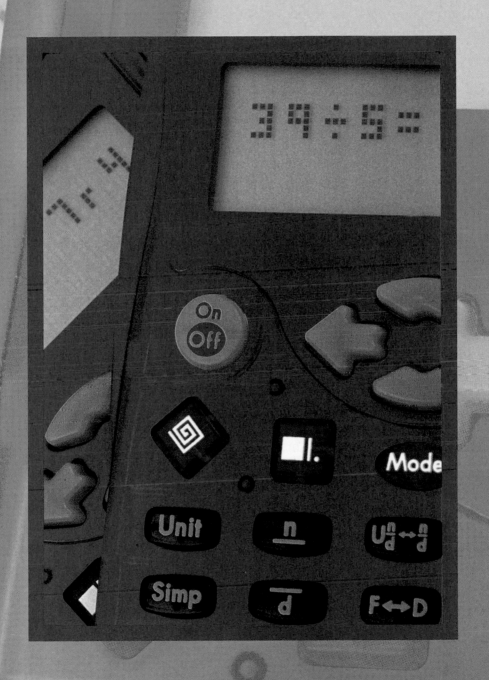

About Calculators

Throughout your study of mathematics you have used tools such as counters, rulers, tape measures, pattern blocks, compasses, protractors, and the Geometry Template. Since kindergarten, you have also used calculators. In earlier grades, you used calculators to help you learn to count. Now you use them for computations with whole numbers, fractions, decimals, and percents.

Although a calculator can help you compute quickly and accurately, you must know when and how to use it. You must decide whether it is best to solve a problem by using mental arithmetic, paper and pencil, or a calculator. When you choose to use a calculator, estimation should always be part of your work. You can use a magnitude estimate of the answer to check whether you have keyed in a wrong number or operation. Always ask yourself if the number in the display makes sense.

There are many different kinds of calculators. Simple four-function calculators do little more than add, subtract, multiply, and divide whole numbers and decimals. Other calculators also perform operations with fractions.

Rather than try to describe how various calculators work, we have chosen one calculator to which we refer throughout this book. If you have a different calculator, don't worry. There are many other calculators that work well with *Everyday Mathematics*. If the instructions in this book don't work for your calculator, you can refer to the directions that came with it, or you can ask your teacher for help.

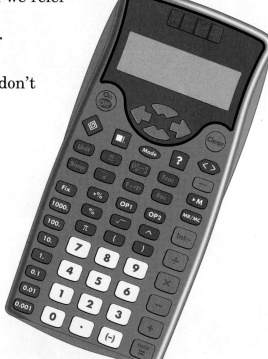

A reminder: Just as carpenters, dentists, and people in many other occupations must take care of their tools if they expect them to work properly, you must take care of your calculator. Dropping it, leaving it in the sun, or other carelessness may break it or make it less reliable.

Basic Operations

Pressing a key on a calculator is called "keying in" or "entering." In this book, calculator keys, except numbers, are shown in rectangular boxes: ⊕ , Enter , ⊗ , and so on. A set of instructions for performing a calculation is called a "key sequence." The key sequences in this book are for the calculator shown on the previous page, but many of them also work for other calculators.

On/Off turns the calculator on and off. When you turn the calculator on, you will see a blinking triangle that looks like this: ◁. This is the cursor.

Simple Arithmetic: On/Off , ⊕ , ⊖ , ⊗ , ÷ , Enter

165–166

You probably already know how to use a calculator for basic arithmetic. Usually, you can just enter the numbers and operations and press Enter to see the answer. Solve each problem on your calculator.

Key	Problem	Key Sequence	Display
⊕	$4.7 + 6.8$	4 · 7 ⊕ 6 · 8 Enter	$4.7 + 6.8 = 11.5$
	$\frac{3}{8} + \frac{1}{4}$	3 n 8 d ⊕ 1 n 4 d Enter	$\frac{3}{8} + \frac{1}{4} = \frac{5}{8}$
⊖	$12.3 - 5.9$	12 · 3 ⊖ 5 · 9 Enter	$12.3 - 5.9 = 6.4$
	$\frac{7}{8} - \frac{1}{3}$	7 n 8 d ⊖ 1 n 3 d Enter	$\frac{7}{8} - \frac{1}{3} = \frac{13}{24}$
⊗	$3.5 * 7.4$	3 · 5 ⊗ 7 · 4 Enter	$3.5 \times 7.4 = 25.9$
	$\frac{4}{5} * \frac{3}{8}$	4 n 5 d ⊗ 3 n 8 d Enter	$\frac{N}{D} \to \frac{n}{d}$ $\frac{4}{5} \times \frac{3}{8} = \frac{12}{40}$
÷	$24.9 / 1.6$	24 · 9 ÷ 1 · 6 Enter	$24.9 \div 1.6 =$ 15.5625
	$\frac{5}{6} / \frac{1}{2}$	5 n 6 d ÷ 1 n 2 d Enter	$\frac{N}{D} \to \frac{n}{d}$ $\frac{5}{6} \div \frac{1}{2} = 1\frac{4}{6}$

Calculators

Correcting and Clearing: ⊖ , [Clear] , ⇐ , ⇒

⊖ erases the character to the left of the cursor.

| EXAMPLE | Enter 123.444. Change it to 123.456. |

Key Sequence	Display
1 2 3 ⊙ 4 4 4	123.444
⊖ ⊖	123.4
5 6	123.456

You can use ⇐ and ⇒ to move the cursor to the left and right. This is useful for correcting mistakes in the middle of expressions you have entered.

| EXAMPLE | Enter 123.567. Change it to 123.4567. | | Enter 123.4456. Change it to 123.456. |

Key Sequence	Display	Key Sequence	Display
1 2 3 ⊙ 5 6 7	123.567	1 2 3 ⊙ 4 4 5 6	123.4456
⇐ ⇐ ⇐ 4 [Enter]	123.4567 = 123.4567	⇐ ⇐ ⇐ ⊖ [Enter]	123.456 = 123.456

[Clear] erases the entire display. If the cursor is in the middle of a display, you will need to press [Clear] twice to clear the entire display. Holding [On/Off] and [Clear] down together for a few moments will clear the calculator completely. Whenever you use the calculator, you should first clear it completely.

> **NOTE**
>
> The calculator remembers its settings and problems it has solved even when it is turned off. If you don't start by clearing it completely, it may not work properly.

Order of Operations and Parentheses: ⌈(⌉ , ⌈)⌉

The calculator shown on page 160 follows the rules for the order of operations.

If you have a different calculator, check whether it follows the rules of the order of operations. To do so, key in 5 ⊕ 6 ⊗ 2 ⌈Enter⌉ . If your calculator follows the order of operations, it will multiply first, then add, and the display will show 17. A calculator that does not follow the order of operations will probably do the operations in the order they are entered, adding first, then multiplying, and will display 22.

If you want the calculator to do operations in an order different from the usual order, use ⌈(⌉ and ⌈)⌉ .

EXAMPLE   Evaluate. $7 - (2 + 1)$

Key Sequence	Display
7 ⊖ ⌈(⌉ 2 ⊕ 1 ⌈)⌉ ⌈Enter⌉	$7 - (2 + 1) = 4$

$7 - (2 + 1) = 4$

Sometimes expressions are given without all of the multiplication signs. Remember to press the multiplication key even when it is not written.

EXAMPLE   Evaluate. $9 - 2(1 + 2)$

Key Sequence	Display
9 ⊖ 2 ⊗ ⌈(⌉ 1 ⊕ 2 ⌈)⌉ ⌈Enter⌉	$9 - 2 \times (1 + 2)$ $= 3$

$9 - 2(1 + 2) = 3$

CHECK YOUR UNDERSTANDING

Use your calculator to evaluate each problem.

1. $28 - (5 + 7)$ **2.** $93 - 5 * (4 + 9)$ **3.** $5 * (7 + 8) - 12$ **4.** $9 * (14 - 7) + 18$

Check your answers on page 284.

Negative Numbers: $\ominus$

Use $\ominus$ to enter a negative number.

> **EXAMPLE** Enter -45.
>
> | Key Sequence | Display |
> |---|---|
> | $\ominus$ 4 5 [Enter] | -45 =   -45 |

Notice that $\ominus$ is not an operation. The key for subtraction is $\ominus$. If you try to use $\ominus$ to do subtraction, you will get an error.

> **EXAMPLE** $38 - 9 = ?$
>
> | Key Sequence | Display |
> |---|---|
> | 3 8 $\ominus$ 9 [Enter] | SYN ERROR |
> | 3 8 $\ominus$ 9 [Enter] | 38 - 9 =   29 |
>
> $38 - 9 = 29$

Division with Remainders: [Int÷]

The result of a division with whole numbers is often not a whole number. Most calculators display such a result as a decimal. Many calculators also have another division key, [Int÷], that displays the results of a division as a whole number quotient with a whole number remainder.

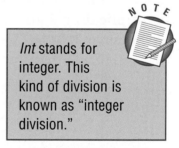

> **NOTE**
>
> *Int* stands for integer. This kind of division is known as "integer division."

> **EXAMPLE** $39 \div 5 = ?$ Use the [Int÷] key.
>
> | Key Sequence | Display |
> |---|---|
> | 3 9 [Int÷] 5 [Enter] | 39 ÷ 5 = 7 r 4 |
>
> $39 \div 5 = 7$ R4

Integer division only works with whole numbers. If you try to use a negative number or a fraction you will get an error.

Fractions and Percent

Certain calculators can handle fractions. Once fractions have been entered on such calculators, they can be added, subtracted, multiplied, and divided using the $+$, $-$, $\times$, or $\div$ keys.

Entering Fractions and Mixed Numbers: [n], [d], [Unit], [U$\frac{n}{d}$↔$\frac{n}{d}$]
Use [n], [d], and [Unit] to enter fractions and mixed numbers.

EXAMPLE $\frac{3}{4} + \frac{7}{8} = ?$

Key Sequence	Display
3 [n] 4 [d] $+$ 7 [n] 8 [d] [Enter]	$\frac{3}{4} + \frac{7}{8} = 1\frac{5}{8}$

$\frac{3}{4} + \frac{7}{8} = 1\frac{5}{8}$

NOTE

You do not need to press [d] after you enter the denominator.

EXAMPLE $1\frac{1}{2} \div 2\frac{1}{2} = ?$

Key Sequence	Display
1 [Unit] 1 [n] 2 [d] $\div$ 2 [Unit] 1 [n] 2 [d] [Enter]	$1\frac{1}{2} \div 2\frac{1}{2} = \frac{6}{10}$

$1\frac{1}{2} \div 2\frac{1}{2} = \frac{6}{10}$

46

Use [U$\frac{n}{d}$↔$\frac{n}{d}$] to change between mixed numbers and improper fractions.

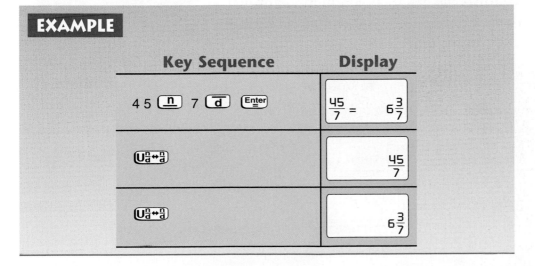

EXAMPLE

Key Sequence	Display
4 5 [n] 7 [d] [Enter]	$\frac{45}{7} = 6\frac{3}{7}$
[U$\frac{n}{d}$↔$\frac{n}{d}$]	$\frac{45}{7}$
[U$\frac{n}{d}$↔$\frac{n}{d}$]	$6\frac{3}{7}$

53–56

Simplifying Fractions: [Simp], [Fac]

Ordinarily, the calculator on page 160 does not simplify fractions automatically. The message $\frac{N}{D} \to \frac{n}{d}$ in the display means that the fraction shown is not yet in simplest form.

Use [Simp] to simplify fractions. When you press [Simp] [Enter], the calculator divides the numerator and the denominator by a common factor. To see what number the calculator used, press [Fac]. You may have to press [Simp] [Enter] several times to put a fraction in simplest form.

The [Simp] key simplifies fractions.

| **EXAMPLE** | Change $\frac{18}{24}$ to simplest form. |

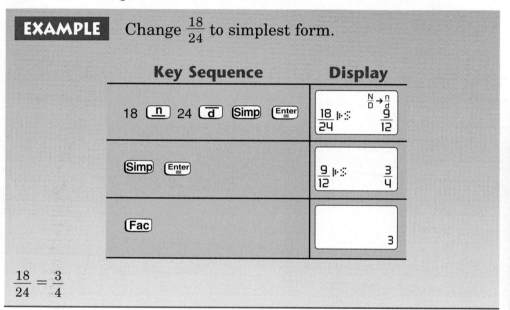

Key Sequence	Display
18 [n] 24 [d] [Simp] [Enter]	$\frac{18}{24} \triangleright \overset{\frac{N}{D} \to \frac{n}{d}}{\frac{9}{12}}$
[Simp] [Enter]	$\frac{9}{12} \triangleright \quad \frac{3}{4}$
[Fac]	3

$$\frac{18}{24} = \frac{3}{4}$$

If you want to tell the calculator to divide the numerator and the denominator by a certain number, then enter that number after you press [Simp]. If you use the greatest common factor of the numerator and the denominator, then you can simplify the fraction in one step.

The [Fac] key tells what common factor the calculator used when simplifying fractions.

| **EXAMPLE** | Change $\frac{18}{24}$ to simplest form in one step by |

dividing the numerator and the denominator by their greatest common factor, 6.

Key Sequence	Display
18 [n] 24 [d] [Simp] 6 [Enter]	$\frac{18}{24} \triangleright 6 \quad \frac{3}{4}$
[Fac]	6

Percent: %, ▸%

On the calculator shown here % divides the number before it by 100. % can be used to change percents into decimals.

EXAMPLE

Key Sequence	Display
85 % Enter	85% = 0.85
250 % Enter	250% = 2.5
1 % Enter	1% = 0.01

% can also be used to solve problems with percents.

EXAMPLE Find 25% of 180.

Key Sequence	Display
2 5 % ✕ 1 8 0 Enter	25% × 180 = 45

25% of 180 = 45

The ▸% key multiplies a number by 100.

The % key divides a number by 100.

▸% does the opposite of % . That is, ▸% multiplies the number before it by 100. ▸% can be used to change a number into an equivalent percent.

EXAMPLES

Key Sequence	Display
0 · 2 5 ▸% Enter	0.25 ▸·: 25%
1 ▸% Enter	1 ▸·: 100%

0.25 = 25%   1 = 100%

Fraction/Decimal/Percent Conversions: F↔D

Calculators can be used to convert between fractions, decimals, and percents. Conversions of fractions to decimals and percents can be done on any calculator. For example, to rename $\frac{3}{5}$ as a decimal, simply enter 3 ÷ 5 Enter. The display will show 0.6. To rename a decimal as a percent, just multiply by 100.

Conversions of decimals and percents to fractions can only be done directly on calculators that have special keys to handle fractions. Such calculators usually have special keys for changing a fraction to its decimal equivalent or a decimal to an equivalent fraction.

Use F↔D to change between fractions and decimals. When decimals are changed to fractions, they may need to be simplified.

EXAMPLE Convert $\frac{3}{8}$ to a decimal and back to a fraction in simplest form.

Key Sequence	Display
3 [n] 8 [d] [Enter]	$\frac{3}{8} = \frac{3}{8}$
[F↔D]	0.375
[F↔D]	$\frac{N}{D} \to \frac{n}{d}$ $\frac{375}{1000}$
[Simp] [Enter]	$\frac{N}{D} \to \frac{n}{d}$ $\frac{375}{1000} \mapsto \frac{75}{200}$
[Simp] [Enter]	$\frac{N}{D} \to \frac{n}{d}$ $\frac{75}{200} \mapsto \frac{15}{40}$
[Simp] [Enter]	$\frac{15}{40} \mapsto \frac{3}{8}$

The table shows examples of various conversions. Although only one key sequence is shown for each conversion, there are other ways to do most of these conversions.

Conversion	Starting Number	Key Sequence	Display
Fraction to decimal	$\frac{3}{5}$	3 [n] 5 [d] [Enter] [F↔D]	0.6
Decimal to fraction	0.125	0 [.] 1 2 5 [Enter] [F↔D]	$\frac{N}{D}$→$\frac{n}{d}$ $\frac{125}{1000}$
Decimal to percent	0.75	0 [.] 7 5 [▶%] [Enter]	0.75 ▶◌ 75%
Percent to decimal	125%	1 2 5 [%] [Enter]	125% = 1.25
Fraction to percent	$\frac{5}{8}$	5 [n] 8 [d] [▶%] [Enter]	$\frac{5}{8}$ ▶◌ 62.5%
Percent to fraction	35%	3 5 [%] [Enter] [F↔D]	$\frac{N}{D}$→$\frac{n}{d}$ $\frac{35}{100}$

CHECK YOUR UNDERSTANDING

Use your calculator to convert between fractions, decimals, and percents.

1. $\frac{5}{8}$ to a decimal
2. 0.175 to a fraction
3. 0.64 to a percent

4. 275% to a decimal
5. $\frac{5}{12}$ to a percent
6. 45% to a fraction

7. $\frac{3}{4}$ to a decimal
8. $\frac{5}{6}$ to a decimal
9. 0.556 to a fraction

10. 67% to a fraction
11. 325% to a decimal
12. $\frac{3}{7}$ to a decimal

Check your answers on page 284.

Advanced Operations

Your calculator can do more than simple arithmetic with whole numbers, fractions, and decimals. The following pages explain some of the other things your calculator can do.

Scrolling: ⬆ , ⬇

⬆ and ⬇ allow you to see previous entries and results. Moving up and down to previous displays is called **scrolling.** Small arrows in the display tell you which directions you can scroll.

You can use ⬆ and ⬇ to see problems you entered before. Then you can use ⬅ , ➡ , and ⬉ to change those problems if you wish.

⬆ and ⬇ are also used with menus.

Menus: Mode

The calculator shown on page 160 has several menus for changing how it works. In each menu, the current choice is underlined. Use ⬅ and ➡ to change what is underlined. Then press Enter to make your new choice active. If you don't press Enter , then the old menu choice will still be active.

Most of the menus are reached by pressing Mode . The fraction menus are reached by pressing Frac .

Key Sequence	Display	Purpose
Mode	⌐ N/d ÷	Controls whether quotients are shown as decimals or as mixed numbers.
Mode ⬇	+1 ? OP	Controls whether the operation is shown or hidden when Op1 and Op2 are used.
Mode ⬇ ⬇	OP1 OP2 CLEAR	Used for clearing a constant operation.
Mode ⬇ ⬇ ⬇	N Y RESET	Used for resetting the calculator.

EXAMPLE Divide. Find the quotient as a mixed number.

$56 / 3 = ?$

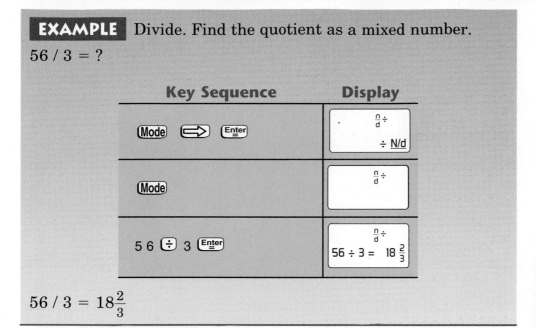

Key Sequence	Display
(Mode) ⇒ (Enter)	$\frac{n}{d}÷$ ÷ N/d
(Mode)	$\frac{n}{d}÷$
5 6 ÷ 3 (Enter)	$\frac{n}{d}÷$ $56 ÷ 3 = 18\frac{2}{3}$

$56 / 3 = 18\frac{2}{3}$

EXAMPLE Reset the calculator.

Key Sequence	Display
(Mode) ⬇ ⬇ ⬇ ⇒	n Y RESET
(Enter)	MEM CLEARED

Fraction Menus: (Frac)

There are two menus for changing how the calculator handles fractions. Use (Frac) to reach these menus. As with other menus, use ⇐ and ⇒ to change what is underlined. Then press (Enter) to make your new choice active. If you don't press (Enter), then the old choice will still be active.

Key Sequence	Display	Purpose
(Frac)	U n/d n/d	Controls whether results are shown as mixed numbers or improper fractions.
(Frac) ⬇	MAN AUTO	Controls whether simplifying fractions is done manually or automatically.

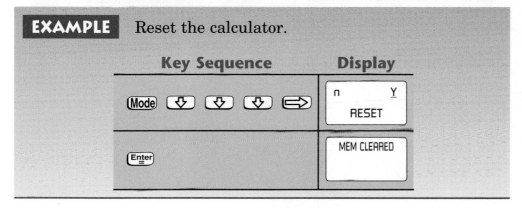

EXAMPLE Solve $\frac{4}{5} * \frac{1}{2}$ with the calculator in MAN mode and again in AUTO mode.

Key Sequence	Display
4 [n] 5 [d] [×] 1 [n] 2 [d] [Enter]	$\frac{4}{5} \times \frac{1}{2} = \frac{N}{D} \to \frac{n}{d}$ $\frac{4}{10}$
[Simp] [Enter]	$\frac{4}{10}$ ▸⁘ $\frac{2}{5}$
[Frac] [⬇] [⮕] [Enter]	Auto MAN **AUTO**
[Frac] [Clear]	Auto
4 [n] 5 [d] [×] 1 [n] 2 [d] [Enter]	Auto $\frac{4}{5} \times \frac{1}{2} = \frac{2}{5}$

$\frac{4}{5} * \frac{1}{2} = \frac{2}{5}$

EXAMPLE Change to improper fraction mode and solve $\frac{5}{2} + \frac{8}{3}$. Then change the answer to a mixed number.

Key Sequence	Display
[Frac] [⮕] [Enter]	U n/d n/d
5 [n] 2 [d] [+] 8 [n] 3 [d] [Enter]	$\frac{5}{2} + \frac{8}{3} = \frac{31}{6}$
[U n/d ↔ n/d]	$5\frac{1}{6}$

$\frac{5}{2} + \frac{8}{3} = 5\frac{1}{6}$

Rounding

To set the calculator to round, press $\boxed{\text{Fix}}$ and one of the numbers on the red keys below the $\boxed{\text{Fix}}$ key.

The calculator can be set to round to any place from thousands $\boxed{\text{1000.}}$ to thousandths $\boxed{\text{0.001}}$. To turn off rounding, press $\boxed{\text{Fix}}$ $\boxed{.}$.

EXAMPLE First set the calculator to round to hundreds. Then round 1,376, 79, and 23 to the nearest hundred.

Key Sequence	Display
$\boxed{\text{Fix}}$ $\boxed{\text{100.}}$	Fix
1376 $\boxed{\text{Enter}}$	Fix 1376 = 1400.
79 $\boxed{\text{Enter}}$	Fix 79 = 100.
23 $\boxed{\text{Enter}}$	Fix 23 = 000.

EXAMPLE Solve 73 * 19 and 1,568 + 399. Find the exact answers. Then find the answers rounded to the nearest hundred.

Key Sequence	Display
73 $\boxed{\times}$ 19 $\boxed{\text{Enter}}$	73 × 19 = 1387
1568 $\boxed{+}$ 399 $\boxed{\text{Enter}}$	1568 + 399 = 1967

Key Sequence	Display
$\boxed{\text{Fix}}$ $\boxed{\text{100.}}$	Fix
73 $\boxed{\times}$ 19 $\boxed{\text{Enter}}$	Fix 73 × 19 = 1400.
1568 $\boxed{+}$ 399 $\boxed{\text{Enter}}$	Fix 1568 + 399 = 2000.

CHECK YOUR UNDERSTANDING

Use your calculator to round 8,578 to the nearest:

1. ten
2. hundred
3. thousand

Check your answers on page 284.

Powers and Square Roots: $\boxed{\wedge}$, $\boxed{\sqrt{}}$

$\boxed{\wedge}$ is used for raising numbers to powers on many calculators. Sometimes $[y^x]$ or some other key is used. Negative exponents are allowed, but be careful to use $\boxed{\ominus}$ when you enter a negative number. If you use $\boxed{\ominus}$, you may get an error.

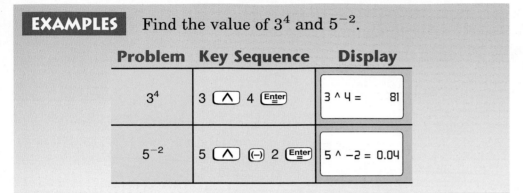

EXAMPLES   Find the value of 3^4 and 5^{-2}.

Problem	Key Sequence	Display
3^4	3 $\boxed{\wedge}$ 4 $\boxed{\text{Enter}}$	3 ^ 4 = 81
5^{-2}	5 $\boxed{\wedge}$ $\boxed{\ominus}$ 2 $\boxed{\text{Enter}}$	5 ^ −2 = 0.04

> **NOTE**
> The symbol ^ is called a "caret." It is often used in computer programming for raising numbers to powers.
>
> 5^2 means
> $5^2 = 5 * 5 = 25$

To find the reciprocal of a number, raise the number to the -1 power.

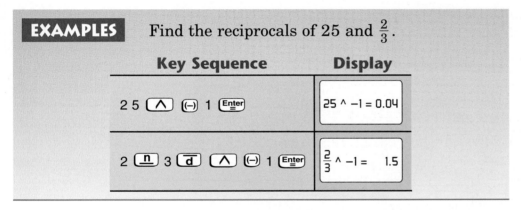

EXAMPLES   Find the reciprocals of 25 and $\frac{2}{3}$.

Key Sequence	Display
25 $\boxed{\wedge}$ $\boxed{\ominus}$ 1 $\boxed{\text{Enter}}$	25 ^ −1 = 0.04
2 $\boxed{\text{n}}$ 3 $\boxed{\text{d}}$ $\boxed{\wedge}$ $\boxed{\ominus}$ 1 $\boxed{\text{Enter}}$	$\frac{2}{3}$ ^ −1 = 1.5

Note: To see the reciprocal of $\frac{2}{3}$ as a fraction, key in $\boxed{\text{F↔D}}$, $\boxed{\text{Simp}}$, $\boxed{\text{Enter}}$, and $\boxed{\text{U}\frac{n}{d}\text{↔}\frac{n}{d}}$. The reciprocal of $\frac{2}{3}$, written as a fraction, is $\frac{3}{2}$.

Many calculators have a special key for finding square roots. Notice that before you press $\boxed{\text{Enter}}$, you have to press $\boxed{)}$.

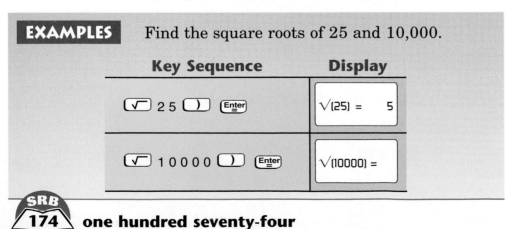

EXAMPLES   Find the square roots of 25 and 10,000.

Key Sequence	Display
$\boxed{\sqrt{}}$ 2 5 $\boxed{)}$ $\boxed{\text{Enter}}$	$\sqrt{(25)}$ = 5
$\boxed{\sqrt{}}$ 1 0 0 0 0 $\boxed{)}$ $\boxed{\text{Enter}}$	$\sqrt{(10000)}$ =

> **NOTE**
> On some calculators the square root key $\boxed{\sqrt{}}$ is entered after the number, and on others, it is entered before the number. On the calculator shown on page 160, the square root key is entered before the number.

Scientific Notation

On many calculators, numbers with more digits than will fit in the display are automatically shown in scientific notation. Calculators differ in the way they show scientific notation.

Scientific notation is a way of writing numbers in which a number is written as the product of a number and a power of 10. The number must be 1 or greater, but less than 10. In scientific notation, 900,000 is written as $9 * 10^5$.

Some calculators can display raised exponents, but most cannot. Some calculators that have scientific notation do not bother to display the base, which is always 10, and use a space or letter to show the exponent. Others, like the one on page 160, do show the base, but use a caret ^ to show the exponent.

EXAMPLES

Key Sequence	Display
7 ⊗ 10 ⌃ 4 (Enter)	7 × 10 ^ 4 = 70000
4 ⊙ 35 ⊗ 10 ⌃ 5 (Enter)	4.35 × 10 ^ 5 = 435000
4 ⊗ 10 ⌃ (-) 3 (Enter)	4 × 10 ^ -3 = 0.004

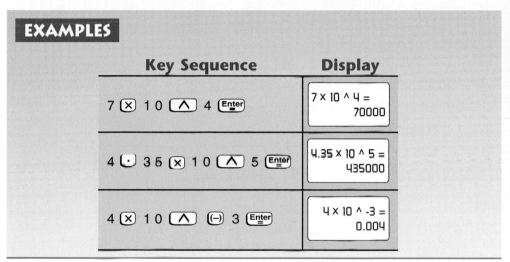

CHECK YOUR UNDERSTANDING

Use your calculator to convert the following to standard notation:

1. $5 * 10^5$ **2.** $9 * 10^{-9}$ **3.** $2.2 * 10^{-2}$ **4.** $5.15 * 10^4$

Check your answers on page 284.

Calculators

Numbers with more than 10 digits can be entered in the calculator on page 160—the maximum number of digits allowed is 88—but answers with more than 10 digits are displayed in scientific notation.

EXAMPLE   Write 123,123,123,123,123,123 in scientific notation.

Key Sequence	Display
1 2 3 1 2 3 1 2 3 1 2 3 1 2 3 1 2 3 [Enter]	1.231 × 10 ^ 17

$123,123,123,123,123,123 = 1.231 * 10^{17}$

EXAMPLE   Write in scientific notation. 1*2*3*4*5*6*7*8*9*10*11*12*13*14*15

Key Sequence	Display
1 [×] 2 [×] 3 [×] 4 [×] 5 [×] 6 [×] 7 [×] 8 [×] 9 [×] 10 [×] 11 [×] 12 [×] 13 [×] 14 [×] 15 [Enter]	1.308 × 10 ^ 12

$1 * 2 * 3 * 4 * 5 * 6 * 7 * 8 * 9 * 10 * 11 * 12 * 13 * 14 * 15 = 1.308 * 10^{12}$

CHECK YOUR UNDERSTANDING

Write in scientific notation.

1. 23 * 624 * 339 * 347 * 528
2. 849 * 796 * 197 * 758 * 64
3. 55 * 2,981 * 34 * 21 * 456
4. 612 * 3,581 * 712 * 314 * 611

Convert from scientific notation to standard notation.

5. $6.55321 * 10^8$
6. $1.59 * 10^{11}$

Check your answers on page 284.

Pi: $\boxed{\pi}$

The formulas for the perimeter, area, and volume of many geometric figures involve pi (π). Pi is a number that is a little more than 3. The first few digits of π are 3.14159265.... Your calculator has a special key for pi, $\boxed{\pi}$. When you need to use π in a calculation, use $\boxed{\pi}$.

Note: To see a decimal for π, press $\boxed{\pi}$ $\boxed{\text{Enter}}$ $\boxed{\text{F↔D}}$.

EXAMPLE Find the area of a circle with a 4-foot radius. Use the formula $A = \pi r^2$.

Key Sequence	Display
$\boxed{\pi}$ $\boxed{\times}$ 4 $\boxed{\wedge}$ 2 $\boxed{\text{Enter}}$	Π×4^2＝16Π

Notice that the display answer is 16π. This is the exact area for a circle with a 4-foot radius. To see 16π as a decimal, press $\boxed{\text{F↔D}}$.

$\boxed{\text{F↔D}}$	50.26548246

This answer, 50.26548246 square feet, has more digits than are significant. Since you know the circle's radius only to one significant digit, it's not appropriate to have 10 digits in the area. You need to round the result to an appropriate number of decimal places. Here, you might say the area is 50 sq ft or perhaps 50.3 square feet.

EXAMPLE Find the circumference of a circle with a 15-foot diameter. Use the formula $c = \pi d$.

Key Sequence	Display
$\boxed{\pi}$ $\boxed{\times}$ 15 $\boxed{\text{Enter}}$	Π×15＝ 15Π
$\boxed{\text{F↔D}}$	47.1238898

The circumference is about 47 feet.

Memory: ▶M , MR/MC

The memory of a calculator is a place where a number can be stored while the calculator is working with other numbers. Later, when you need it, you can recall the number from memory. Most calculators display an M or similar symbol when there is a number other than 0 in the memory.

Key Sequence	Purpose
▶M Enter	Stores the number in the display in the memory, *replacing* any number already in the memory.
MR/MC	Recalls the number stored in memory and shows it in the display.
MR/MC MR/MC	Clears the memory. (This really means that 0 is in the memory.)

The calculator's memory only works with numbers that are the result of calculations. This means that you must press Enter before you can store a number in the memory.

The ▶M key stores the number in the display.

The MR/MC key recalls the number stored in the memory.

EXAMPLE   Store 25 in the memory.

Key Sequence	Display
2 5 ▶M Enter	MEM ERROR
2 5 Enter ▶M Enter	M 25 = 25
Clear	M
MR/MC	M 25

CHECK YOUR UNDERSTANDING

Store each number in the memory. To check that the nuber has been stored, clear the calculator screen. Then recall the stored number from memory.

1. 79

2. $\frac{5}{8}$

3. −36

EXAMPLE   Compute a 15% tip on a $25 bill. Store the tip in the memory and then find the total bill.

Key Sequence	Display
15 [%] [×] 25 [Enter]	15% × 25 = 3.75
[▶M] [Enter]	M 15% × 25 = 3.75
25 [+] [MR/MC] [Enter]	25 + 3.75 = 28.75

To clear the memory, press [MR/MC] twice. Do not press [MR/MC] more than twice.

Key Sequence	Display	Number in Memory
5 [Enter] [▶M] [Enter]	M 5 = 5	5
[MR/MC]	M 5	5
[MR/MC]	M 5	0

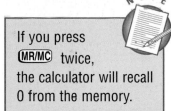

NOTE

If you press [MR/MC] twice, the calculator will recall 0 from the memory.

CHECK YOUR UNDERSTANDING

Use your calculator to solve each problem.

1. Compute a 15% tip on a $100 bill.

2. Compute a 20% tip on a bill totaling $55.75.

Check your answers on page 284.

You can use the memory of a calculator to solve problems that have several steps.

EXAMPLE   Marguerite ordered the following food at the food court: 2 hamburgers at $1.49 each and 3 hot dogs at $0.89 each. How much change will she receive from a $10 bill?

Key Sequence	Display
2 × 1 [.] 4 9 (Enter) (▶M) (Enter)	M 2 × 1.49 = 2.98
3 (×) [.] 8 9 (Enter) (▶M) (+)	M 3 × .89 = 2.67
1 0 (−) (MR/MC) (Enter)	M 10 − 5.65 = 4.35

Marguerite will receive $4.35 cash back.

EXAMPLE   Mr. Beckman bought 2 adult tickets at $8.25 each and 3 child tickets at $4.75 each. He redeemed a $5 gift certificate. How much did he pay for the tickets?

Key Sequence	Display
2 (×) 8 [.] 2 5 (Enter) (▶M) (Enter)	M 2 × 8.25 = 16.5
3 (×) 4 [.] 7 5 (Enter) (▶M) (+)	M 3 × 4.75 = 14.25
(MR/MC) (−) 5 (Enter)	M 30. 75 − 5 = 25.75

Mr. Beckman paid $25.75 for the tickets.

Repeating an Operation: (Op1) , (Op2)

Most calculators have a way to let you repeat an operation. This is called the **constant function.** (*Constant* means *unchanging*.)

To use the constant function of your calculator, follow these steps.

1. Press (Op1) .
2. Press the keys that define the constant function.
3. Press (Op1) .
4. Enter a number.
5. Press (Op1) .

The (Op1) and (Op2) keys allow you to program and repeat operations.

You can repeat Steps 4 and 5 for as many different numbers as you wish.

EXAMPLE   Set up the calculator to multiply numbers by 7. Then multiply several numbers by 7.

Key Sequence	Display
(Op1) (×) 7 (Op1)	Op1 × 7
8 (Op1)	Op1 8 × 7 1 56
20 (Op1)	Op1 20 × 7 1 140

Use (Mode) to clear the constant operation(s).

Key Sequence	Display
(Mode) (⇩) (⇩) (Enter)	OP1 OP2 CLEAR

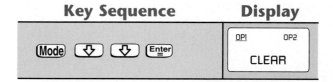

In earlier grades, you may have used the constant function to practice counting by a certain number.

Calculators

EXAMPLE Count by 7s, starting at 3.

Key Sequence	Display
(Op1) (+) 7 (Op1)	Op1 + 7
3 (Op1)	Op1 3 + 7 1 10
(Op1)	Op1 10 + 7 2 17
(Op1)	Op1 17 + 7 3 24
(Op1)	Op1 24 + 7 4 31
(Op1)	Op1 31 + 7 5 38

> **NOTE**
> The numbers in the lower left corner of the display show how many counts you have made.

You can use (Op2) to define a second constant operation.
(Op2) works exactly the same way as (Op1).

Other Features

The calculator shown on page 160 has several features not discussed in this book. Most of these have to do with the red keys: ◈, ▣, ②, and so on. Some of these keys are for place value. Others make the calculator give you problems so you can practice arithmetic. For details, ask your teacher or read the instructions that came with the calculator.

CHECK YOUR UNDERSTANDING

Use your calculator to do the following counts. Write five counts each.

1. Count by 11s, starting at 8.
2. Count by 3s, starting at 6.

Check your answers on page 284.

Games

Games

Throughout the year, you will play games that help you practice important math skills. Playing mathematics games gives you a chance to practice math skills in a way that is different and enjoyable.

In this section of your *Student Reference Book,* you will find the directions for many games. The numbers in most games are generated randomly. This means that the games can be played over and over without repeating the same problems.

Many students have created their own variations to these games to make them more interesting. We encourage you to do this. We hope that you will play often and have fun!

Materials

You need a deck of number cards for many of the games. You can use an Everything Math Deck, a regular deck of cards, or make your own deck out of index cards.

An Everything Math Deck includes 54 cards. There are four cards each for the numbers 0–10. And there is one card for each of the numbers 11–20.

You can also use a regular deck of playing cards to play, with a few changes. A deck of playing cards includes 54 cards (52 regular cards, plus 2 jokers). To create a deck of number cards from it, use a permanent marker to mark these cards in the following way:

* Mark each of the four aces with the number 1.
* Mark each of the four queens with the number 0.
* Mark the four jacks and four kings with the numbers 11 through 18.
* Mark the two jokers with the numbers 19 and 20.

For some games you will have to make a game board, or a score sheet, or a set of cards that are not number cards. The instructions for doing this are included with the game directions. More complicated game boards and card decks are available from your teacher.

Baseball Multiplication (1 to 6 Facts)

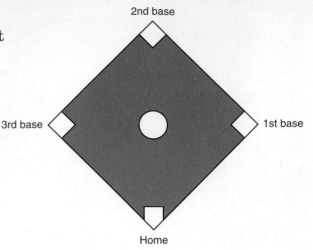

2nd base

3rd base

1st base

Home

Materials ☐ *Baseball Multiplication* Game Mat
(*Math Masters*, p. 31)
☐ 2 six-sided dice
☐ 4 pennies
☐ calculator or a
multiplication/division table

Players   2 or 2 teams

Object of the game To score the most runs in
a 3-inning game.

Directions

Advance Preparation: Draw a diamond and label *Home plate,*
1st base, 2nd base, and *3rd base.* Make a Scoreboard
sheet that looks like the one shown at the right.

Take turns being the *pitcher* and the *batter.* The rules
are similar to the rules of baseball, but this game lasts
only three innings.

Inning		1	2	3	Total
Team 1	outs				
	runs				
Team 2	outs				
	runs				

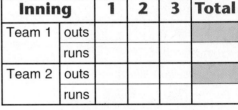

Hitting Table 1 to 6 Facts	
1 to 9	Out
10 to 18	Single (1 base)
20 to 28	Double (2 bases)
30 to 35	Triple (3 bases)
36	Home Run (4 bases)

1. At the start of the inning, the batter puts a penny
    on home plate. The pitcher rolls the dice. The batter
    multiplies the numbers rolled and gives the answer. The
    pitcher checks the answer and may use a calculator to do so.

2. If the answer is correct, the batter looks up the product in
    the Hitting Table at the right. If it is a hit, the batter
    moves all pennies on the field the number of bases shown
    in the table. If a product is not a hit, it is an out.

3. An incorrect answer is a strike and another pitch (dice roll)
    is thrown. Three strikes make an out.

4. A run is scored each time a penny crosses home plate. The
    batter tallies each run scored on the Scoreboard.

5. After each hit or out, the batter puts a penny on home plate.
    A player remains the batter for three outs. Then the players
    switch roles. The inning is over when both players have
    made three outs.

The player who has more runs at the end of three innings wins
the game. If the game is tied at the end of three innings, play
continues into extra innings until one player wins.

Baseball Multiplication (Advanced Versions)

1 to 10 Facts
Materials ☐ number cards 1–10 (4 of each)

Follow the basic rules. The pitcher draws two cards from the deck. The batter finds their product and uses the Hitting Table at the right to find out how to move the pennies.

2 to 12 Facts
Materials ☐ 4 six-sided dice

Follow the basic rules. The pitcher rolls four dice. The batter separates them into two pairs, adds the numbers in each pair, and multiplies the sums. Use the Hitting Table at the right.

How you pair the numbers can determine the kind of hit you get or whether you get an out. For example, suppose you roll a 1, 2, 3, and 5. You could add pairs in different ways and multiply as follows:

one way	a second way	a third way
1 + 2 = 3	1 + 3 = 4	1 + 5 = 6
3 + 5 = 8	2 + 5 = 7	2 + 3 = 5
3 * 8 = 24	4 * 7 = 28	6 * 5 = 30
Out	Single	Single

Three-Factors Game
Materials ☐ 3 six-sided dice

The pitcher rolls three dice. The batter multiplies the three numbers (factors) and uses the Hitting Table at the right.

10s * 10s Game
Materials ☐ 4 six-sided dice

The rules for this game are the same as for the **2 to 12 Facts** game with two exceptions:

1. A sum 2 through 9 represents 20 through 90. A sum 10 through 12 represents itself. For example,
   Roll 1, 2, 3, and 5. Get sums 6 and 5. Multiply 60 * 50.
   Roll 3, 4, 6, and 6. Get sums 12 and 7. Multiply 12 * 70.
2. Use the Hitting Table at the right.

Hitting Table
1 to 10 Facts

1 to 21	Out
24 to 45	Single (1 base)
48 to 70	Double (2 bases)
72 to 81	Triple (3 bases)
90 to 100	Home Run (4 bases)

Hitting Table
2 to 12 Facts

4 to 24	Out
25 to 49	Single (1 base)
50 to 64	Double (2 bases)
66 to 77	Triple (3 bases)
80 to 144	Home Run (4 bases)

Hitting Table
Three-Factors Game

1 to 54	Out
60 to 90	Single (1 base)
96 to 120	Double (2 bases)
125 to 150	Triple (3 bases)
180 to 216	Home Run (4 bases)

Hitting Table
10s * 10s Game

100 to 2,000	Out
2,100 to 4,000	Single (1 base)
4,200 to 5,400	Double (2 bases)
5,600 to 6,400	Triple (3 bases)
7,200 to 8,100	Home Run (4 bases)

Beat the Calculator

Multiplication Facts

Materials ☐ *Beat the Calculator* Gameboard
(*Math Masters*, p. 69)
☐ number cards 1–10 (4 of each)
☐ 1 calculator

Players   3

Directions

1. One player is the "Caller," one is the "Calculator," and one is the "Brain."

2. Shuffle the deck of cards and place it facedown.

3. The Caller draws two cards from the number deck and asks for their product.

4. The Calculator solves the problem with a calculator. The Brain solves it without a calculator. The Caller decides who got the answer first.

5. The Caller continues to draw two cards at a time from the number deck and asks for their product.

6. Players trade roles every 10 turns or so.

> **EXAMPLE**   The Caller draws a 10 and 7 and calls out "10 times 7." The Brain and the Calculator solve the problem.
>
> The Caller decides who got the answer first.
>
> 10   7

Extended Multiplication Facts

In this version of the game, the Caller:

• Draws two cards from the number deck.

• Attaches a 0 to either one of the factors or to both factors, before asking for the product.

> **EXAMPLE**   If the Caller turns over a 4 and a 6, he or she may make up any one of the following problems:
>
> 4 * 60   40 * 6   40 * 60
>
> The Brain and the Calculator solve the problem. The Caller decides who got the answer first.
>
> 4   6

Broken-Calculator Games

Broken Number Keys

Materials ☐ *Broken Calculator* Record Sheet
(*Math Master*, p. 43)
☐ 1 calculator

Players 2

Directions

1. Partners pretend that one of the number keys is broken.
2. One partner says a number.
3. The other partner tries to display that number on the calculator without using the "broken" key.

> **EXAMPLE** Suppose the 8 key is "broken."
> The number 18 can be displayed by pressing
> 9 ⊕ 7 ⊕ 2 (Enter) , or 9 ⊗ 2 (Enter) , or 72 ÷ 4 (Enter) .

Scoring: A player's score is the number of keys pressed to display the number. Scores for five rounds are totaled. The player with the lowest total wins.

Broken Operation Keys
Directions

1. Partners pretend that one of the operation keys is broken.
2. One partner says an open sentence.
3. The other tries to solve the sentence on the calculator without using the "broken" key.

> **EXAMPLE** Pretend the ⊖ key is broken. What is the solution
> to the open sentence $452 + x = 735$?
>
> Replace the variable x with   Try 400: 452 ⊕ 400 (Enter) Answer: 852   400 is too big.
> a number and see if you get   Try 300: 452 ⊕ 300 (Enter) Answer: 752   300 is 17 away.
> a true number sentence. If it   Try 317: 452 ⊕ 317 (Enter) Answer: 769   Wrong way!
> is not true, try other numbers   Try 283: 452 ⊕ 283 (Enter) Answer: 735   True sentence.
> until you get a true sentence.
>
> 283 is the answer.

Scoring: A player's score is the number of guesses it took to get a true number sentence. Scores for five rounds are totaled. The player with the lowest total wins.

Buzz Games

Buzz

Materials   none

Players   5–10

Directions

1. Players sit in a circle, and choose a leader. The leader names any whole number from 3 to 9. This number is the BUZZ number. The leader also chooses the STOP number. The STOP number should be at least 30.

2. The player to the left of the leader begins the game by saying "one." Play continues clockwise with each player saying either the next whole number or "BUZZ."

3. A player must say "BUZZ" instead of the next number if:
   - The number is the BUZZ number or a multiple of the BUZZ number; or
   - The number contains the BUZZ number as one of its digits.

4. If a player makes an error, the next player starts with 1.

5. Play continues until the STOP number is reached.

6. For the next round, the player to the right of the leader becomes the new leader.

> **EXAMPLE**   The BUZZ number is 4. Play should proceed as follows: 1, 2, 3, BUZZ, 5, 6, 7, BUZZ, 9, 10, 11, BUZZ, 13, BUZZ, 15, and so on.

Bizz-Buzz

Bizz-Buzz is played like *Buzz*, except the leader names two numbers: a BUZZ number and a BIZZ number.

Players say:

1. "BUZZ" if the number is a multiple of the BUZZ number.

2. "BIZZ" if the number is a multiple of the BIZZ number.

3. "BIZZ–BUZZ" if the number is a multiple of both the BUZZ number and the BIZZ number.

> **NOTE**
>
> The numbers 6 and 12 in the example below are replaced by the word "BIZZ-BUZZ" since 6 and 12 are multiples of both 6 and 3.

> **EXAMPLE**   The BUZZ number is 6, and the BIZZ number is 3. Play should proceed as follows: 1, 2, BIZZ, 4, 5, BIZZ-BUZZ, 7, 8, BIZZ, 10, 11, BIZZ-BUZZ, 13, 14, BIZZ, 16, and so on.

Calculator 10,000

Materials ☐ calculator

Object of the game To get from a starting number to 10,000, or as close as possible. Each operation—addition, subtraction, multiplication, and division—must be used exactly one time.

One-player Game

1. Form a starting number. Pick any number from 1 to 12. Cube it. For example, Pick 5. Cube it. 5 ⊗ 5 ⊗ 5 (Enter) 125. 125 is the starting number.

2. Pick a number. Add, subtract, multiply, or divide your starting number with it. For example, Pick 100. Multiply it with your starting number. 125 ⊗ 100 (Enter) 12,500.

3. Pick a different number. Add, subtract, multiply, or divide your result in Step 2 with it. Use a **different** operation from the one in Step 2. For example, Pick 2. Divide the result in Step 2 by 2. 12,500 ÷ 2 (Enter) 6,250.

4. Continue to pick numbers and use operations until you have used each of the four operations once. You can use the operations in any order, but may *use each operation only one time.* You must pick a different number for each operation.

5. You can choose the numbers you add, subtract, multiply, and divide with from Level 1 or Level 2. Decide which level to use before playing. (Level 2 is harder.)
   - Level 1: any number except 0
   - Level 2: only numbers from 2 to 100

For each game, record what you did.

A sample game record (using Level 1) is shown at the right. The final result is 10,150.

Pick a Number	Key in	Result
5	5 ⊗ 5 ⊗ 5 (Enter)	125 (starting number)
100	⊗ 100 (Enter)	12,500
2	÷ 2 (Enter)	6,250
3,000	− 3000 (Enter)	3,250
6,900	+ 6900 (Enter)	10,150

Two-player Game

Each player plays 3 games using the rules above. Find the difference between your final result and 10,000 for each game. Add the 3 differences to find your total score. The player with the lowest total score wins the game.

Credits/Debits Game

Materials ☐ 1 complete deck of number cards
☐ recording sheet for each player
(*Math Masters,* p. 166)

Players 2

Directions

Pretend that you are an accountant for a business. Your job is to keep track of the company's current balance. The current balance is also called the "bottom line." As credits and debits are reported, you will record them and then adjust the bottom line.

Recording Sheet			
	Start	**Change**	**End/next start**
1	+$10		
2			
3			
4			
5			
6			
7			
8			
9			
10			

1. Shuffle the deck and lay it facedown between the players.

2. The black-numbered cards are the "credits," and the blue- or red-numbered cards are the "debits."

3. Each player begins with a bottom line of +$10.

4. Players take turns. On your turn, do the following:
   - Draw a card. The card tells you the dollar amount and whether it is a credit or debit to the bottom line. Record the credit or debit in the "Change" column.
   - Use the credit or debit to adjust the bottom line.
   - Record the result in the table.

EXAMPLE Beth has a "Start" balance of +$20. She draws a black 9. This is a credit of $9, so she records +$9 in the "Change" column. She adds $9 to the bottom line: $20 + $9 = $29. Beth then records +$29 in the "End" column. She also records +$29 in the "Start" column on the next line.

Alex has a "Start" balance of +$10. He draws a red 12. this is a debit of $12, so he records −$12 in the "Change" column. He subtracts $12 from the bottom line: $10 − $12 = −$2. Alex then records −$2 in the "End" column. He also records −$2 in the "Start" column on the next line.

Scoring: At the end of 10 draws each, the player with the most money is the winner of the round. If both players have negative dollar amounts, the player whose amount is closest to 0 wins.

Credits/Debits Game (Advanced Version)

Materials
☐ 1 complete deck of number cards
☐ 1 penny
☐ recording sheet for each player
(*Math Masters*, p. 187)

		Recording Sheet		
	Start	**Change**		**End, and next start**
		Addition or Subtraction	**Credit or Debit**	
1	+$10			
2				
3				
4				
5				
6				
7				
8				
9				
10				

Players 2

Directions
Pretend that you are an accountant for a business. Your job is to keep track of the company's current balance, also called the "bottom line."

1. Shuffle the deck and lay it facedown between the players.

2. The black-numbered cards are the "credits," and the blue- or red-numbered cards are the "debits."

3. The heads side of the coin tells you to **add** a credit or debit to the bottom line. The tails side of the coin tells you to **subtract** a credit or debit from the bottom line.

4. Each player begins with a bottom line of +$10.

5. Players take turns. On your turn, do the following:
   • Flip the coin. This tells you whether to add or subtract.
   • Draw a card. The card tells you what amount in dollars (positive or negative) to add or subtract from the bottom line. Red or blue numbers are negative numbers.
   • Record the result in the table.

> **EXAMPLE** Max has a "Start" balance of $5. He draws a red 8 and records −$8 in the "Credit or Debit" column. His coin lands heads-side up and he records + in the "Addition or Subtraction" column. Max adds: $5 + (−$8) = −$3. He records −$3 in the "End" balance column and in the "Start" column on the next line.
>
> Beth has a "Start" balance of −$20. Her coin lands tails-side up, which means subtract. She draws a black 11 (+$11). She subtracts: −$20 − (+$11) = −$31. Her "End" balance is −$31.

Scoring: After 10 turns each, the player with more money is the winner of the round. If both players have negative dollar amounts, the player whose amount is closer to 0 wins.

Division Arrays

Materials   ☐ number cards 6–18 (1 of each)
                 ☐ 1 six-sided die
                 ☐ 18 counters

Players   2 to 4

Directions

1. Shuffle the cards. Place the deck number-side down on the playing surface.

2. Take turns. When it is your turn, draw a card and take the number of counters shown on the card. You will use the counters to make an array.

3. Now roll the die. The number on the die is the number of equal rows you must have in your array.

4. Make an array with the counters.

5. Your score is the number of counters in one row. If there are no leftover counters, your score is double the number of counters in one row.

6. Keep track of your scores. The player with the highest total at the end of 5 rounds wins.

EXAMPLE   Dave draws a 14-card and takes 14 counters. He rolls a 3 and makes an array with 3 rows by putting 4 counters in each row. Two counters are left over.

Dave scores 4 because there are four counters in each row.

EXAMPLE   Marsha draws a 15-card and takes 15 counters. She rolls a 3 and makes an array of 15 counters with 3 rows by putting 5 counters in each row.

Her score is 5 * 2 = 10 because there are five counters in each row and none is left over.

Division Dash

Materials ☐ calculator for each player
☐ score sheet

Players   1 or 2

Object of the game To reach 100 in as few
divisions as possible.

Player 1		Player 2	
Quotient	Score	Quotient	Score

Directions

1. On a piece of paper, prepare a score sheet as
   shown at the right.

2. Players clear their calculator memories.
   Each player then chooses a number that is greater
   than 1,000 and enters the following key sequence
   on their calculator:
   [Op1] [∧] [·] 5 [Op1] [selected number] [Op1]

3. Each player uses the final digit in the calculator display as a
   1-digit number, and the two digits before the final digit as a
   2-digit number.

4. Each player divides the 2-digit number by the 1-digit
   number and records the result. (This result is the quotient.
   Remainders are ignored.) Players calculate mentally or on
   paper, not on the calculator.

5. **Players do not clear their calculators.** They just press
   [Op1] and repeat Steps 3 and 4 until the sum of one player's
   quotients is 100 or more. The winner is the first player to
   reach at least 100. If there is only one player, the object of
   the game is to reach 100 or more in as few turns as possible.

EXAMPLE   Quotient   Score

First turn: Press [Op1] [∧] [·] 5 [Op1] 5678 [Op1]
On a 10-digit display, the result is 7 5 . 3 5 2 5 0 <u>4 9</u> <u>4</u>.
Divide 49 by 4. The quotient is 12 with a remainder of 1.   12   12

Second turn: Press [Op1]. The result is 8 . 6 8 0 5 8 2 <u>0 6</u> <u>2</u>.
Divide 06, or 6, by 2. The quotient is 3.   3   15

Third turn: Press [Op1]. The result is 2 . 9 4 6 2 8 2 <u>7 5</u> <u>3</u>.
Divide 75 by 3. The quotient is 25.   25   40
Continue until one player has a total score of 100 or more.

Fraction/Percent Concentration

Materials ☐ 1 set of Fraction/Percent Tiles
(*Math Journal 2*, Activity Sheets 7 and 8)
☐ calculator

Players 2 or 3

Object of the game To match equivalent fraction tiles and percent tiles.

Directions

1. Spread out the tiles facedown on the playing surface. Create two separate piles—a fraction pile and a percent pile. Mix up the tiles in each pile. The backs of the 12 fraction tiles should have the letter *F* showing. The backs of the 12 percent tiles should have the letter *P* showing.

2. Players take turns. At each turn, a player turns over a fraction tile and a percent tile. If the fraction and percent are equivalent, the player keeps the tiles. If the tiles do not match, the player turns the tiles facedown.

3. Players may use a calculator to check each other's matches.

4. The game ends when all tiles have been taken. The player with the most tiles wins.

Fraction/Percent Tiles			
10%	20%	25%	30%
40%	50%	60%	70%
75%	80%	90%	100%
$\frac{1}{2}$	$\frac{1}{4}$	$\frac{3}{4}$	$\frac{1}{5}$
$\frac{2}{5}$	$\frac{3}{5}$	$\frac{4}{5}$	$\frac{1}{10}$
$\frac{3}{10}$	$\frac{7}{10}$	$\frac{9}{10}$	$\frac{2}{2}$

Fraction Top-It

Materials ☐ 1 deck of 32 Fraction Cards
(*Math Journal 2*, Activity Sheets 5 and 6)

Players 2 to 4

Object of the game To collect the most cards.

Directions

Advance Preparation: Before beginning the game, write the fraction for the shaded part on the back of each card.

1. Deal the same number of cards, fraction-side up, to each player:
   • 16 cards each, if there are 2 players
   • 10 cards each, if there are 3 players
   • 8 cards each, if there are 4 players

2. Place the cards on the playing surface in front of each player, fraction-side up.

3. Starting with the dealer and going in a clockwise direction, each player plays one card.

4. Place cards on the table with the fraction-side showing.

5. The player with the largest fraction wins the round and takes the cards. Players may check who has the largest fraction by turning over the cards and comparing the amount shaded.

6. If there is a tie for the largest fraction, each player plays another card. The player with the largest fraction takes all the cards.

7. The player who takes the cards starts the next round. The game is over when all cards have been played.

The player who takes the most cards wins.

Fraction Cards 1

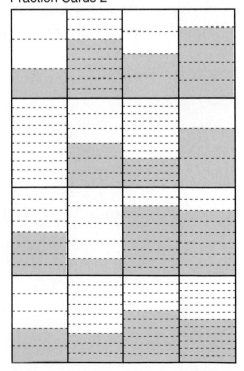

Fraction Cards 2

Getting to One

Materials ☐ 1 calculator

Players 2

Object of the game To guess a mystery number in as few tries as possible.

Directions

1. Player A chooses a mystery number that is less than 100. Suppose the mystery number is 65.

2. Player B guesses the mystery number.

3. Player A uses a calculator to divide the guessed number by the mystery number. Player A then reads the answer that appears in the calculator display. If the answer has more than two decimal places, only the first two decimal places are read.

4. Player B continues to guess until the result is 1. Player B keeps track of the number of guesses.

5. When Player B has guessed the mystery number, players trade roles and follow Steps 1–4. The player who guesses the mystery number in the fewest number of guesses wins the round. The first player to win three rounds wins the game.

EXAMPLE Player A chooses the mystery number 65.

Player B guesses: 55. Player A keys in: 55 ÷ 65 Enter. Answer: 0.8461538462 Too small.

Player B guesses: 70. Player A keys in: 70 ÷ 65 Enter. Answer: 1.076923077 Too big.

Player B guesses: 65. Player A keys in: 65 ÷ 65 Enter. Answer: 1 Just right!

Advanced Version Allow mystery numbers up to 1,000.

Grid Search

Materials ☐ 2 playing grids for each player
(*Math Masters,* p. 96)

Players 2

Directions

Players sit so neither player can see what the other player is
doing. Each player uses two grids (see the margin).

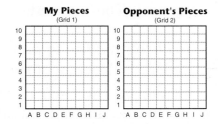

Advance Preparation: Before the start of the game, each
player secretly decides where to place a queen and 6 knights
on Grid 1. They write the letter Q to record the location of the
queen and the letter K to record the location of a knight.

• The queen may be placed on any square.
• The knights may also be placed on any of the squares,
provided that the queen and the knights can all be connected,
without skipping squares.

These are acceptable
arrangements of
the pieces:

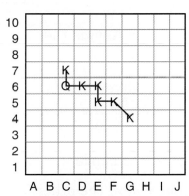

These arrangements
are *not* acceptable
because the pieces
cannot be connected
without skipping
squares.

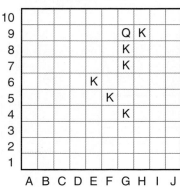

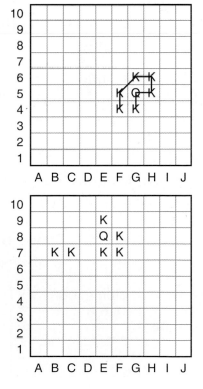

Each square is named by a letter-number coordinate pair.

Each piece and each square has a value.

- A queen is worth 5 points; each knight is worth 1 point.

- The value of a square is equal to the sum of the values of the piece on the square itself and the pieces on the surrounding squares. These include squares on a diagonal.

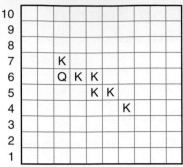

Examples of square values for the grid above:
G-4 is worth 2: 1 + 1 = 2
E-6 is worth 4: 1+1+1+1 = 4
C-7 is worth 7: 1 + 5 + 1 = 7
B-6 is worth 6: 5 + 1 = 6
A-6 is worth 0

Searching for the opponent's queen: Once players have recorded the location of their pieces on Grid 1, they take turns searching for the other player's queen. They use Grid 2 to record the results of their search. The object is to develop a search strategy that will locate the queen in as few turns as possible

Directions

1. At the start of the game: Player A names a square on Player B's Grid 1.

   - If Player B's queen is on that square, Player A wins the game.

   - If Player B's queen is not on that square, Player B tells the value of the square. Player A then records the value of the square on his or her Grid 2.

2. Players A and B reverse roles. Play proceeds as above.

3. Play continues until one player figures out where the other player's queen is located.

EXAMPLE   Suppose Player B has arranged the pieces as shown.

Player A: "I guess E-6."

Player B: "You didn't find the queen. Square E-6 is worth 4 points."

Player A writes 4 in square E-6 on Grid 2.

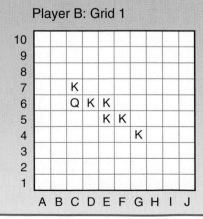

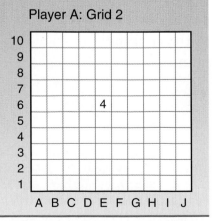

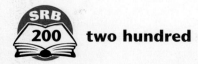

High-Number Toss

Materials ☐ 1 six-sided die

Players 2

Object of the game To make the largest number possible.

Directions

If you don't have a die, you can use a deck of number cards. Use the numbers 1 through 6. Instead of rolling the die, draw the top card from the facedown deck.

1. Each player draws four blank lines on a sheet of paper to record the numbers that come up on the rolls of the die.

   Player 1: ____ ____ ____ | ____

   Player 2: ____ ____ ____ | ____

2. Player 1 rolls the die and writes the number on any one of his or her four blanks. It does not have to be the first blank—it can be any of them. *Keep in mind that the larger number wins!*

3. Player 2 then rolls the die and writes the number on one of his or her blanks.

4. Players take turns rolling the die and writing the numbers three more times each.

5. Each player then uses the four numbers on his or her blanks to build a number.
   - The numbers on the first three blanks are the first three digits of the number the player builds.
   - The number on the fourth blank tells the number of zeros that come after the first three digits.

Each player reads his or her number. (See the place-value chart below.) The player with the larger number wins the round. The first player to win four rounds wins the game.

Hundred-Millions	Ten-Millions	Millions	,	Hundred-Thousands	Ten-Thousands	Thousands	,	Hundreds	Tens	Ones

EXAMPLE

First three digits   Number of zeros

Player 1: _1_ _3_ _2_ | _6_ = 132,000,000 (132 million)

Player 2: _3_ _5_ _6_ | _4_ =   3,560,000 (3 million, 560 thousand)

Player 1 wins.

Multiplication Wrestling

Materials ☐ *Multiplication Wrestling* Worksheet
(*Math Masters*, p. 72)
☐ number cards 0–9 (4 of each)

Players 2

Object of the game To get the largest product of two 2-digit numbers.

Directions

1. Shuffle the deck of cards and place it facedown.

2. Each player draws four cards and forms two 2-digit numbers. There are many possible ways to form 2-digit numbers using the four cards. Each player should form their two numbers so that their product is as large as possible.

3. Players create two "wrestling teams" by writing each of their numbers as a sum of tens and ones.

4. Next, each player's two teams wrestle. Each member of the first team (for example, 70 and 5) is multiplied by each member of the second team (for example, 80 and 4). Then the four products are added.

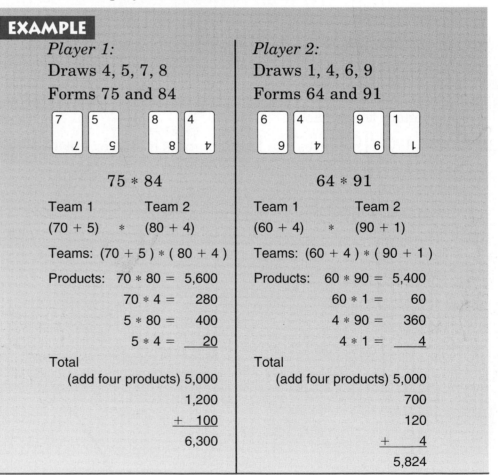

EXAMPLE

Player 1:
Draws 4, 5, 7, 8
Forms 75 and 84

75 * 84

Team 1		Team 2
(70 + 5)	*	(80 + 4)

Teams: (70 + 5) * (80 + 4)

Products: 70 * 80 = 5,600
70 * 4 =   280
5 * 80 =   400
5 * 4 =   20

Total
(add four products) 5,000
1,200
+ 100
6,300

Player 2:
Draws 1, 4, 6, 9
Forms 64 and 91

64 * 91

Team 1		Team 2
(60 + 4)	*	(90 + 1)

Teams: (60 + 4) * (90 + 1)

Products: 60 * 90 = 5,400
60 * 1 =   60
4 * 90 =   360
4 * 1 =   4

Total
(add four products) 5,000
700
120
+   4
5,824

5. **Scoring:** The player with the larger product wins the round and receives 1 point.

6. To begin a new round, each player draws four new cards to form two new numbers. A game consists of three rounds.

Name That Number

Materials ☐ 1 complete deck of number cards

Players   2 or 3

Object of the game To collect the most cards.

Directions

1. Shuffle the cards and deal five cards to each player. Place the remaining cards number-side down. Turn over the top card and place it beside the deck. This is the **target number** for the round.

2. Players try to match the target number by adding, subtracting, multiplying, or dividing the numbers on as many of their cards as possible. A card may only be used once.

3. Players write their solutions on a sheet of paper or a slate. When players have written their best solutions:

   • They set aside the cards they used to name the target number.

   • Replace them by drawing new cards from the top of the deck.

   • Put the old target number on the bottom of the deck.

   • Turn over a new target number, and play another hand.

4. Play continues until there are not enough cards left to replace all of the players' cards. The player who sets aside more cards wins the game.

EXAMPLE   Target number: 16   A player's cards:

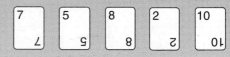

Some possible solutions:

   $10 + 8 - 2 = 16$ (three cards used)

   $7 * 2 + 10 - 8 = 16$ (four cards used)

   $8/2 + 10 + 7 - 5 = 16$ (all five cards used)

The player sets aside the cards used to make a solution and draws the same number of cards from the top of the deck.

Number Top-It (7-Digit Numbers)

Materials ☐ number cards 0–9 (4 of each)
☐ Place-Value Mat (*Math Masters,* pp. 18 and 19)

Players 2 to 5

Object of the game To make the largest 7-digit number.

Directions

1. Shuffle the cards. Place the deck number-side down on the playing surface.

2. The Place-Value Mat has rows of boxes. Each player uses one row of boxes on the game mat.

3. In each round, players take turns turning over the top card from the deck and placing it on any one of their empty boxes. Each player takes seven turns, and places seven cards on his or her row of the game mat.

4. At the end of each round, players read their numbers aloud and compare them to the other players' numbers. The player with the largest number for the round scores 1 point. The player with the next-larger number scores 2 points, and so on.

5. Players play five rounds for a game. Shuffle the deck between each round. The player with the smallest total number of points at the end of five rounds wins the game.

EXAMPLE Andy and Barb played 7-digit *Number Top-It.*
Here is the result for one complete round of play.

Place-Value Mat

	Millions	Hundred-Thousands	Ten-Thousands	Thousands	Hundreds	Tens	Ones
Andy	7	6	4	5	2	0	1
Barb	4	9	7	3	5	2	4

Andy's number is larger than Barb's number. So Andy scores
1 point for this round. Barb scores 2 points.

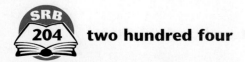

Number Top-It (Decimals)

Materials ☐ number cards 0–9 (4 of each)
☐ Place-Value Mat for Decimals
(*Math Masters,* pp. 51 and 59)

Players 2 or more

Object of the game To make the largest 2-digit decimal number.

Directions

1. This game is played using the same directions as those for *Number Top-It* (7-Digit Numbers). The only difference is that players use the Place-Value Mat for decimals.

2. In each round, players take turns turning over the top card from the deck and placing it on any one of their empty boxes. Each player takes two turns, and places two cards on his or her row of the game mat.

3. Players play five rounds for a game. Shuffle the deck between each round. The player with the smallest total number of points at the end of the five rounds wins the game.

EXAMPLE Kent and Kari played *Number Top-It* using the Place-Value Mat for Decimals. Here is the result.

Place-Value Mat for Decimals

	Ones	.	Tenths	Hundredths
Kent	0	.	3	5
Kari	0	.	6	4

Kari's number is larger than Kent's number. So Kari scores 1 point for this round, and Kent scores 2 points.

Variation: Use a place-value mat that has empty boxes in the tenths, hundredths, and thousandths places. Each player takes three turns, and places three cards on his or her row of the game mat.

Subtraction Target Practice

Materials ☐ number cards 0–9 (4 of each)
           ☐ calculator for each player

Players   1 or more

Object of the game To get as close to 0 as possible, without
going below 0.

Directions

1. Shuffle the cards and place the deck facedown on the playing
   surface. Each player starts at 250.

2. Players take turns doing the following:

   • Turn over the top two cards and make a 2-digit number.
     (You can place the cards in either order.) Subtract this
     number from 250 on scratch paper. Check the answer on
     a calculator.

   • Turn over the next two cards and make another 2-digit
     number. Subtract this number from the result obtained in
     the previous subtraction. Check the answer on a calculator.

   • Do this three more times: take two cards; make a 2-digit
     number; subtract it from the last result; check the answer
     on a calculator.

3. The player whose final result is closest to 0, without going
   below 0, is the winner. If the final results for all players are
   below 0, no one wins.

If there is only one player, the object of the game is to get as
close to 0 as possible, without going below 0.

EXAMPLE

Turn 1: Draw 4 and 5. Subtract 45 or 54. $250 - 45 = 205$

Turn 2: Draw 0 and 6. Subtract 6 or 60. $205 - 60 = 145$

Turn 3: Draw 4 and 1. Subtract 41 or 14. $145 - 41 = 104$

Turn 4: Draw 3 and 2. Subtract 32 or 23. $104 - 23 = 81$

Turn 5: Draw 6 and 9. Subtract 69 or 96. $81 - 69 = 12$

Variation: Each player starts at 100 instead of 250.

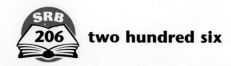

Top-It Games

The materials, number of players, and object of the game are the same for all *Top-It Games*.

Materials   □ number cards 1–10 (4 of each)

Players   2 to 4

Object of the game To collect the most cards.

Addition Top-It
Directions

1. Shuffle the cards and place the deck number-side down.

2. Each player turns over two cards and calls out the sum of the numbers. The player with the highest sum takes all the cards. In case of a tie for the highest sum, each tied player turns over two more cards and calls out the sum. The player with the highest sum takes all the cards from both plays.

3. Check answers using an Addition Table or a calculator.

4. Play ends when not enough cards are left for each player to have another turn.

5. The player who took the most cards wins.

Variation: Each player turns over three cards and finds their sum.

Advanced Version Use only the number cards 1–9. Each player turns over four cards, forms two 2-digit numbers, and finds the sum. Players should carefully consider how they form their numbers since different arrangements have different sums. For example, 74 + 52 has a greater sum than 25 + 47.

Subtraction Top-It
Directions

1. Each player turns over three cards, finds the sum of any two of the numbers, then finds the difference between the sum and the third number.

2. The player with the largest difference takes all the cards.

> **EXAMPLE** A 4, an 8, and a 3 are turned over. There are three ways to form the numbers. Always subtract the smaller number from the larger one.
>
> | $4 + 8 = 12$ | or | $3 + 8 = 11$ | or | $3 + 4 = 7$ |
> |---|---|---|---|---|
> | $12 - 3 = 9$ | | $11 - 4 = 7$ | | $8 - 7 = 1$ |

Advanced Version Use only the number cards 1–9. Each player turns over four cards, forms two 2-digit numbers, and finds their difference. Players should carefully consider how they form their numbers. For example, $75 - 24$ has a greater difference than $57 - 42$.

Multiplication Top-It
Directions

1. The rules are the same as for *Addition Top-It*, except that players find the product of the numbers instead of the sum.

2. The player with the largest product takes all the cards. Answers can be checked with a Multiplication Table or a calculator.

Variation: Use only the number cards 1–9. Each player turns over three cards, forms a 2-digit number, then multiplies the 2-digit number by the remaining number.

Division Top-It
Directions

1. Use only the number cards 1–9. Each player turns over three cards and uses them to generate division problems as follows:
   - Choose two cards to form the dividend.
   - Use the remaining card as the divisor.
   - Divide and drop the remainder.

2. The player with the largest quotient takes all the cards.

Advanced Version Use only the number cards 1–9. Each player turns over four cards, chooses three of them to form a 3-digit number, then divides the 3-digit number by the remaining number. Players should carefully consider how they form their 3-digit numbers. For example, 462 / 5 is greater than 256 / 4.

World Tour

Introduction
About the World Tour

For the rest of the school year, you and your classmates will go on an imaginary tour of the world. As you visit various countries, you will learn about the customs of people in other parts of the world and about the ways their lives are like yours and different from yours. You will practice globe and map skills to help you locate the places you visit. As you collect and examine numerical information for the countries you visit, you will have many opportunities to apply your knowledge of mathematics.

How the World Tour Is Organized

You will first fly from your hometown to Washington, D.C. The class will then visit five regions of the world: Africa, Europe, South America, Asia and Australia, and, finally, North America.

A Chinese farmer waters crops by hand.

The class will first visit the continent of Africa, landing in Cairo, Egypt. From there, you will fly to the second region, Europe, landing in Budapest, Hungary. This pattern will be repeated for each of the other regions. The class will complete the tour by flying back to Washington, D.C.

As you visit each country, you will collect information about that country and record it in a set of Country Notes pages in your journal. The World Tour section of your *Student Reference Book* will serve as a major source for that information.

Women in Guatemala sell fruits and vegetables at a market.

As you make your world tour, there will be opportunities to learn about countries you have not visited. This World Tour section includes detailed information for ten selected countries within each of the five regions of the world. It includes a Fascinating Facts insert that lists interesting facts about world geography, population, and climate. And it includes a collection of games played in different parts of the world that require logical or mathematical thinking. You can also look up additional information in a world almanac, *National Geographic* magazines, travel brochures, guidebooks, and newspapers.

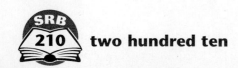

Washington, D.C., Facts

Washington, D.C., is the **capital** of the United States of America. The capital is where our country's laws are made. It is also where our president lives.

Washington, D.C., has been the capital of the United States since 1791. Before that, the capital was in Philadelphia, Pennsylvania. President George Washington decided to move the capital to an area between Virginia and Maryland. The capital city was named "Washington, the District of Columbia" in honor of George Washington and Christopher Columbus. "District of Columbia" is usually abbreviated as D.C.

Washington, D.C., has an area of 68 square miles. With a population of about 525,000 people, more people live in our capital city than in the state of Wyoming!

There are many interesting things to do in Washington, D.C. The facts below will help you plan your visit.

The White House

Every U.S. president except George Washington has lived here. The White House sits on 18 acres of land. It has 132 rooms, five of which can be seen on a 20-minute public tour. Every year more than 1,500,000 people tour the White House. Web site: http://www.whitehouse.gov

Washington Monument

This 555-foot-tall monument was built to honor George Washington. It is the tallest building in Washington, D.C., and is one of the tallest masonry structures in the world. You can take an elevator to a viewing area at the 500-foot level of the monument. The monument's cornerstone was laid in 1848, but building was interrupted by the Civil War (1861–1865). At that time, the monument was only 150 feet tall. Construction workers started building again in 1880 and completed the Washington Monument in 1884. It receives more than 800,000 visitors each year. Web site: http://www.nps.gov/wamo

Washington Metrorail

This system of underground electric trains opened in 1976. There are 78 stations in the Washington area; some are decorated with beautiful artworks. They are connected by more than 96 miles of train lines. On an average weekday, about 500,000 people ride these trains. Web site: http://www.wmata.com

Average High/Low Temperatures (°F)			Average Precipitation (in.)	
Month	High	Low	Month	Precipitation
Jan	43	27	Jan	2.7
Feb	46	28	Feb	2.8
Mar	55	35	Mar	3.2
Apr	67	45	Apr	3.1
May	76	55	May	4.0
Jun	84	64	Jun	3.9
Jul	88	69	Jul	3.5
Aug	86	67	Aug	3.9
Sep	80	61	Sep	3.4
Oct	69	49	Oct	3.2
Nov	57	38	Nov	3.3
Dec	45	29	Dec	3.2

More Washington, D.C., Facts

Jefferson Memorial

This memorial was built in honor of Thomas Jefferson. Jefferson was the third president of the United States and the author of the *Declaration of Independence.* The memorial was dedicated in 1943, exactly 200 years after Jefferson was born. Inside the memorial, a statue of Jefferson stands 19 feet tall. Web site: http://www.nps.gov/thje/home.htm

Lincoln Memorial

This memorial was built in 1922 in honor of Abraham Lincoln. Lincoln was the 16th U.S. president. Inside the memorial is a 19-foot-high statue of Lincoln, seated in a large armchair. The statue is made of 28 blocks of white marble from the state of Georgia. Web site: http://www.nps.gov/linc/home.htm

The United States Capitol

The Capitol Building is where the senators and representatives in Congress meet to make laws. George Washington laid its cornerstone in 1793. The building's cast iron dome weighs 9 million pounds. Brass doors that weigh 10 tons lead to the rotunda, which is 180 feet high and 96 feet in diameter.

Web site: http://www.aoc.gov

Library of Congress

The Library of Congress is the world's largest library. It contains more than 115 million items in 450 languages. It has about 535 miles of bookshelves. The Library is composed of three buildings. One of these, the James Madison Building, encloses an area greater than 35 football fields. The Library has more than 18 million books, 12 million photographs, 2 million sound recordings, and 4 million maps. It also has about 125,000 telephone books and 100,000 comic books. The Library of Congress collection grows by more than 10,000 items every day.

Web site: http://www.loc.gov

National Museum of Natural History

Exhibits in the National Museum of Natural History include the 45.5-carat Hope Diamond, a 360-million-year-old fossilized fish, a 90-foot-long skeleton of a diplodocus, a 30-foot-long giant squid, a stuffed 857 pound Bengal Tiger, moon rocks, a mural of a 3.5-billion-year-old shoreline, and a 92 foot life-size model of a blue whale. The Insect Zoo has live insects, including scorpions and tarantulas. In the Discovery Room, you can try on costumes from around the world. The museum is part of the Smithsonian Institution. Web site: http://www.mnh.si.edu

National Air and Space Museum

The National Air and Space Museum is the most popular museum in the world. Every year more than 7.5 million people visit it. Its collection includes the *Wright Flyer,* which is the original plane flown by the Wright brothers at Kitty Hawk, North Carolina, in 1903. It also includes the *Spirit of St. Louis,* the plane in which Charles Lindbergh made the first nonstop flight across the Atlantic in 1927. *Columbia,* the Apollo 11 command module that brought back the first men to walk on the moon in 1969, is also on display. Web site: http://www.nasm.si.edu

Map of the National Mall in Washington, D.C.

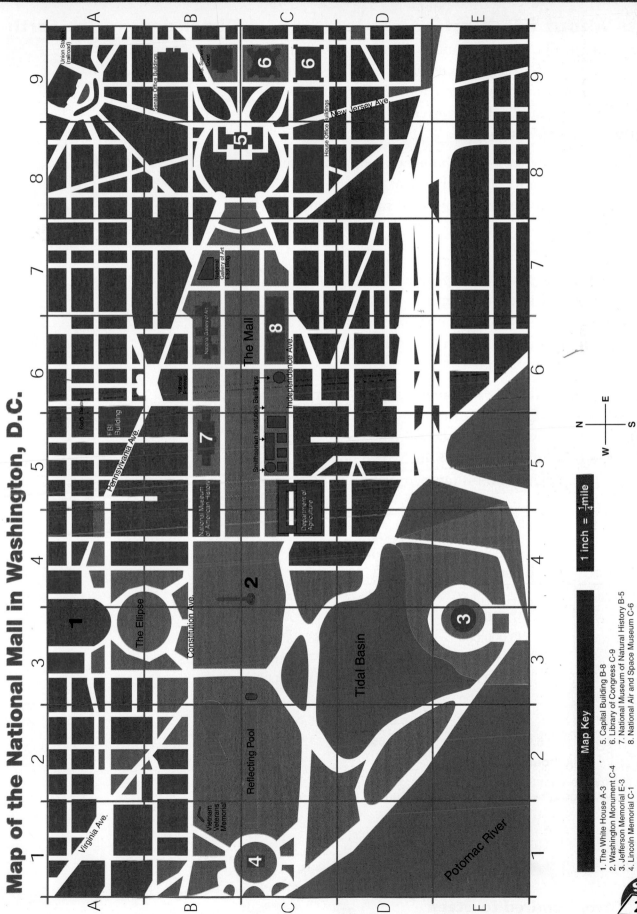

1 inch = $\frac{1}{4}$ mile

Map Key

1. The White House A-3
2. Washington Monument C-4
3. Jefferson Memorial E-3
4. Lincoln Memorial C-1
5. Capital Building B-8
6. Library of Congress C-9
7. National Museum of Natural History B-5
8. National Air and Space Museum C-6

Facts about the World

Continents are large land masses. There are seven continents on the Earth, although Europe and Asia are sometimes thought of as one continent. Most continents contain many countries, but there are no countries at all in Antarctica.

A **country** is a territory and the people who live there under one government. The number of countries in the world often changes as countries split apart or join with other countries. At this time, there are about 200 countries in the world.

Population is the number of people who live in a certain region. Population growth is the change in the population every year after all births and deaths are accounted for. The **population growth rate** is the percent of change in the population.

The world's population is now increasing by about 210,000 people per day, or about 77 million people per year. Over the last 40 years, the world's population has about doubled. It reached the 6 billion mark in 1999. World population is expected to reach about 9 billion people by the year 2050.

Dimensions of the Earth

Equatorial circumference*:
about 24,900 miles
(40,000 kilometers)

Equatorial diameter**:
about 7,930 miles
(12,760 kilometers)

Volume: 2.6×10^{11} cubic miles
(1.1×10^{12} cubic kilometers)

Weight (mass): 6.6×10^{21} tons
(6.0×10^{21} metric tons)

Total world water area:
about 139,433,000 square miles
(361,129,000 square kilometers)

*Circumference is the distance around a circle or sphere.

**Diameter is the distance measured by a straight line passing from one side of a circle or sphere, through the center, to the other side.

The Continents

Continent	Population*	Percent of World Population	Area (sq miles)	Percent of Land Area
North America	482,000,000	7.9%	9,400,000	16.2%
South America	347,000,000	5.7	6,900,000	11.9
Europe	736,000,000	12.1	3,800,000	6.6
Asia	3,688,000,000	60.7	17,400,000	30.1
Africa	788,000,000	13.0	11,700,000	20.2
Australia	30,000,000	0.5	3,300,000	5.7
Antarctica	0	0.0	5,400,000	9.3
World Totals	**6,071,000,000** (about 6.1 billion)	**100.0%**	**57,900,000**	**100.0%**

*Data are for the year 2000.
  World population growth rate for the year 2000: about 1.3% per year

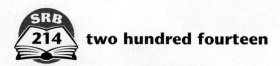

National Flags

Region 1	Region 2	Region 3	Region 4	Region 5
Algeria	France	Argentina	Australia	Canada
Egypt	Greece	Bolivia	Bangladesh	Costa Rica
Ethiopia	Hungary	Brazil	China	Cuba
Ghana	Iceland	Chile	India	El Salvador
Kenya	Italy	Colombia	Iran	Guatemala
Liberia	Netherlands	Ecuador	Japan	Haiti
Morocco	Norway	Paraguay	Russia	Jamaica
Senegal 	Poland	Peru	Thailand	Mexico
South Africa	Spain	Uruguay	Turkey	Panama
Zimbabwe 	United Kingdom	Venezuela	Vietnam	United States

Latitude and Longitude

You sometimes use a world globe or a flat map to locate countries, cities, rivers, and so forth. Reference lines are drawn on globes and maps to make places easier to find.

Latitude

Lines that go east and west around the Earth are called **lines of latitude**. The **equator** is a special line of latitude. Every point on the equator is the same distance from the North Pole and the South Pole. Lines of latitude are called **parallels** because each one is a circle that is parallel to the equator.

Lines of latitude are measured in **degrees**. The symbol for degrees is (°). Lines north of the equator are labeled °N. Lines south of the equator are labeled °S. The number of degrees tells how far north or south of the equator a place is. The area north of the equator is called the **Northern Hemisphere.** The area south of the equator is called the **Southern Hemisphere.**

EXAMPLES   The latitude of Cairo, Egypt, is 30°N. We say that Cairo is 30 degrees north of the equator.

The latitude of Durban, South Africa, is 30°S. Durban is in the Southern Hemisphere.

The latitude of the North Pole is 90°N. The latitude of the South Pole is 90°S. The poles are the points farthest north and farthest south on Earth.

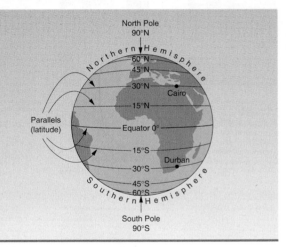

Longitude

A second set of lines runs from north to south. These are semicircles (half-circles) that connect the poles. They are called **lines of longitude** or **meridians.** The meridians are not parallel since they meet at the poles.

The **prime meridian** is the special meridian labeled 0°. The prime meridian crosses near London, England. Another special meridian falls on, or close to, the **international date line**. This meridian is labeled 180° and is exactly opposite the prime meridian on the other side of the world.

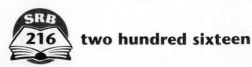

Longitude is measured in degrees. Lines west of the prime meridian are labeled °W. Lines east of the prime meridian are labeled °E. The number of degrees tells how far west or east of the prime meridian a place is located. The area west of the prime meridian is called the **Western Hemisphere.** The area east of the prime meridian is called the **Eastern Hemisphere.**

EXAMPLES The longitude of London is 0° because London lies close to the prime meridian.

The longitude of Durban, South Africa, is 30°E. Durban is in the Eastern Hemisphere.

The longitude of Gambia (a small country in Africa) is about 15°W. We say that Gambia is 15 degrees west of the prime meridian.

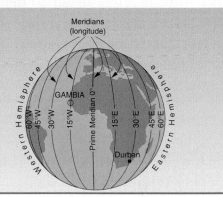

When both latitude and longitude lines are shown on a globe or map, they form a pattern of crossing lines called a **grid.** The grid can help you locate places on the globe or map. Any place on the map can be located by naming its latitude and longitude.

CHECK YOUR UNDERSTANDING

Use the grid below to find the approximate latitude and longitude for the cities shown. For example, Denver, Colorado, is about 40° North and 105° West.

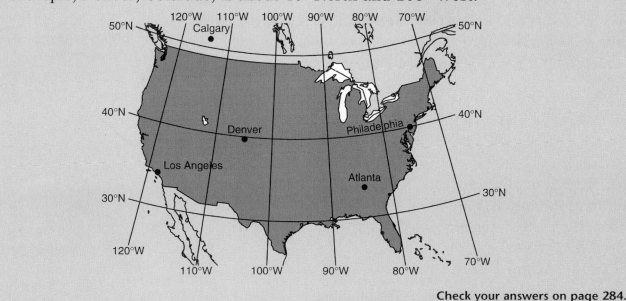

Check your answers on page 284.

Map Projections

A **world globe** shows the Earth accurately. All of the distances and directions are shown correctly. The sizes and shapes of countries, bodies of water, and other features are all as correct as possible.

A **flat map** is often easier to use than a globe. But all flat maps have a common problem. Since the Earth is a sphere, no flat map can show the whole Earth as it really is in the same way that a globe can. Some features will be distorted on a flat map.

Pretend you are a map maker trying to turn a world globe into a flat map of the world. Imagine peeling the Earth map off the globe and laying it flat. That would be like peeling an orange and then flattening the peel. You can almost do this if you tear the peel into many small pieces. But even those pieces are rounded and will not lie perfectly flat.

Map makers have invented many ways to show the spherical world as a flat map. These flat views of the Earth are called **map projections.** Every map projection has some distortions because the map maker must cut and stretch the shape of the globe to make it flat.

The Mercator Projection

One of the most common types of flat maps is the **Mercator projection.** It was invented by Gerardus Mercator in 1569. Mercator's map projection was useful to sailors, but as a picture of our world, it creates many false impressions.

A Mercator map exaggerates areas that are nearer to the poles. For example, Greenland looks about the same size as Africa. But, Africa is actually about 15 times the size of Greenland.

The Robinson Projection

Another kind of flat map is the **Robinson projection.** It makes the world look somewhat like a globe. Areas near the poles are distorted, but they are distorted a lot less than they are on a Mercator map.

The National Geographic Society and many map companies use the Robinson projection.

> **N O T E**
>
> Look at the Mercator map on the opposite page.
>
> - Notice that the meridians (lines of longitude) are an equal distance apart. On a globe, the meridians get closer as they get near the poles.
>
> - Notice that the parallels (lines of latitude) are farther apart toward the poles. On a globe, the parallels are an equal distance apart.

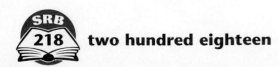

MERCATOR PROJECTION

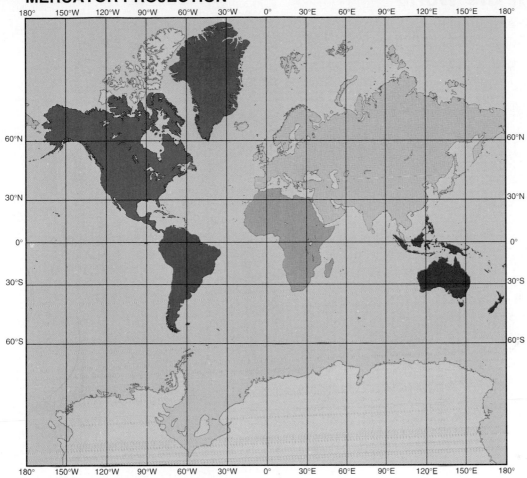

ROBINSON PROJECTION

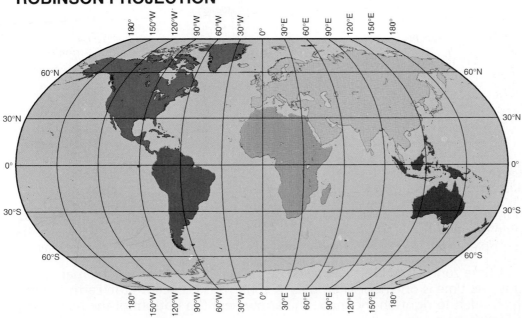

Time Zones of the World

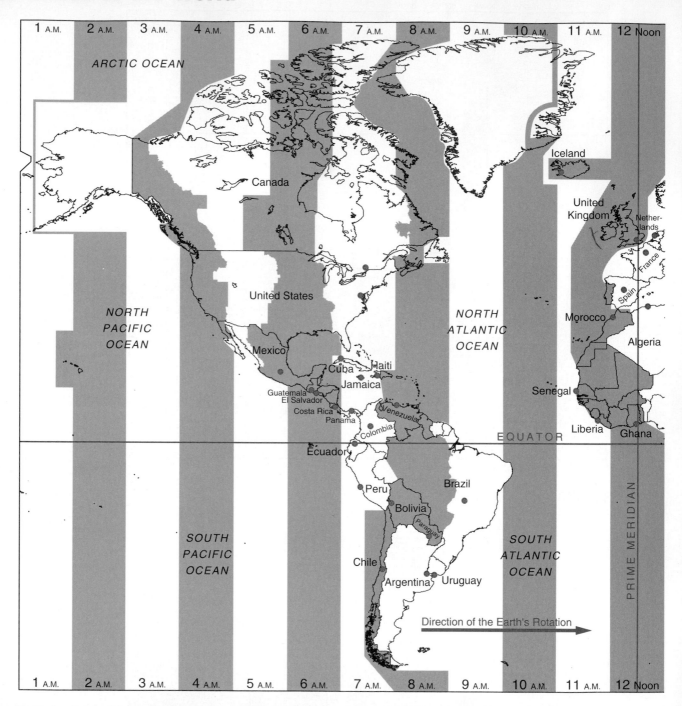

The Earth is divided into 24 time zones. We need time zones because the Earth is spinning, and the sun does not shine on all of the Earth at the same time. It takes one day, or 24 hours, for the Earth to make one complete spin. Each time zone represents one of the 24 hours of that day.

This map shows all 24 time zones. The times are given at the top and bottom of the map. As you read from left to right, the time is one hour later in each zone. This is because the Earth rotates toward the east, which is left to right on the map. The arrow near the bottom of the map shows the direction of the Earth's rotation.

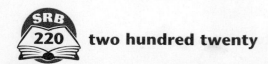

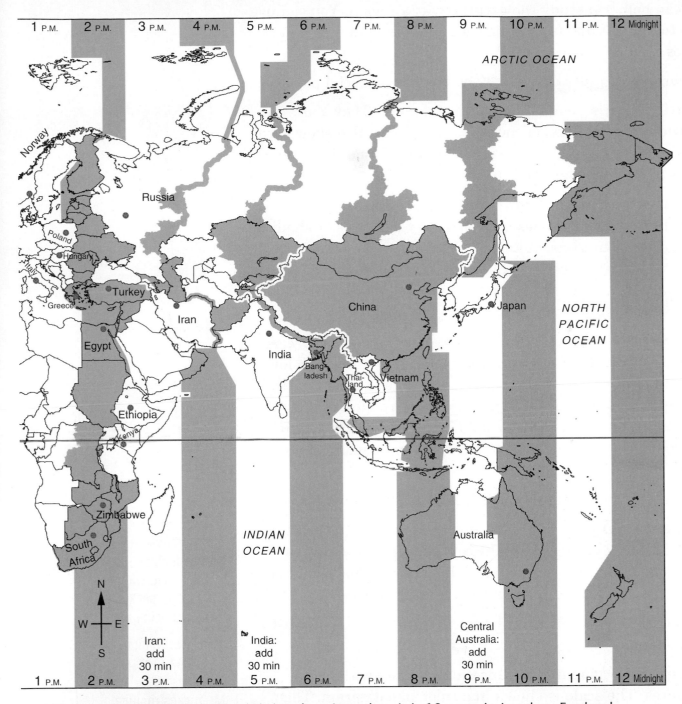

The map tells you what time it is in a location when it is 12 noon in London, England.
- Put your finger on the place you want to find the time for. See if it is in a pink strip or a white strip.
- Keep your finger in the strip you start in. Follow it up to the top of the map or down to the bottom. Read the time.

If you know the time in one location, you can find the time in another location.
- Put your finger on the place that is farther west.
- Slide your finger to the right until you reach the place that is farther east.
- Count the number of pink and white time zones you enter as you slide your finger.
- The number of time zones you enter is the number of hours that the place to the east is ahead of the place to the west.

two hundred twenty-one

Political and Physical Maps

Maps can help you study the geography of a region. You can use a map to find out about a region's size and its land and water features.

There are many types of maps. Each one has a special purpose.

- **Political maps** identify countries and cities. They show the **boundaries** (borders) of countries. They may also show areas within a country such as states or counties. Sometimes these maps also show rivers and lakes.

- **Physical maps** show features such as rivers, lakes, mountain ranges, and deserts. They may use lines or shading to identify mountains, valleys, and low spots. Some physical maps use different colors to show **elevation** (height above sea level) on a map. Many physical maps do not include country boundaries or city names.

The maps in this World Tour section of your *Student Reference Book* are both political *and* physical maps. There is a map for every continent except Antarctica. Countries and capital cities are identified. Major rivers, lakes, mountain ranges, and deserts are shown. The maps use different colors to help you locate countries more easily, but colors are not used to show elevations.

Each map has three features which are found on most maps:

- A **legend** or **key** explains the symbols and markings on the map. Several **symbols** and **abbreviations** that are often used in map legends are listed in the margin. The legend is one of the first places to look when reading a map.

- A **direction symbol** identifies north, south, east, and west on the map.

- A **map scale** compares distances on the map with actual distances. The scale is shown in a ruler-like diagram. The scale is also given in words such as "1 inch represents 400 miles."

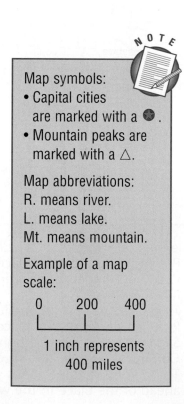

Map symbols:
- Capital cities are marked with a ⬤.
- Mountain peaks are marked with a △.

Map abbreviations:
R. means river.
L. means lake.
Mt. means mountain.

Example of a map scale:

```
0      200     400
├───────┼───────┤
```

1 inch represents 400 miles

Country Profiles

The countries you can visit on your world tour are listed below by geographical region. Languages in bold type are the official languages of a country. Some countries have no official language, while others have more than one. All measurements in the country profiles are approximate.

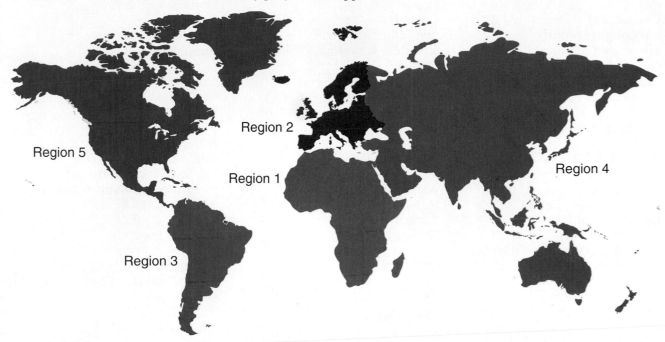

REGION 1   Africa

Algeria
Area: 919,600 sq mi
Population: 31,133,000
Capital: Algiers (**Pop.** 3,705,000)
Languages: Arabic, French, Berber
Monetary unit: Dinar

Egypt
Area: 386,700 sq mi
Population: 67,274,000
Capital: Cairo (**Pop.** 6,789,000)
Languages: Arabic, English, French
Monetary unit: Pound

Ethiopia
Area: 435,200 sq mi
Population: 59,680,000
Capital: Addis Ababa (**Pop.** 2,431,000)
Languages: Amharic, Tigrinya, Orominga
Monetary unit: Birr

Ghana
Area: 92,100 sq mi
Population: 18,888,000
Capital: Accra (**Pop.** 1,673,000)
Languages: English, Akan, Ewe, Ga, Moshi-Dagomba
Monetary unit: Cedi

Kenya
Area: 225,000 sq mi
Population: 28,809,000
Capital: Nairobi (**Pop.** 2,000,000)
Languages: Swahili, English, numerous indigenous languages
Monetary unit: Shilling

Liberia
Area: 43,000 sq mi
Population: 2,924,000
Capital: Monrovia (**Pop.** 962,000)
Languages: English, tribal languages
Monetary unit: Dollar

Morocco
Area: 172,400 sq mi
Population: 29,662,000
Capital: Rabat (**Pop.** 1,220,000)
Languages: Arabic, Berber
Monetary unit: Dirham

Senegal
Area: 75,700 sq mi
Population: 10,052,000
Capital: Dakar (**Pop.** 1,641,000)
Languages: French, Pulaar, Wolof, Diola, Mandingo
Monetary unit: CFA franc

South Africa
Area: 471,000 sq mi
Population: 43,426,000
Capitals: Pretoria (**Pop.** 1,080,000), administrative; Cape Town (**Pop.** 2,350,000), legislative; Bloemfontein, judicial
Languages: 11 official languages including Afrikaans, English, Ndebele, Sotho, Pedi
Monetary unit: Rand

Zimbabwe
Area: 150,800 sq mi
Population: 11,163,000
Capital: Harare (**Pop.** 1,410,000)
Languages: English, Sindebele, Shona
Monetary unit: Dollar

REGION 2 Europe

France
Area: 211,200 sq mi
Population: 58,978,000
Capital: Paris (**Pop.** 2,152,000)
Language: French
Monetary unit: Franc

Greece
Area: 50,900 sq mi
Population: 10,707,000
Capital: Athens (**Pop.** 3,073,000)
Languages: Greek, English, French
Monetary unit: Drachma

Hungary
Area: 35,900 sq mi
Population: 10,186,000
Capital: Budapest (**Pop.** 1,885,000)
Language: Hungarian (Magyar)
Monetary unit: Forint

Iceland
Area: 40,000 sq mi
Population: 273,000
Capital: Reykjavik (**Pop.** 105,000)
Language: Icelandic
Monetary unit: Krona

Italy
Area: 116,300 sq mi
Population: 56,735,000
Capital: Rome (**Pop.** 2,645,000)
Languages: Italian, German, French, Slovene
Monetary unit: Lira

Netherlands
Area: 16,000 sq mi
Population: 15,808,000
Capital: Amsterdam (**Pop.** 717,000)
Language: Dutch
Monetary unit: Guilder

Norway
Area: 125,200 sq mi
Population: 4,439,000
Capital: Oslo (**Pop.** 492,000)
Language: Norwegian
Monetary unit: Krona

Poland
Area: 120,700 sq mi
Population: 38,609,000
Capital: Warsaw (**Pop.** 1,633,000)
Language: Polish
Monetary unit: Zloty

Spain
Area: 194,900 sq mi
Population: 39,168,000
Capital: Madrid (**Pop.** 2,867,000)
Languages: Castilian Spanish, Basque, Catalan, Galician
Monetary unit: Peseta

United Kingdom
Area: 94,500 sq mi
Population: 59,113,000
Capital: London (**Pop.** 7,074,000)
Languages: English, Welsh, Scottish, Gaelic
Monetary unit: Pound

REGION 3 South America

Argentina
Area: 1,068,300 sq mi
Population: 36,738,000
Capital: Buenos Aires (**Pop.** 11,802,000)
Languages: Spanish, English, Italian
Monetary unit: Peso

Bolivia
Area: 424,200 sq mi
Population: 7,983,000
Capital: La Paz (**Pop.** 739,000)
Languages: Spanish, Quechua, Aymara
Monetary unit: Boliviano

Brazil
Area: 3,286,500 sq mi
Population: 171,853,000
Capital: Brasília (**Pop.**1,738,000)
Languages: Portuguese, English, Spanish, French
Monetary unit: Real

Chile
Area: 292,300 sq mi
Population: 14,974,000
Capital: Santiago (Pop. 4,641,000)
Language: Spanish
Monetary unit: Peso

Colombia
Area: 439,700 sq mi
Population: 39,309,000
Capital: Bogota (**Pop.** 6,005,000)
Language: Spanish
Monetary unit: Peso

Ecuador
Area: 109,500 sq mi
Population: 12,562,000
Capital: Quito (**Pop.** 1,444,000)
Languages: Spanish, Quechua, other Amerindian
Monetary unit: Sucre

Paraguay
Area: 157,000 sq mi
Population: 5,434,000
Capital: Asunción (**Pop.** 547,000)
Languages: Spanish, Guarani
Monetary unit: Guarani

Peru
Area: 496,200 sq mi
Population: 26,625,000
Capital: Lima (**Pop.** 6,743,000)
Languages: Spanish, Quechua, Aymara
Monetary unit: New Sol

Uruguay
Area: 68,000 sq mi
Population: 3,309,000
Capital: Montevideo (**Pop.** 1,303,000)
Language: Spanish
Monetary unit: Peso

Venezuela
Area: 352,100 sq mi
Population: 23,203,000
Capital: Caracas (**Pop.** 3,673,000)
Language: Spanish
Monetary unit: Bolivar

REGION 4   Asia and Australia

Australia
Area: 2,967,900 sq mi
Population: 18,784,000
Capital: Canberra (**Pop.** 325,000)
Languages: English, aboriginal languages
Monetary unit: Dollar

Bangladesh
Area: 55,600 sq mi
Population: 127,118,000
Capital: Dhaka (**Pop.** 8,545,000)
Languages: Bangla, English
Monetary unit: Taka

China
Area: 3,705,400 sq mi
Population: 1,246,872,000
Capital: Beijing (**Pop.** 11,299,000)
Languages: Mandarin, Gan, Wu, Haka, Yue, Minbei, Xiang, Minnan
Monetary unit: Renminbi (Yuan)

India
Area: 1,269,300 sq mi
Population: 1,000,849,000
Capital: New Delhi (**Pop.** 9,948,000)
Languages: Hindi, English, 14 regional languages
Monetary unit: Rupee

Iran
Area: 636,000 sq mi
Population: 65,180,000
Capital: Tehran (**Pop.** 6,750,000)
Languages: Farsi, Kurdish, Turkic, Luri
Monetary unit: Rial

Japan
Area: 145,900 sq mi
Population: 126,182,000
Capital: Tokyo (**Pop.** 7,968,000)
Language: Japanese
Monetary unit: Yen

Russia
Area: 6,592,800 sq mi
Population: 146,394,000
Capital: Moscow (**Pop.** 8,368,000)
Languages: Russian, many others
Monetary unit: Ruble

Thailand
Area: 198,500 sq mi
Population: 60,609,000
Capital: Bangkok (**Pop.** 6,547,000)
Languages: Thai, English
Monetary unit: Baht

Turkey
Area: 301,400 sq mi
Population: 65,599,000
Capital: Ankara (**Pop.** 2,938,000)
Languages: Turkish, Arabic, Kurdish
Monetary unit: Lira

Vietnam
Area: 127,200 sq mi
Population: 77,311,000
Capital: Hanoi (**Pop.** 1,236,000)
Languages: Vietnamese, Chinese, French, English
Monetary unit: Dong

REGION 5   North America

Canada
Area: 3,851,800 sq mi
Population: 31,006,000
Capital: Ottawa (**Pop.** 1,000,000)
Languages: English, French
Monetary unit: Dollar

Costa Rica
Area: 19,700 sq mi
Population: 3,674,000
Capital: San José (**Pop.** 324,000)
Language: Spanish
Monetary unit: Colon

Cuba
Area: 42,800 sq mi
Population: 11,096,000
Capital: Havana (**Pop.** 2,185,000)
Language: Spanish
Monetary unit: Peso

El Salvador
Area: 8,100 sq mi
Population: 5,839,000
Capital: San Salvador (**Pop.** 1,214,000)
Language: Spanish
Monetary unit: Colon

Guatemala
Area: 42,000 sq mi
Population: 12,336,000
Capital: Guatemala City (**Pop.** 2,205,000)
Languages: Spanish, Mayan languages
Monetary unit: Quetzal

Haiti
Area: 10,700 sq mi
Population: 6,884,000
Capital: Port-au-Prince (**Pop.** 844,000)
Languages: French, Haitian Creole
Monetary unit: Gourde

Jamaica
Area: 4,200 sq mi
Population: 2,652,000
Capital: Kingston (**Pop.** 104,000)
Languages: English, Jamaican Creole
Monetary unit: Dollar

Mexico
Area: 761,600 sq mi
Population: 100,294,000
Capital: Mexico City (**Pop.** 8,489,000)
Languages: Spanish, Mayan dialects
Monetary unit: New Peso

Panama
Area: 30,200 sq mi
Population: 2,779,000
Capital: Panama City (**Pop.** 465,000)
Languages: Spanish, English
Monetary unit: Balboa

United States of America
Area: 3,717,800 sq mi
Population: 272,640,000
Capital: Washington, D.C. (**Pop.** 523,000)
Languages: English, Spanish
Monetary unit: Dollar

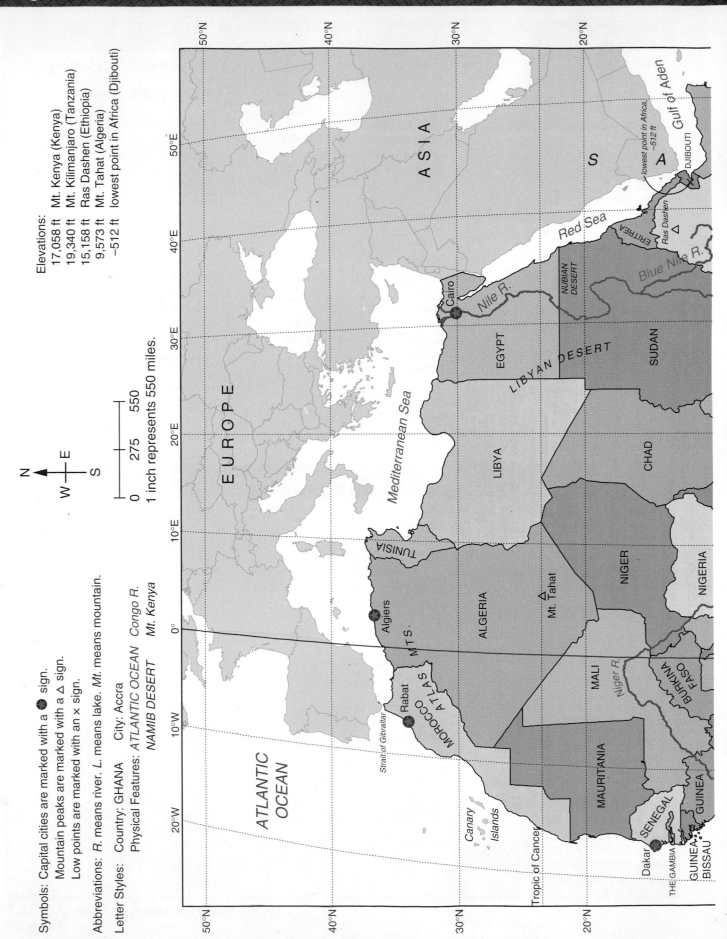

Symbols: Capital cities are marked with a ● sign.
Mountain peaks are marked with a △ sign.
Low points are marked with an × sign.

Abbreviations: *R.* means river. *L.* means lake. *Mt.* means mountain.

Letter Styles: Country: GHANA   City: Accra
Physical Features: *ATLANTIC OCEAN Congo R.*
NAMIB DESERT   Mt. Kenya

Elevations:
17,058 ft   Mt. Kenya (Kenya)
19,340 ft   Mt. Kilimanjaro (Tanzania)
15,158 ft   Ras Dashen (Ethiopia)
9,573 ft   Mt. Tahat (Algeria)
−512 ft   lowest point in Africa (Djibouti)

0   275   550

1 inch represents 550 miles.

N
W — E
S

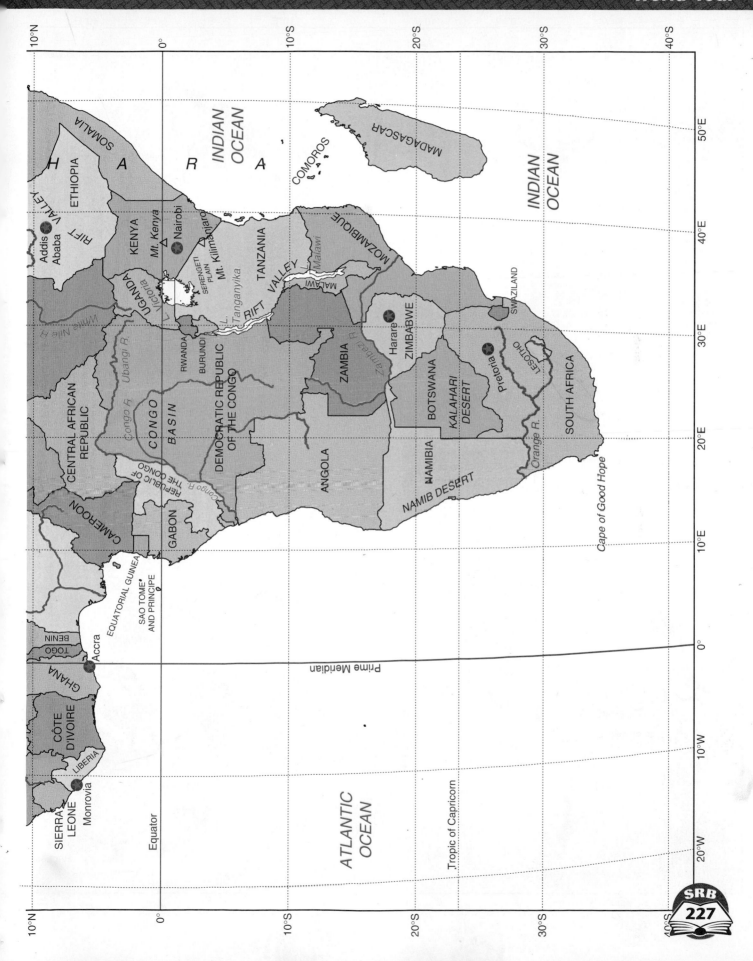

10°N

0°

10°S

20°S

30°S

40°S

50°E

40°E

30°E

20°E

10°E

0°

10°W

20°W

INDIAN OCEAN

INDIAN OCEAN

ATLANTIC OCEAN

SOMALIA

ETHIOPIA

RIFT VALLEY

Addis Ababa

White Nile R.

KENYA

Mt. Kenya

Nairobi

UGANDA

L. Victoria

SERENGETI PLAIN

Mt. Kilimanjaro

L. Tanganyika

TANZANIA

RIFT VALLEY

COMOROS

MADAGASCAR

MOZAMBIQUE

L. Malawi

MALAWI

CENTRAL AFRICAN REPUBLIC

Ubangi R.

CONGO BASIN

Congo R.

RWANDA

BURUNDI

DEMOCRATIC REPUBLIC OF THE CONGO

ZAMBIA

Zambezi R.

Harare

ZIMBABWE

SWAZILAND

Pretoria

LESOTHO

SOUTH AFRICA

CAMEROON

GABON

REPUBLIC OF THE CONGO

Congo R.

ANGOLA

NAMIBIA

NAMIB DESERT

BOTSWANA

KALAHARI DESERT

Orange R.

Cape of Good Hope

EQUATORIAL GUINEA

SAO TOME AND PRINCIPE

Accra

BENIN

TOGO

GHANA

CÔTE D'IVOIRE

LIBERIA

SIERRA LEONE

Monrovia

Prime Meridian

Equator

Tropic of Capricorn

10°N

0°

10°S

20°S

30°S

40°S

30°W 20°W 10°W 0° 10°E 20°E 30°E 40°E

Barents

70°N

Reykjavik

ICELAND

Arctic Circle

Hvannadalshnúkur

Norwegian Sea

60°N

SWEDEN

FINLAND

Glittertind

NORWAY

Helsinki

Oslo

Stockholm

ESTONIA

Scotland

LATVIA

N. Ireland

North Sea

DENMARK

Baltic Sea

LITHUANIA

Daugava R.

UNITED KINGDOM

RUSSIA

50°N

IRELAND

NETHERLANDS

POLAND

BELARUS

Wales

Amsterdam

GERMANY

Berlin

England

London

BELGIUM

Rhine R.

Elbe R.

Warsaw

Vistula R.

Oder R.

UKRAINE

Kiev

LUXEMBOURG

CZECH REPUBLIC

CARPATHIAN

Dniester

ATLANTIC OCEAN

Seine R.

Paris

Danube R.

LIECHTEN-STEIN

SLOVAKIA

MOLDOVA

Loire R.

SWITZERLAND

Vienna

Budapest

HUNGARY

MOUNTAINS

FRANCE

AUSTRIA

SLOVENIA

ROMANIA

Rhône R.

Mont Blanc

ALPS

Matterhorn

Po R.

CROATIA

Serbia

Belgrade

Danube R.

40°N

Pico de Aneto

ANDORRA

DINARIC

BOSNIA AND HERZEGOVINA

YUGO-SLAVIA

PORTUGAL

Ebro R.

PYRENEES

MONACO

APENNINES

SAN MARINO

ALPS

Monte negro

BULGARIA

Madrid

Tagus R.

Corsica

Adriatic Sea

BALKAN

MTS.

Lisbon

Rome

VATICAN CITY

ITALY

MACE-DONIA

SPAIN

Sardinia

Vesuvius

ALBANIA

Olympus

Majorca

GREECE

Aegean Sea

Strait of Gibraltar

Athens

M e d i t e r r a n e a n

Prime Meridian

Sicily

Etna

Rhodes

A F R I C A

MALTA

S e a

Crete

0° 10°E 20°E 30°E

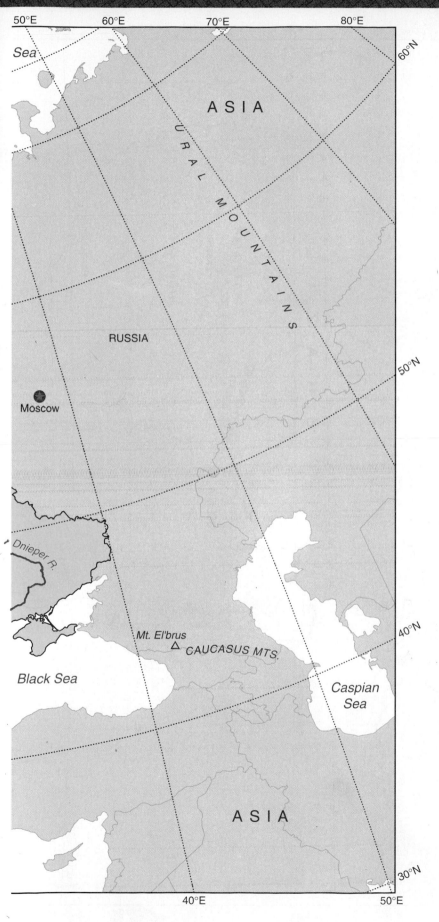

Symbols: Capital cities are marked with a ● sign.

Mountain peaks are marked with a △ sign.

Abbreviations: *R.* means river.
Mt. means mountain.
Mts. means mountains.

Letter Styles: Country: ITALY

City: Rome

Physical Features:
ATLANTIC OCEAN
Seine R.
ALPS
Mont Blanc

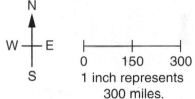

N
W — E
S

0   150   300
1 inch represents
300 miles.

Elevations:
18,510 ft   Mt. El'brus (Russia)
11,053 ft   Etna (Italy)
8,104 ft   Glittertind (Norway)
6,952 ft   Hvannadalshnúkur (Iceland)
14,690 ft   Matterhorn
(Italy– Switzerland border)
15,771 ft   Mont Blanc (France–Italy border)
9,570 ft   Olympus (Greece)
11,168 ft   Pico de Aneto (Spain)
4,202 ft   Vesuvius (Italy)

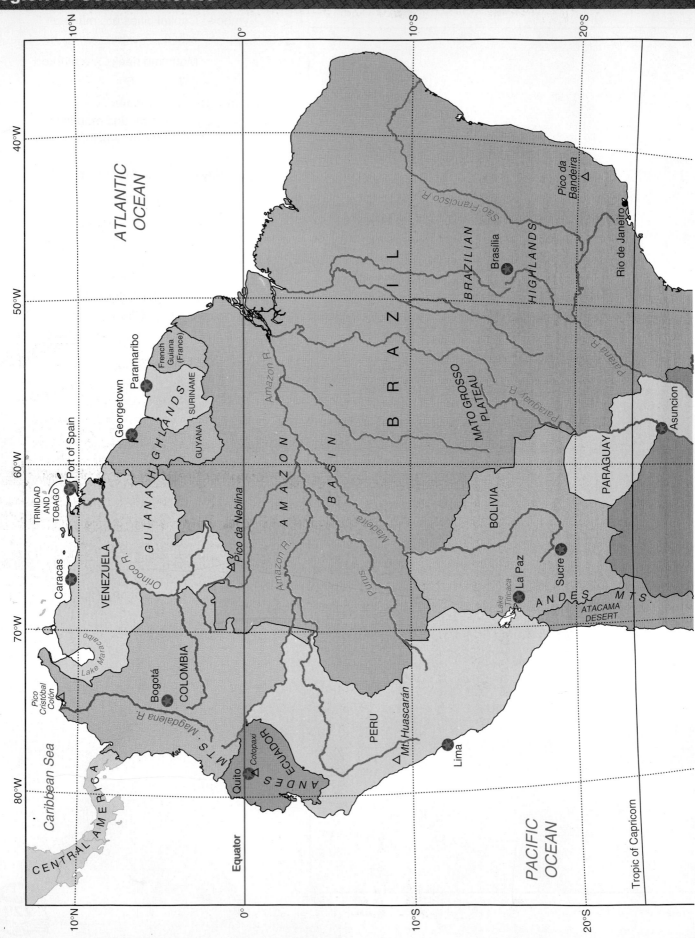

ATLANTIC OCEAN

PACIFIC OCEAN

Caribbean Sea

CENTRAL AMERICA

VENEZUELA

Caracas

Port of Spain

TRINIDAD AND TOBAGO

Pico Cristobal Colón

Lake Maracaibo

COLOMBIA

Bogotá

ANDES MTS.

Magdalena R.

Orinoco R.

GUIANA HIGHLANDS

Georgetown

Paramaribo

GUYANA

SURINAME

French Guiana (France)

Pico da Neblina

Quito

ECUADOR

Cotopaxi

PERU

Mt. Huascarán

Lima

Amazon R.

Amazon R.

Purus

Madeira

AMAZON BASIN

BRAZIL

BRAZILIAN HIGHLANDS

Brasília

São Francisco R.

Pico da Bandeira

Rio de Janeiro

MATO GROSSO PLATEAU

BOLIVIA

La Paz

Sucre

Lake Titicaca

ANDES MTS.

ATACAMA DESERT

Paraguay R.

Paraná R.

PARAGUAY

Asuncion

Equator

Tropic of Capricorn

0°

10°N

10°S

20°S

40°W

50°W

60°W

70°W

80°W

0°

10°N

10°S

20°S

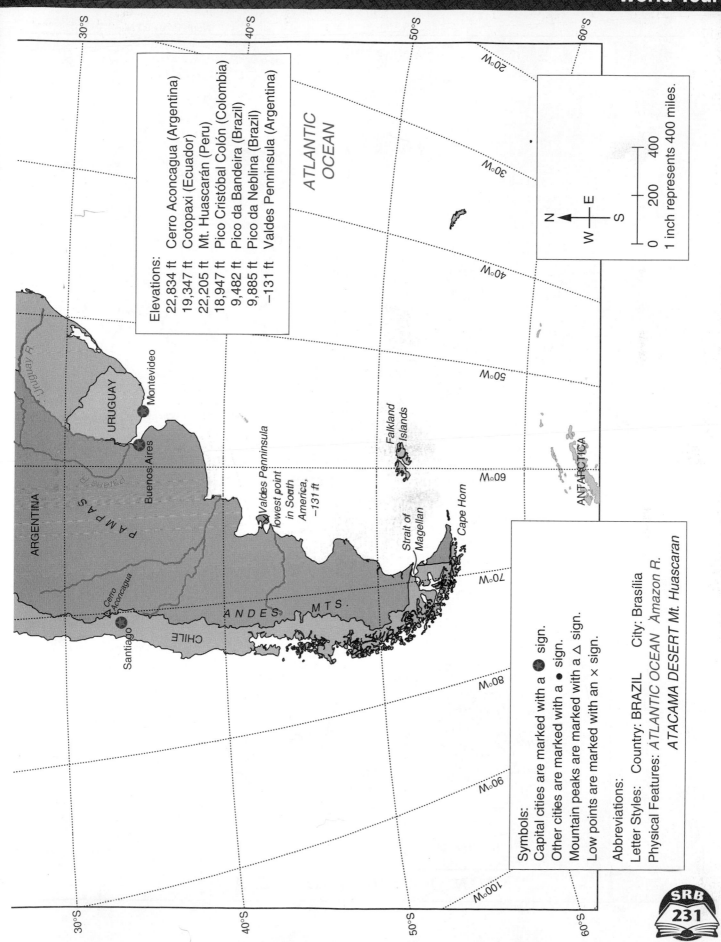

Elevations:
22,834 ft Cerro Aconcagua (Argentina)
19,347 ft Cotopaxi (Ecuador)
22,205 ft Mt. Huascarán (Peru)
18,947 ft Pico Cristóbal Colón (Colombia)
9,482 ft Pico da Bandeira (Brazil)
9,885 ft Pico da Neblina (Brazil)
−131 ft Valdes Penninsula (Argentina)

ATLANTIC OCEAN

1 inch represents 400 miles.
0   200   400

N
W   E
S

Uruguay R.
URUGUAY
Montevideo
Buenos Aires
ARGENTINA
PAMPAS
Patagonia
Valdes Penninsula
lowest point
in South
America,
−131 ft
Falkland
Islands
Strait of
Magellan
Cape Horn
ANTARCTICA
Cerro
Aconcagua
Santiago
CHILE
A N D E S   M T S.

Symbols:
Capital cities are marked with a ⊛ sign.
Other cities are marked with a ● sign.
Mountain peaks are marked with a △ sign.
Low points are marked with an × sign.

Abbreviations:
Letter Styles: Country: BRAZIL   City: Brasília
Physical Features: *ATLANTIC OCEAN* *Amazon R.*
                   ATACAMA DESERT *Mt. Huascaran*

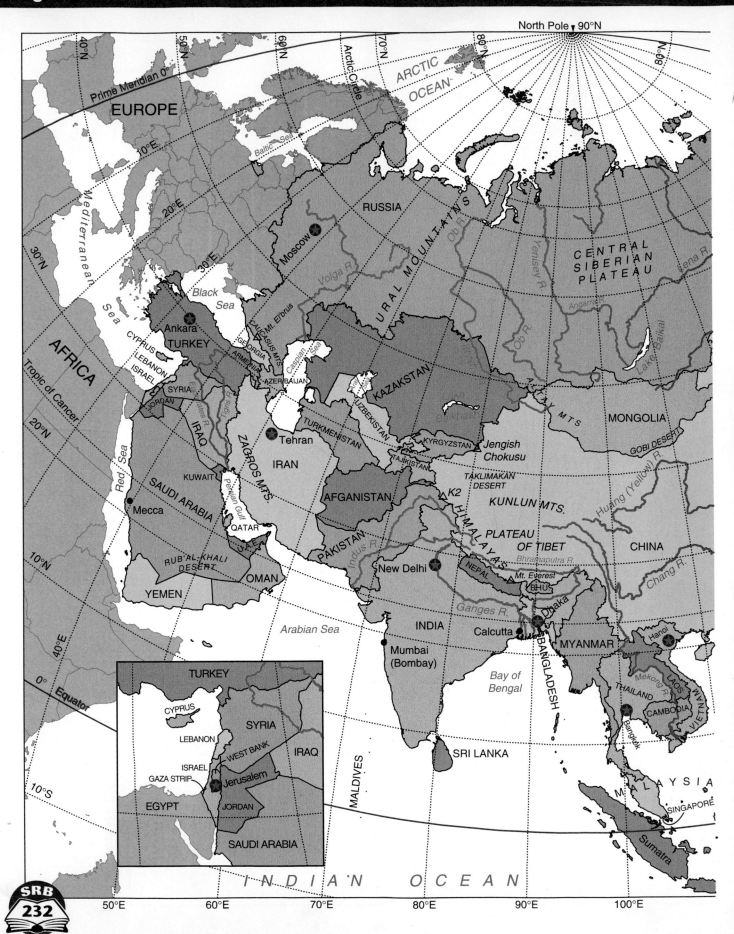

North Pole 90°N

ARCTIC OCEAN

EUROPE

Prime Meridian 0°

Arctic Circle

Baltic Sea

RUSSIA

Moscow

CENTRAL SIBERIAN PLATEAU

Volga R.

Lena R.

URAL MOUNTAINS

Ob R.

Yenisey R.

Angara R.

Mediterranean Sea

Black Sea

Ankara

TURKEY

CYPRUS

LEBANON

ISRAEL

SYRIA

JORDAN

AFRICA

Tropic of Cancer

CAUCASUS MTS.

Mt. El'brus

GEORGIA

ARMENIA

AZERBAIJAN

Caspian Sea

Euphrates R.

Tigris R.

IRAQ

ZAGROS MTS.

Tehran

IRAN

TURKMENISTAN

UZBEKISTAN

KAZAKSTAN

Lake Balkhash

Aral Sea

ALTAY MTS

MONGOLIA

Lake Baikal

GOBI DESERT

Red Sea

KUWAIT

SAUDI ARABIA

Mecca

QATAR

U.A.E.

Persian Gulf

AFGHANISTAN

TAJIKISTAN

KYRGYZSTAN

Jengish Chokusu

TAKLIMAKAN DESERT

KUNLUN MTS.

K2

Huang (Yellow) R.

PLATEAU OF TIBET

CHINA

Chang R.

RUB'AL-KHALI DESERT

OMAN

PAKISTAN

Indus R.

New Delhi

HIMALAYAS

NEPAL

Mt. Everest

BHUTAN

Bhramaputra R.

YEMEN

Ganges R.

Dhaka

Calcutta

BANGLADESH

MYANMAR

Hanoi

40°E

Arabian Sea

INDIA

Mumbai (Bombay)

Bay of Bengal

THAILAND

LAOS

Mekong R.

CAMBODIA

VIETNAM

Bangkok

Equator

MALDIVES

SRI LANKA

MALAYSIA

SINGAPORE

Sumatra

INDIAN OCEAN

Inset map:

TURKEY

CYPRUS

SYRIA

LEBANON

WEST BANK

IRAQ

ISRAEL

GAZA STRIP

Jerusalem

JORDAN

EGYPT

SAUDI ARABIA

50°E   60°E   70°E   80°E   90°E   100°E

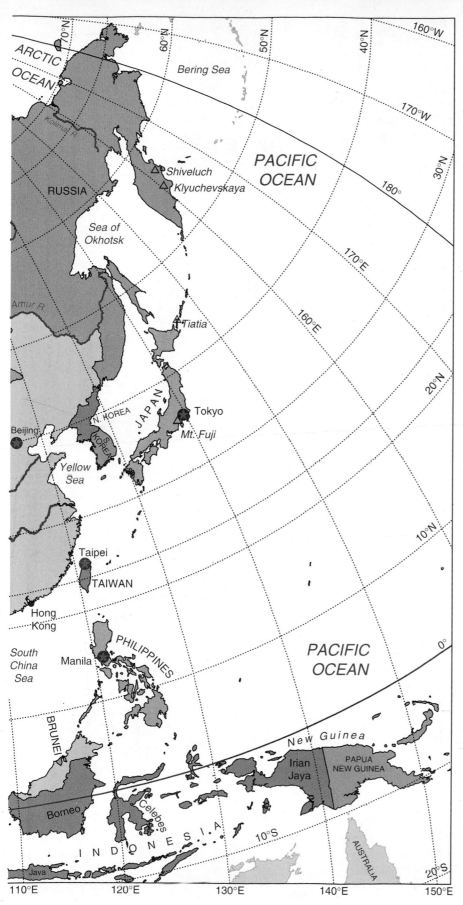

Symbols:
Capital cities are marked with a ⬟ sign.
Other cities are marked with a ● sign.
Mountain peaks are marked with a △ sign.

Abbreviations:
R. means river.
Mt. means mountain.
Mts. means mountains.
U.A.E. means United Arab Emirates.
BHU. means Bhutan.

Letter Styles:

Country: CHINA

City: Beijing

Physical Features:
PACIFIC OCEAN
Ganges R.
HIMALAYAS
Mt. Everest

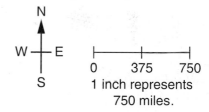

0   375   750
1 inch represents
750 miles.

Elevations:
18,510 ft Mt. El'brus (Russia)
29,028 ft Mt. Everest (China–Nepal border)
12,388 ft Mt. Fuji (Japan)
24,406 ft Jengish Chokusu (Kyrgyzstan)
19,584 ft Klyuchevskaya (Russia)
28,250 ft K2 (China–Pakistan border)
10,771 ft Shiveluch (Russia)
6,013 ft Tiatia (Russia)

Symbols: Capital cities are marked
with a ✹ sign.
Other major cities are marked
with a ● sign.
Smaller cities are marked
with a ○ sign.
Mountain peaks are marked
with a △ sign.
Low points are marked
with an × sign.

Abbreviations: *R.* means river.
Mt. means mountain.

Letter Styles: Country: AUSTRALIA
State: Victoria
City: Canberra

Physical Features:

PACIFIC OCEAN

Darling R.

GREAT SANDY DESERT

Mt. Kosciusko

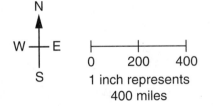

N
W —|— E
S

0   200   400

1 inch represents
400 miles

Elevations:

2,844 ft	Ayers Rock (Australia)
5,322 ft	Mt. Bartle (Australia)
4,052 ft	Mt. Bruce (Australia)
12,349 ft	Mt. Cook (New Zealand)
4,131 ft	Mt. Dalrymple (Australia)
2,546 ft	Mt. Hann (Australia)
7,310 ft	Mt. Kosciusko (Australia)
5,305 ft	Mt. Ossa (Australia)
16,500 ft	Puncak Jaya (Indonesia)
5,276 ft	Round Mountain (Australia)
9,175 ft	Ruapehu (New Zealand)
14,793 ft	Mt. Wilhelm (Paupua New Guinea)
4,724 ft	Mt. Woodroffe (Australia)
4,957 ft	Mt. Ziel (Australia)
−52 ft	Lake Eyre (Australia)

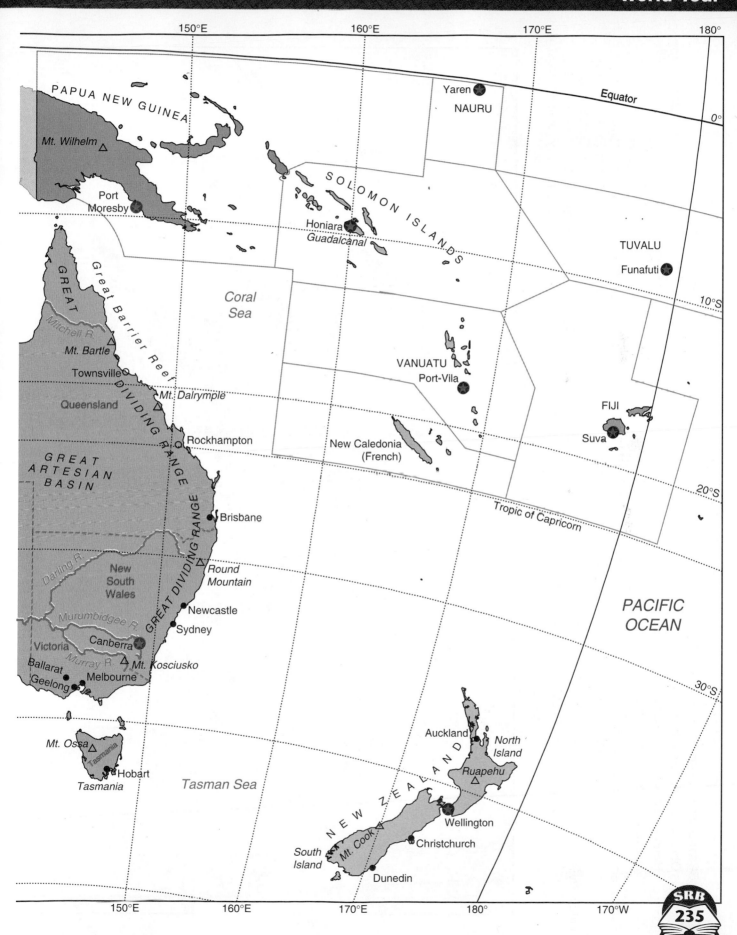

PAPUA NEW GUINEA

Mt. Wilhelm

Port
Moresby

Yaren
NAURU

Equator

0°

S O L O M O N   I S L A N D S

Honiara
Guadalcanal

TUVALU

Funafuti

10°S

Coral
Sea

GREAT

Great Barrier Reef

Mitchell R.

Mt. Bartle

Townsville

Queensland

GREAT
DIVIDING RANGE

Mt. Dalrymple

Rockhampton

VANUATU

Port-Vila

FIJI

Suva

GREAT
ARTESIAN
BASIN

New Caledonia
(French)

20°S

Tropic of Capricorn

Darling R.

New
South
Wales

GREAT DIVIDING RANGE

Brisbane

Round
Mountain

PACIFIC
OCEAN

Murrumbidgee R.

Newcastle

Sydney

Victoria

Canberra

Murray R.

Mt. Kosciusko

Ballarat

Geelong

Melbourne

30°S

Mt. Ossa

Tasmania

Hobart

Tasmania

Tasman Sea

Auckland

North
Island

Ruapehu

N E W   Z E A L A N D

Wellington

South
Island

Mt. Cook

Christchurch

Dunedin

150°E

160°E

170°E

180°

170°W

150°E

160°E

170°E

180°

SRB
235

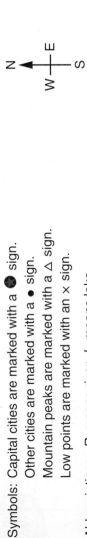

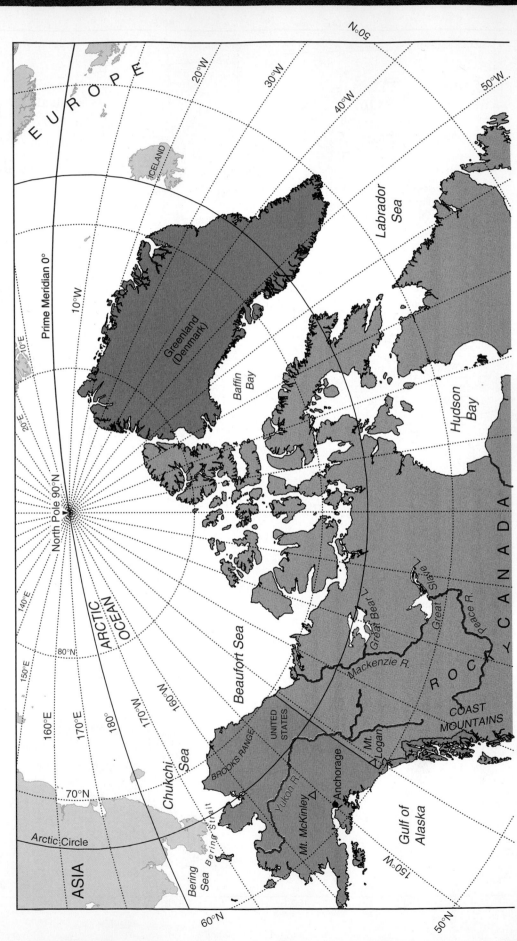

Symbols: Capital cities are marked with a ● sign.
Other cities are marked with a ● sign.
Mountain peaks are marked with a △ sign.
Low points are marked with an × sign.

Abbreviations: *R.* means river. *L.* means lake.
Mt. means mountain. *Mts.* means mountains.

Letter Styles: Country: CANADA   City: Ottawa
Physical Features: *ATLANTIC OCEAN Mississippi R.*
GREAT PLAINS   *Mt. Whitney*

Elevations:
19,850 ft   Mt. Logan (Canada)
20,320 ft   Mt. McKinley (United States)
6,684 ft   Mt. Mitchell (United States)
18,855 ft   Pico de Orizaba (Mexico)
14,110 ft   Pikes Peak (United States)
14,410 ft   Mt. Rainier (United States)
13,845 ft   Tajumulco (Guatemala)
14,494 ft   Mt. Whitney (United States)
−282 ft   Death Valley (United States)

N
W ← → E
S

0   250   500
1 inch represents 500 miles.

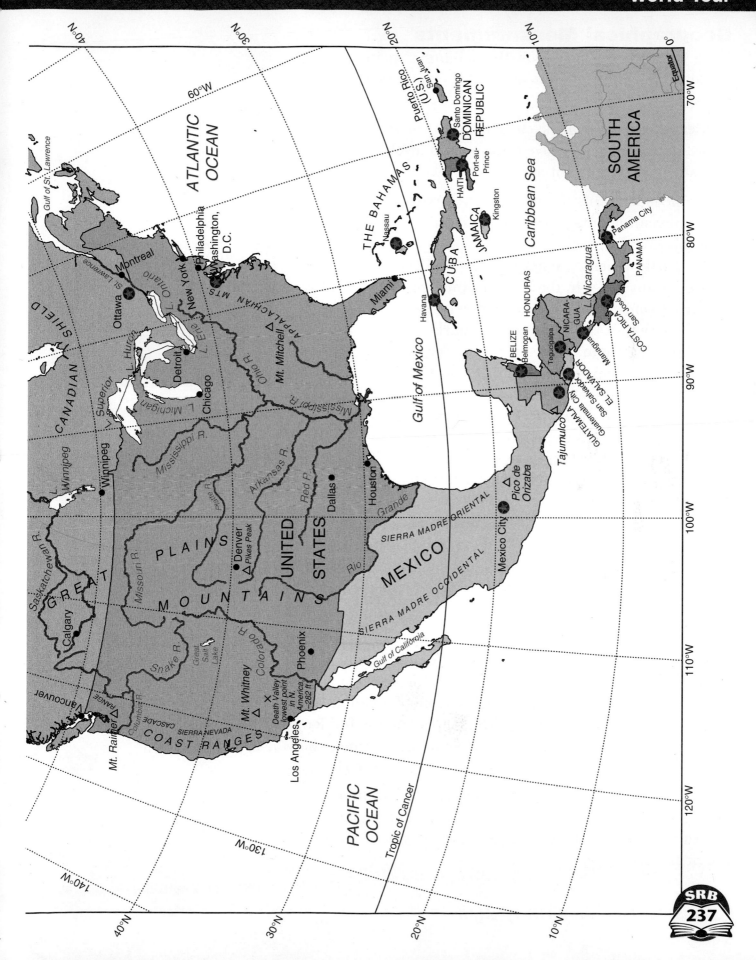

Geographical Measurements

Have you ever wondered how the heights of mountains or the lengths of rivers are measured? How accurate are these measurements?

Vertical measurements, such as heights and depths, are recorded as distances above or below sea level. The term **elevation** means height above sea level.

Many measurements are made with surveying instruments. These measurements can be made more accurate by using data collected by satellites.

- The parts of a city are not all the same height above sea level. Many cities in the United States have an elevation marker somewhere in the downtown area. The elevation of the city tells the height of the marker above sea level and is accurate to the nearest foot. For example, Denver, Colorado, has an elevation of 5,260 feet. Since 1 mile = 5,280 feet, Denver is almost exactly 1 mile high.

- The height of a mountain is the elevation at its highest point. The land around mountains is often very rugged. So the reported heights of mountains may be less accurate than the reported elevations of cities.
- The depth of an ocean is measured by sending sound signals to the ocean floor. The time it takes for these signals to reach the bottom and bounce back is used to determine the ocean's depth. Depth measurements are usually accurate to the nearest 10 feet.

Other measurements are made without measuring the object.

- The length of a river is usually measured using very accurate maps, created with the help of satellite photographs. The instrument used to measure length is the size of a ballpoint pen but with a very small wheel instead of a ball at its tip. This instrument is moved on the map along the full length of the river. Using the map scale, the number of times the wheel rotates is converted into the actual length of the river.

Length-of-river measurements are usually accurate to the nearest mile for each 1,000 miles of river. For example, the length of a 3,000-mile-long river is probably accurate to the nearest 3 miles.

Geographical Area Measurements

The heights of mountains and the depths of oceans are obtained *directly*. We find heights and depths by measuring the Earth itself.

The areas of countries and the areas of oceans are found *indirectly*. We measure very accurate maps or satellite pictures. The countries and oceans themselves are not measured.

Countries, oceans, and deserts have irregular boundaries. To measure their areas, scientists count grid squares. They place a transparent grid of squares on a map. Then they count the squares and parts of squares that cover the region being measured. The squares are drawn to the same scale as the map.

There are several reasons that it is hard to measure the following regions accurately:

Area of a country. Sometimes people disagree about the exact boundary of a country. So the area may depend on which boundary is being used to measure.

Area of a lake, sea, or ocean. Some bodies of water have shorelines that shift greatly depending on the level of the water. So it is very hard to accurately measure the area that is covered by water.

The world's oceans are not separated from one another by shorelines. Sometimes people disagree on the boundaries between the oceans. This makes it difficult to measure the areas of oceans.

Area of a desert. Measuring desert areas is very hard. Desert boundaries may change because the climate changes. When land is cultivated, a desert boundary shifts. Also, scientists do not agree on what a desert actually is. Some define a desert as land that cannot be used for raising crops. Others define it as land that cannot be used for either crops or grazing. There are deserts that are hot and dry only part of the year. Some deserts are dry all year because it is very hot. Other deserts are dry all year because it is very cold and the water is always frozen. Very cold deserts are known as *tundras*.

Climate and Elevation of Capital Cities

The **climate** of a city or a country refers to the average weather conditions in that place. Two kinds of weather data are shown on the opposite page: temperature and rainfall. Elevation data are also shown.

Temperature Data

Average temperatures are given in degrees Fahrenheit (°F).
- Each column lists average temperatures for a 3-month period.
- The first number is the average high temperature for that period. The second number is the average low temperature for that period.

> **EXAMPLES** The average high and low temperatures for Cairo, Egypt, for March through May are about 83°F and 57°F. The highest temperature listed for Santiago, Chile, is 84°F. This is the average high temperature for December through February. Santiago is in the Southern Hemisphere. Countries south of the equator have summer in December, January, and February.

Rainfall Data

Average rainfall is given in inches per month. All moisture that falls as rain or as snow is counted as rainfall. When snow falls, a sample is melted and the depth of the water is measured.

> **EXAMPLES** The average rainfall in Monrovia, Liberia, is 30.7 inches *per month* from June through August. That's about 1 inch per day, on average. The average rainfall in Rome, Italy, is 1 inch *per month* from June through August. The total rainfall during these 3 months is about 1 in. + 1 in. + 1 in., or 3 inches.

Elevation Data

The table also lists the elevation for each capital city. A city's **elevation** is its height above sea level.

> **EXAMPLES** The highest elevation listed is 12,001 feet for La Paz, Bolivia. The elevation listed for Amsterdam, Netherlands, is 0 feet. Amsterdam is exactly at sea level.

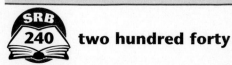

Climate and Elevation of Capital Cities

	Capital, Country	Average Monthly Temps (°F) in Capital City (High/Low)				Average Monthly Rainfall (in.) in Capital City				Elevation of capital (ft)
		Dec/Feb	Mar/May	Jun/Aug	Sept/Nov	Dec/Feb	Mar/May	Jun/Aug	Sept/Nov	
Region 1	Algiers, Algeria	60/50	68/55	82/72	74/63	4.4	2.1	0.3	3.3	194
	Cairo, Egypt	67/48	83/57	95/70	85/64	0.2	0.1	0.0	0.0	381
	Addis Ababa, Ethiopia	75/44	77/50	70/50	73/46	0.7	3.1	9.4	3.0	8,038
	Accra, Ghana	88/74	88/76	82/73	84/74	0.9	3.7	3.1	1.8	88
	Nairobi, Kenya	77/55	75/57	70/51	75/54	2.5	6.5	1.1	2.5	5,971
	Monrovia, Liberia	86/73	87/73	80/73	83/72	2.8	10.9	30.7	23.0	75
	Rabat, Morocco	64/47	71/52	81/62	76/58	2.8	1.8	0.1	1.9	213
	Dakar, Senegal	80/65	87/66	88/75	88/75	0.1	0.0	4.7	2.3	131
	Pretoria, South Africa	78/58	71/49	64/40	77/52	4.8	2.4	0.4	2.7	4,491
	Harare, Zimbabwe	78/60	77/54	71/45	81/57	7.0	2.1	0.1	1.7	4,831
Region 2	Paris, France	44/35	61/44	75/57	50/46	2.0	1.8	2.3	2.1	246
	Athens, Greece	57/45	68/53	90/71	75/60	2.2	1.2	0.4	1.6	351
	Budapest, Hungary	37/28	61/44	80/60	61/45	1.7	2.0	2.3	2.1	456
	Reykjavik, Iceland	36/28	44/34	56/47	45/38	3.0	2.1	2.0	3.1	59
	Rome, Italy	54/42	66/50	85/66	70/55	3.0	2.0	1.0	4.1	56
	Amsterdam, Netherlands*	41/32	56/40	71/54	57/44	2.4	1.9	2.9	2.8	0*
	Oslo, Norway	30/21	50/34	70/53	49/38	1.9	1.5	3.2	2.9	308
	Warsaw, Poland	33/24	54/38	74/56	54/41	1.4	1.5	3.0	1.5	361
	Madrid, Spain	49/36	65/45	84/61	66/49	1.6	1.8	0.7	1.8	2,165
	London, United Kingdom	44/37	56/42	70/55	58/47	1.9	1.6	2.1	2.2	16
Region 3	Buenos Aires, Argentina	83/62	72/53	58/42	70/51	3.3	3.6	2.3	3.3	89
	La Paz, Bolivia	64/43	64/40	63/35	66/40	4.1	1.5	0.4	1.5	12,001
	Brasília, Brazil	87/63	90/62	90/57	93/63	10.6	5.1	0.2	5.7	3,297
	Santiago, Chile	84/52	73/45	60/38	72/45	0.1	1.1	2.8	0.7	1,706
	Bogota, Columbia	67/49	67/51	65/50	66/50	2.5	4.8	2.3	4.5	8,678
	Quito, Ecuador	72/46	70/47	72/45	72/45	3.8	6.0	1.2	3.6	9,446
	Asunción, Paraguay	94/71	84/64	75/54	86/62	5.6	4.7	2.1	4.8	456
	Lima, Peru	81/65	79/63	67/57	71/58	0.1	0.1	0.3	0.2	394
	Montevideo, Uruguay	81/61	71/53	60/43	68/50	2.9	3.7	3.1	2.8	72
	Caracas, Venezuela	77/57	80/60	78/61	79/61	1.0	1.7	4.2	4.1	3,418
Region 4	Canberra, Australia	81/54	68/44	53/34	68/43	1.9	1.9	2.0	1.9	1,837
	Dhaka, Bangladesh	79/55	93/70	89/79	87/73	0.7	4.7	14.0	5.9	26
	Beijing, China	37/17	68/43	87/67	65/43	0.2	0.8	6.1	1.1	171
	New Delhi, India	73/46	96/68	87/81	90/64	0.7	0.4	5.6	1.7	714
	Tehran, Iran	49/31	71/49	96/70	76/53	1.5	1.2	0.1	0.4	4,002
	Tokyo, Japan	49/31	63/45	82/68	72/55	2.3	5.1	6.0	7.1	19
	Moscow, Russia	20/7	49/37	72/53	48/36	1.7	1.7	2.9	2.0	512
	Bangkok, Thailand	89/69	94/77	90/76	88/74	0.4	3.8	6.5	7.6	7
	Ankara, Turkey	41/26	62/40	84/57	68/44	1.5	1.5	0.6	0.9	2,825
	Hanoi, Vietnam	89/71	93/75	88/75	88/74	1.0	3.6	12.0	9.4	30
Region 5	Ottawa, Canada	22/5	50/30	78/56	54/37	2.6	2.7	3.2	3.0	339
	San José, Costa Rica	75/59	79/61	78/62	78/60	0.8	3.9	9.1	9.8	3,760
	Havana, Cuba	79/66	84/69	89/75	85/72	2.3	2.9	5.6	5.3	80
	San Salvador, El Savador	90/60	93/65	88/66	87/65	0.3	3.3	12.0	7.7	2,238
	Guatemala City, Guatemala	74/54	82/58	79/60	76/59	0.2	2.6	8.9	5.6	4,855
	Port-au-Prince, Haiti	87/68	89/71	93/73	90/72	1.6	6.3	4.2	5.7	121
	Kingston, Jamaica	86/68	87/70	90/73	88/72	1.0	2.0	3.5	4.6	110
	Mexico City, Mexico	67/43	77/51	74/54	71/56	0.3	1.1	5.8	2.6	7,575
	Panama City, Panama	88/72	88/73	87/74	85/73	2.1	3.9	7.8	9.5	118
	Washington, D.C., United States	44/28	64/44	85/66	67/48	3.2	3.5	4.2	3.1	72

*Parts of Amsterdam are as much as 13 ft below sea level.

Literacy and Standard of Living Data

The table on the opposite page lists information about TVs, radios, telephones, and cars. Each number in the table shows what you would expect to find for a group of 1,000 people.

> **EXAMPLES**   There are only 122 radios in Algeria for every 1,000 people. But there are 2,122 radios in the U.S. for every 1,000 people. That's more than 2 radios for each person in the U.S. Many people in the U.S. have more than 1 radio.

Suppose that you know the number of people in a city or other large area. You can use the table to estimate the total number of TVs, radios, phones, and cars the people in that area have.

> **EXAMPLE**   A town in Ethiopia has about 25,000 people. How many cars would you expect to find in that town? The table shows 1 car for every 1,000 people in Ethiopia.
>
> So, we would expect to find about 25 cars where there are 25,000 people.

You can use the data table to draw graphs and compare countries. The bar graph below shows TV data for Region 1 (Africa). The graph shows that Algeria, Egypt, Morocco, and South Africa all have many more TVs per 1,000 people than the other six countries have.

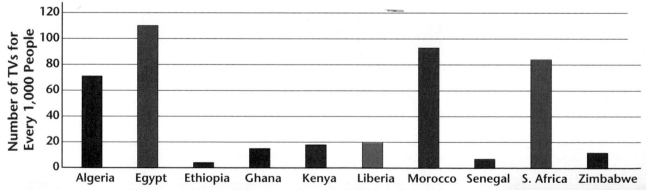

The last column in the table tells about the level of education in each country. A **literate** person is one who can read and write. The **percent of literacy** is the number of people out of 100 who are literate.

> **EXAMPLE**   In Mexico, 90% of the people are literate. This means that about 90 of every 100 people can read and write.

Literacy and Standard of Living Data

Per 1,000 People

	Country	Televisions	Radios	Telephones	Cars	Percent Literate*
Region 1	Algeria	71	122	51	16	62
	Egypt	110	312	59	19	51
	Ethiopia	4	153	3	1	35
	Ghana	15	249	6	5	64
	Kenya	18	103	9	9	78
	Liberia	20	263	2	6	38
	Morocco	93	222	51	37	44
	Senegal	7	93	13	11	33
	South Africa	84	268	107	100	82
	Zimbabwe	12	113	19	22	85
Region 2	France	579	869	576	432	99
	Greece	442	402	517	219	95
	Hungary	444	590	304	224	99
	Iceland	285	733	615	486	100
	Italy	436	790	458	546	97
	Netherlands	495	877	591	368	100
	Norway	459	763	616	397	100
	Poland	250	263	228	195	99
	Spain	490	306	416	391	97
	United Kingdom	612	1,194	539	433	100
Region 3	Argentina	347	614	199	130	96
	Bolivia	202	560	67	25	83
	Brazil	193	348	116	81	85
	Chile	280	305	176	60	95
	Colombia	188	151	164	29	91
	Ecuador	79	277	80	20	90
	Paraguay	144	141	40	13	92
	Peru	85	221	62	19	89
	Uruguay	191	586	249	144	97
	Venezuela	183	372	117	65	91
Region 4	Australia	641	1,148	513	463	100
	Bangladesh	5	65	2	1	38
	China	189	177	68	4	82
	India	21	117	18	4	52
	Iran	117	213	100	25	79
	Japan	619	799	479	370	100
	Russia	379	341	184	94	99
	Thailand	56	167	80	26	94
	Turkey	171	141	259	50	82
	Vietnam	43	106	26	1	94
Region 5	Canada	647	919	621	429	97
	Costa Rica	102	224	159	13	95
	Cuba	200	327	33	1	96
	El Salvador	91	373	83	6	71
	Guatemala	45	52	35	8	56
	Haiti	4	41	9	5	45
	Jamaica	306	739	158	16	85
	Mexico	192	227	99	82	90
	Panama	13	5	132	52	91
	United States	776	2,122	633	476	97

* Data are hard to measure and may vary greatly.

Population Data

The table on the opposite page lists population information for each country.

Life expectancy is the average number of years a person can expect to live. It is listed separately for males and females because women usually live longer than men.

> **EXAMPLES**   In the United States, women live an average of 80 years, and men live an average of 73 years. In Russia, women live an average of 13 years longer than men. Bangladesh is the only country where men on average live longer than women.

The **percent of people ages 0–14** is the number of people out of every 100 who are very young.

> **EXAMPLES**   In Liberia, 45% of the people are 14 or younger. That's nearly 50%, or one-half, of the people who are very young. In Italy, only 14% of the people are very young. Italy's fraction of very young people is much smaller than Liberia's fraction.

Percent urban is the number of people out of 100 who live in towns or cities. **Percent rural** is the number of people out of 100 who live in the country. These two percents add up to 100%.

> **EXAMPLE**   In the United States, 76 of 100 people live in towns or cities, while 24 out of 100 people live in the country. 76% + 24% = 100%.

The population in most countries grows larger each year. The **percent population growth** is one way to measure how fast the population is growing.

> **EXAMPLE**   The population in Mexico rises by 2% each year.

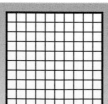 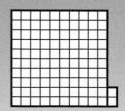

For every 100 Mexicans at the beginning of the year,   there are 102 Mexicans at the end of the year.

Population Data

	Country	Percent of Population Ages 0–14	Life Expectancy Males	Life Expectancy Females	Percent Population Growth in 1 Year	Percent Urban	Percent Rural
Region 1	Algeria	37	68	70	2.1	56	44
	Egypt	36	60	64	1.9	45	55
	Ethiopia	46	39	42	2.3	16	84
	Ghana	42	55	59	2.1	36	64
	Kenya	43	47	47	1.6	30	70
	Liberia	45	57	63	3.0	46	54
	Morocco	36	67	71	2.0	53	47
	Senegal	48	55	61	3.3	44	56
	South Africa	34	53	57	1.3	50	50
	Zimbabwe	43	39	39	1.0	33	67
Region 2	France	19	75	83	0.2	74	26
	Greece	16	76	81	0.1	59	41
	Hungary	17	67	76	−0.2	65	35
	Iceland	23	77	81	0.8	92	8
	Italy	14	75	82	−0.1	67	33
	Netherlands	18	75	81	0.3	89	11
	Norway	20	76	81	0.2	73	27
	Poland	20	69	77	0.1	64	36
	Spain	15	74	82	0	77	23
	United Kingdom	19	75	80	0.1	89	11
Region 3	Argentina	27	71	79	1.2	88	12
	Bolivia	39	59	65	2.1	61	39
	Brazil	30	59	69	1.2	79	21
	Chile	28	72	79	1.2	84	16
	Colombia	33	67	75	1.9	73	27
	Ecuador	35	70	75	1.7	60	40
	Paraguay	39	70	75	2.7	53	47
	Peru	35	68	73	2.0	71	29
	Uruguay	24	73	79	0.8	91	9
	Venezuela	33	70	76	1.7	86	14
Region 4	Australia	21	77	83	0.6	85	15
	Bangladesh	38	61	60	1.7	19	81
	China	26	69	71	0.8	29	71
	India	34	63	64	1.7	27	73
	Iran	36	68	71	1.5	60	40
	Japan	15	77	83	0.2	78	22
	Russia	19	59	72	−0.5	76	24
	Thailand	24	66	73	0.9	20	80
	Turkey	30	71	76	1.6	71	29
	Vietnam	33	66	71	1.4	19	81
Region 5	Canada	20	76	83	0.5	77	23
	Costa Rica	33	74	79	1.8	50	50
	Cuba	22	73	78	0.6	76	24
	El Salvador	37	67	74	2.0	45	55
	Guatemala	43	64	69	2.9	39	61
	Haiti	42	50	54	1.9	32	68
	Jamaica	31	73	78	1.5	54	46
	Mexico	35	69	75	2.0	74	26
	Panama	32	72	78	1.7	56	44
	United States	22	73	80	0.6	76	24

Fascinating Facts

Smallest Countries

Country	Area (sq miles)	Population
Vatican City	0.17	860
Monaco	0.75	32,000
Nauru	8.2	11,000
Tuvalu	10	11,000
San Marino	23	25,000
Liechtenstein	62	32,000

Largest Cities by Population

City, Country	Population
Tokyo, Japan	26,959,000
Mexico City, Mexico	16,562,000
Sao Paulo, Brazil	16,533,000
New York City, United States	16,332,000
Mumbai (Bombay), India	15,138,000
Shanghai, China	13,584,000
Los Angeles, United States	12,410,000

Tokyo, Japan

Languages with the Most Speakers (in millions)

Language	Native Speakers	Total Speakers
Mandarin	885	1,075
Hindi	375	496
Spanish	358	425
English	347	514
Arabic	211	256
Bengali	210	215

Cellular Telephone Use

Country or Region	Number of Cellular Telephone Users (in millions)	Percent of Population Using Cellular Telephones
Finland	2.9	57
Norway	2.1	48
Sweden	4.1	46
Hong Kong	2.9	43
Israel	2.1	37
Italy	20.5	36
Denmark	1.9	35
Singapore	1.0	32
Portugal	3.1	31
Australia	5.9	31
Japan	39.0	31
South Korea	14.0	30
Austria	2.3	29
United States	69.8	26

World's Tallest Buildings

Name	Place	Year Built	Height (feet)
Petronas Towers, I and II	Kuala Lumpur, Malaysia	1998	1,483*
Sears Tower	Chicago, United States	1974	1,450
Jin Mao	Shanghai, China	1998	1,381*
One World Trade Center	New York, United States	1972	1,368
Two World Trade Center	New York, United States	1973	1,362
CITIC Plaza	Guangzhou, China	1996	1,283*
Shun Hing Square	Shenzhen, China	1996	1,250
Empire State Building	New York, United States	1931	1,250
Central Plaza	Hong Kong, China	1992	1,227*
Bank of China	Hong Kong, China	1989	1,209*

* height measurement includes a spire

Sears Tower

Petronas Towers, I and II

English Channel Tunnel

For more information and ongoing updates, go to the *World's Tallest Buildings* Web site at http://www.worldstallest.com.

World's Longest Railway Tunnels

Tunnel	Place	Year Built	Length (miles)
Seikan	Japan	1985	33.5
English Channel Tunnel	United Kingdom–France	1994	31
Dai-shimizu	Japan	1979	14
Simplon Nos. 1 and 2	Switzerland–Italy	1906, 1922	12
Kanmon	Japan	1975	12
Apennine	Italy	1934	11
Rokko	Japan	1972	10

Largest Oceans and Seas

Name	Area (sq miles)	Average Depth (feet)
Pacific Ocean	64,186,300	12,925
Atlantic Ocean	33,420,000	11,730
Indian Ocean	28,350,500	12,598
Arctic Ocean	5,105,700	3,407
South China Sea	1,148,500	4,802
Caribbean Sea	971,400	8,448
Mediterranean Sea	969,100	4,926
Bering Sea	873,000	4,893
Gulf of Mexico	582,100	5,297
Okhotsk Sea	537,500	3,192

Longest Rivers

Name	Location	Length (miles)
Nile	Africa	4,160
Amazon	S. America	4,000
Chang (Yangtze)	Asia	3,964
Huang (Yellow)	Asia	3,395
Ob-Irtysh	Asia	3,362
Congo	Africa	2,900
Lena	Asia	2,734
Niger	Africa	2,590
Parana	S. America	2,485
Mississippi	N. America	2,340

Largest Deserts

Name	Location	Area (sq miles)
Sahara	Africa	3,500,000
Gobi	Asia	500,000
Libyan	Africa	450,000
Patagonia	S. America	300,000
Rub al Khali	Asia	250,000
Kalahari	Africa	225,000
Great Sandy	Australia	150,000
Great Victory	Australia	150,000
Chihuahuan	N. America	140,000

Largest Freshwater Lakes

Name	Location	Area (sq miles)
Superior	N. America	31,700
Victoria	Africa	26,828
Huron	N. America	23,000
Michigan	N. America	22,300
Tanganyika	Africa	12,700
Baykal	Asia	12,162
Great Bear	N. America	12,096
Malawi (Nyasa)	Africa	11,150

Tallest Mountains

Name	Location	Height (feet)
Everest	Nepal–Tibet	29,028
K-2 (Godwin-Austen)	Kashmir	28,250
Kanchenjunga	Nepal–India	28,208
Lhotse I (Everest)	Nepal–Tibet	27,923
Makalu I	Nepal–Tibet	27,824
Lhotse II (Everest)	Nepal–Tibet	27,560
Dhaulagiri I	Nepal	26,810
Manaslu I	Nepal	26,760
Cho Oyu	Nepal–Tibet	26,750
Nanga Parbat	Kashmir	26,660

Highest/Lowest Elevation Points

Continent	Highest/Lowest Point	Elevation (feet)
Africa	Mt. Kilimanjaro, Tanzania	19,340
	Lake Assal, Djibouti	−512
Antarctica	Vinson Massif	16,864
	Bentley Subglacial Trench	−8,327
Asia	Mt. Everest, Nepal–Tibet	29,028
	Dead Sea, Israel–Jordan	−1,312
Australia	Mt. Kosciusko, New S. Wales	7,310
	Lake Eyre, South Australia	−52
Europe	Mt. El'brus, Russia	18,510
	Caspian Sea, Russia, Azerbaijan	−92
N. America	Mt. McKinley (Denali), Alaska	20,320
	Death Valley, California	−282
S. America	Mt. Aconcagua, Argentina	22,834
	Valdés Penninsula, Argentina	−131

Temperature and Rainfall Extremes

Hottest single days	136°F, Azizia (Alaziziyah), Libya	134°F, Death Valley, California
Hottest yearly average	95°F, Dalol Depression, Ethiopia	
Coldest single days	−129°F, Vostok, Antarctica	−90°F, Oimekon, Russia
Coldest yearly average	−72°F, Plateau Station, Antarctica	
Highest average yearly rainfall	467 in., Mawsynram, India	460 in., Mt. Waialeale, Kauai, Hawaii
Lowest average yearly rainfall	0.03 in., Arica, Chile	Less than 0.1 in., Wadi Halfa, Sudan

Top Countries for Mammals

Country	Continent	Number of Known Species
Indonesia	Asia	515
Mexico	N. America	439
Zaire	Africa	415
Brazil	S. America	394
China	Asia	394
Colombia	S. America	359
United States	N. America	346
Peru	S. America	344
India	Asia	317
Uganda	Africa	315

Top Countries for Birds

Country	Continent	Number of Known Species
Colombia	S. America	1,721
Peru	S. America	1,705
Brazil	S. America	1,573
Indonesia	Asia	1,519
Ecuador	S. America	1,435
Venezuela	S. America	1,308
Bolivia	S. America	1,257
China	Asia	1,100
Zaire	Africa	1,086
Kenya	Africa	1,067
Tanzania	Africa	1,016

Top Countries for Reptiles and Amphibians

Country	Continent	Number of Known Species
Mexico	N. America	1,001
Brazil	S. America	970
Australia	Australia	880
Colombia	S. America	790
Indonesia	Asia	781
Ecuador	S. America	680
India	Asia	595
Peru	S. America	539
China	Asia	472
Papua New Guinea	Australia	432
Malaysia	Asia	426

Top Countries for Flowering Plants

Country	Continent	Approximate Number of Known Species
Brazil	S. America	52,000
Colombia	S. America	33,000
China	Asia	30,000
Mexico	N. America	25,000
Indonesia	Asia	20,000
Venezuela	S. America	20,000
United States	N. America	20,000

Mancala

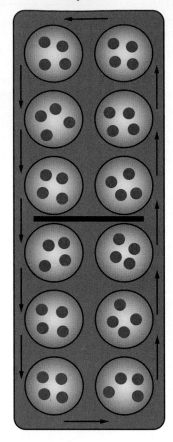

Player 1

Mancala is a 3,000-year-old game of strategy. It is popular throughout Africa and Asia. The game has a variety of names, and the rules vary slightly from country to country. The game is usually played using a wooden board with 12 cups carved into it. Seeds or beans are used as counters.

Materials   ☐ an egg carton or gameboard with 12 cups
☐ 48 counters, beans, or seeds

Players   2

Directions

Players sit at opposite ends of the board. Each player places four counters in each of the six cups on his or her side of the board. (See diagram.)

To begin, Player 1 picks up all of the counters from *one* of the six cups on his or her side. Beginning with the next cup, Player 1 drops the four counters one at a time into each consecutive cup, moving *counterclockwise* around the board.

Player 2 does the same thing with counters from one of the cups on his or her side of the board. (Players always begin by picking up counters from a cup on their side of the board).

Player 2

A player *captures* counters if these two conditions hold true:

• The last counter the player drops in a cup lands on the *other* player's side of the board.
• It lands in a cup with one or two counters already there.

When this happens, the player picks up the counters in that cup, including the one just dropped in. These are then set aside for counting at the end of the game. Players may only capture counters from their opponent's side of the board.

Play continues until one player has no counters left on his or her side of the board. At that time, players tally the number of counters captured, plus the number of counters remaining on the opponent's side of the board. The player with the most counters wins.

Move counterclockwise as you drop counters into the cups.

Tchuka Ruma

(This is a solitaire version of *Mancala*.)

Materials   ☐ an egg carton or gameboard with 5 cups
                ☐ 8 counters

Player   1

Directions

The player places 2 counters in each of the first 4 cups. The cup on the far right remains empty. The empty cup is called the *Ruma*.

The gameboard at the start of play

The player takes all of the counters from any cup and drops them one at a time into each consecutive cup, moving from left to right. If there are still counters in the player's hand after placing a counter in the Ruma, the player goes back to the far-left cup and continues.

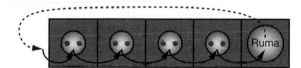

Move in the direction of the arrows as you drop counters into the cups.

If there are counters in the cup where the last counter is dropped, the player takes all of the counters (including the one dropped) and continues as before. The player drops the counters one at a time into consecutive cups, beginning with the next cup to the right. The player always moves from left to right. If there are still counters in the player's hand after placing a counter in the Ruma, the player returns to the far-left cup and continues play.

If the last counter is dropped in the Ruma, the player can select any cup to begin the next move. The player takes all of the counters from this cup and drops them into other cups in the usual way.

If the last counter is dropped in a cup that is *not* the Ruma, and if there are no counters in that cup, the game ends and the player loses.

The player wins if he or she can get all of the counters into the Ruma.

Seega

This is a version of a traditional Egyptian game that is popular among young Egyptians today.

Materials ☐ *Seega* Game Mat (*Math Masters,* p. 480)
☐ 6 markers (3 each of two colors)

Players 2

Directions

Each player takes 3 markers of the same color. To begin, players place their markers on the starting lines at the ends of the game mat. (See diagram.)

Players take turns moving one of their markers one or two squares.

- A marker can be moved to any open square that is next to it. Diagonal moves are OK.

- A marker can be moved two squares in any direction to an open square. Diagonal moves are OK, but a change in direction during the move is NOT allowed. Jumping over another marker is also NOT allowed.

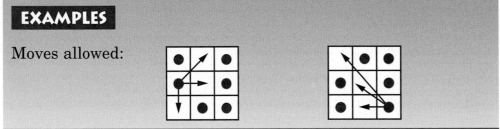

EXAMPLES

Moves allowed:

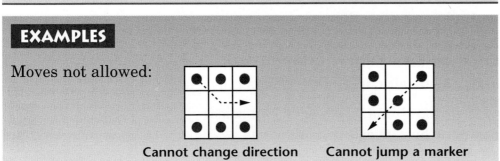

EXAMPLES

Moves not allowed:

Cannot change direction   **Cannot jump a marker**

The first player to get his or her markers in a straight line is the winner. The line can be horizontal, vertical, or diagonal, but it cannot be the player's starting line.

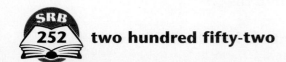

Sz'kwa

This is a Chinese children's game. Its name means "the game of four directions." In China, the game mat is often marked in the dirt or gravel, and pebbles, nuts, or shells are used as markers.

Materials   ☐ *Sz'kwa* Game Mat (*Math Masters*, p. 481)
                 ☐ 40 markers (20 each of two different colors)

Players   2

Directions

The game mat has 21 places where lines meet (called "intersections"). Players take turns. At each turn, a player places one marker on any intersection that is not already covered by a marker.

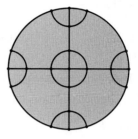

A marker is "captured" if it is surrounded by the opponent's markers. The captured marker is removed from the mat and kept by the opponent.

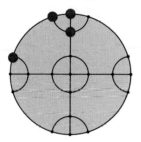   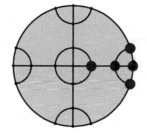

Green marker captured   **Two red markers captured**

Play continues until players run out of markers, or until there is no place left on the mat to put a marker without it being captured. The player who holds the most captured pieces at this time is the winner.

Alleyway

This game is popular in Eastern Europe. The game mat is shaped like a semicircle with 25 numbered spaces. Space 13 is left open and is called the "alleyway."

Materials □ *Alleyway* Game Mat (*Math Masters*, p. 482)
□ 1 marker for each player
□ 1 die

Players any number

Directions

Players place their markers in the Start area. They take turns rolling the die and moving their markers. A player moves his or her marker forward on the game mat by as many spaces as there are dots showing on the die.

A player's marker may land on a space already occupied by another player's marker. If that happens, the opponent's marker must be moved back.

- If the marker is in one of the spaces numbered 1–13, the opponent's marker must move back to the Start area.
- If the marker is in one of the spaces numbered 14–25, the opponent's marker must move back 2 spaces.

If a marker lands on another player's marker when it is moved back, then the marker it lands on must also be moved back. Use the rules given above for moving it back.

If a player's marker lands exactly on space 25, it must go back to space 14.

The winner is the first person to get *beyond* space 25.

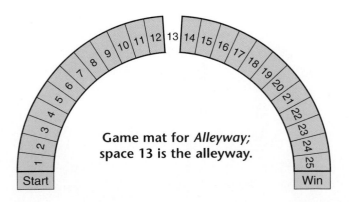

Game mat for *Alleyway*;
space 13 is the alleyway.

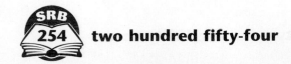

Maltese-Cross Dominoes

In this version of dominoes, the dominoes are played to form a shape called the *Maltese Cross*. Malta is a small country in the Mediterranean Sea south of Italy. The Knights of Malta, who used the Maltese-Cross design on their flag and armor, ruled the country from 1500 to 1800.

Materials   ☐ 28 dominoes from a double-6 set
(If you have a larger set of dominoes, use only dominoes with six or fewer dots on each side).

Players   4

Directions

Each player draws 7 dominoes. The player with the double-6 domino plays first by putting the double-6 piece in the middle of the board.

Players then take turns placing one domino next to any domino that has already been played. If they follow the rules below, the dominoes played will form a cross.

- A domino placed next to the double-6 must have 6 dots on one end. The other end may have any number of dots.

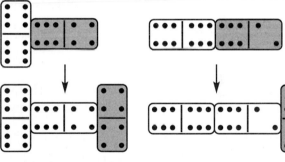

- If a domino is *not* a double, then only a double can be placed next to its open end. The domino played must have double the number of spots at the open end.

- If a domino *is* a double, then a domino placed next to it must have the same number of dots on one end as the double has on one end.

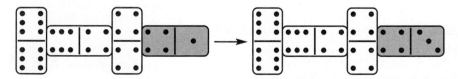

A player passes when he or she cannot play a domino. Play ends when one player plays all of his or her dominoes, or when no one can play. Players then total the number of dots on the dominoes left in their hands. The player with the fewest dots left wins.

Patolli

This game was a favorite of the Aztecs, the native people of central Mexico. The Aztecs lived in and around the Valley of Mexico from about A.D. 1200 until they were conquered by the Spanish in 1521. Today, their capital city, Tenochtitlan, is Mexico City, the capital of Mexico. The Aztecs are the ancestors of many people living in Mexico today. The Aztecs were very serious about playing *Patolli.* Before a game, players made offerings of food to Mecuilxochitl, the god of chance, in hopes of winning his favor in the game.

Materials ☐ *Patolli* Game Mat (*Math Masters*, p. 483)
☐ 5 flat beans (such as limas)
  Mark one side of each bean with a dot.
☐ counters: • for 2 players: 6 counters per
    player
  • for 3 players: 4 counters per player
  • for 4 players: 3 counters per player
Each player should have counters of a different color from the other players.

Players   2–4

Directions

Players each place a counter on the HOME space nearest to them. Each player tosses the 5 beans. The player with the highest number of dots showing goes first.

Players take turns tossing the beans and moving their counters.

• A counter is moved the same number of spaces as the number of dots showing on the beans. If all 5 dots are showing, the count is doubled, and the player moves the counter 10 spaces.

• If exactly one dot is showing, the player may place a new counter on his or her HOME space.

A counter is removed from the mat when it comes back to HOME after going all the way around the mat. The counter must land exactly on HOME.

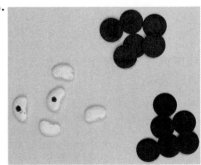

Beans and counters for a 2-player game.

The first player to move all of his or her counters around the mat and back to HOME wins the game.

Sprouts

John Conway, professor of mathematics at Princeton University, invented this paper-and-pencil game in 1967.

Materials □ paper and pencil

Players 2

Directions

On a piece of paper, draw 3 dots that are widely spaced apart. You can start with more dots, but 3 dots is a good number to use when learning how to play.

Players take turns drawing a line (curved or straight) connecting any two dots, or joining a dot to itself. A player completes his or her turn by drawing another dot anywhere on the new line.

These rules must be followed when drawing the connecting lines:
• No line may cross itself.
• No line may cross any other line that has been drawn.
• No line may be drawn through a dot.
• A dot can have no more than 3 lines coming from it. A good way to keep track of this is to draw a box around any dot that has 3 lines coming from it. (See below.)

The winner is the last person who is able to draw a connecting line.

Sample Play (for an incomplete game)

1. 3 dots drawn	2. Player 1's turn	3. Player 2's turn
4. Player 1's turn	5. Player 2's turn	6. Player 1's turn

Place-Value Chart

billions	100 millions	10 millions	millions	100 thousands	10 thousands	thousands	hundreds	tens	ones	.	tenths	hundredths	thousandths
1,000 millions	100,000,000s	10,000,000s	1,000,000s	100,000s	10,000s	1,000s	100s	10s	1s	.	0.1s	0.01s	0.001s
10^9	10^8	10^7	10^6	10^5	10^4	10^3	10^2	10^1	10^0	.	10^{-1}	10^{-2}	10^{-3}

Prefixes

uni-	one	tera-	trillion (10^{12})
bi-	two	giga-	billion (10^9)
tri-	three	mega-	million (10^6)
quad-	four	kilo-	thousand (10^3)
penta-	five	hecto-	hundred (10^2)
hexa-	six	deca-	ten (10^1)
hepta-	seven	uni-	one (10^0)
octa-	eight	deci-	tenth (10^{-1})
nona-	nine	centi-	hundredth (10^{-2})
deca-	ten	milli-	thousandth (10^{-3})
dodeca-	twelve	micro-	millionth (10^{-6})
icosa-	twenty	nano-	billionth (10^{-9})

Multiplication and Division Table

*,/	1	2	3	4	5	6	7	8	9	10	11	12
1	1	2	3	4	5	6	7	8	9	10	11	12
2	2	4	6	8	10	12	14	16	18	20	22	24
3	3	6	9	12	15	18	21	24	27	30	33	36
4	4	8	12	16	20	24	28	32	36	40	44	48
5	5	10	15	20	25	30	35	40	45	50	55	60
6	6	12	18	24	30	36	42	48	54	60	66	72
7	7	14	21	28	35	42	49	56	63	70	77	84
8	8	16	24	32	40	48	56	64	72	80	88	96
9	9	18	27	36	45	54	63	72	81	90	99	108
10	10	20	30	40	50	60	70	80	90	100	110	120
11	11	22	33	44	55	66	77	88	99	110	121	132
12	12	24	36	48	60	72	84	96	108	120	132	144

Metric System
Units of Length

1 kilometer (km)	= 1,000 meters (m)
1 meter	= 10 decimeters (dm)
	= 100 centimeters (cm)
	= 1,000 millimeters (mm)
1 decimeter	= 10 centimeters
1 centimeter	= 10 millimeters

Units of Area

1 square meter (m^2)	= 100 square decimeters (dm^2)
	= 10,000 square centimeters (cm^2)
1 square decimeter	= 100 square centimeters
1 square kilometer	= 1,000,000 square meters

Units of Volume

1 cubic meter (m^3)	= 1,000 cubic decimeters (dm^3)
	= 1,000,000 cubic centimeters (cm^3)
1 cubic decimeter	= 1,000 cubic centimeters

Units of Capacity

1 kiloliter (kL)	= 1,000 liters (L)
1 liter	= 1,000 milliliters (mL)
1 cubic centimeter	= 1 milliliter

Units of Mass

1 metric ton (t)	= 1,000 kilograms (kg)
1 kilogram	= 1,000 grams (g)
1 gram	= 1,000 milligrams (mg)

System Equivalents

1 inch is about 2.5 cm (2.54)
1 kilometer is about 0.6 mile (0.621)
1 mile is about 1.6 kilometers (1.609)
1 meter is about 39 inches (39.37)
1 liter is about 1.1 quarts (1.057)
1 ounce is about 28 grams (28.350)
1 kilogram is about 2.2 pounds (2.205)

U.S. Customary System
Units of Length

1 mile (mi)	= 1,760 yards (yd)
	= 5,280 feet (ft)
1 yard	= 3 feet
	= 36 inches (in.)
1 foot	= 12 inches

Units of Area

1 square yard (yd^2)	= 9 square feet (ft^2)
	= 1,296 square inches ($in.^2$)
1 square foot	= 144 square inches
1 acre	= 43,560 square feet
1 square mile (mi^2)	= 640 acres

Units of Volume

1 cubic yard (yd^3)	= 27 cubic feet (ft^3)
1 cubic foot	= 1,728 cubic inches ($in.^3$)

Units of Capacity

1 gallon (gal)	= 4 quarts (qt)
1 quart	= 2 pints (pt)
1 pint	= 2 cups (c)
1 cup	= 8 fluid ounces (fl oz)
1 fluid ounce	= 2 tablespoons (tbs)
1 tablespoon	= 3 teaspoons (tsp)

Units of Weight

1 ton (T)	= 2,000 pounds (lb)
1 pound	= 16 ounces (oz)

Units of Time

1 century	= 100 years
1 decade	= 10 years
1 year (yr)	= 12 months
	= 52 weeks (plus one or two days)
	= 365 days (366 days in a leap year)
1 month (mo)	= 28, 29, 30, or 31 days
1 week (wk)	= 7 days
1 day (d)	= 24 hours
1 hour (hr)	= 60 minutes
1 minute (min)	= 60 seconds (sec)

Decimal and Percent Equivalents for "Easy" Fractions

"Easy" Fractions	Decimals	Percents
$\frac{1}{2}$	0.50	50%
$\frac{1}{4}$	0.25	25%
$\frac{3}{4}$	0.75	75%
$\frac{1}{5}$	0.20	20%
$\frac{2}{5}$	0.40	40%
$\frac{3}{5}$	0.60	60%
$\frac{4}{5}$	0.80	80%
$\frac{1}{10}$	0.10	10%
$\frac{3}{10}$	0.30	30%
$\frac{7}{10}$	0.70	70%
$\frac{9}{10}$	0.90	90%

The Global Grid

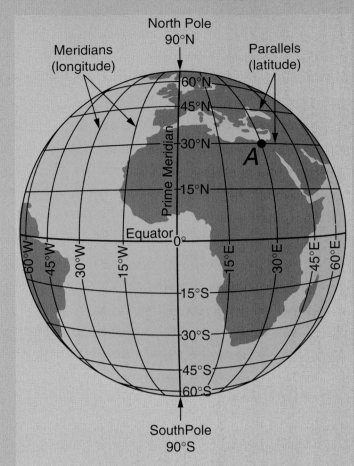

Point A is located at 30°N, 30°E.

Fraction-Decimal Number Line

0	0.125	0.25	0.375	0.5	0.625	0.75	0.875	1
$\frac{0}{2}$	$\frac{1}{8}$	$\frac{1}{4}$	$\frac{3}{8}$	$\frac{1}{2}$	$\frac{5}{8}$	$\frac{3}{4}$	$\frac{7}{8}$	$\frac{2}{2}$
$\frac{0}{4}$		$\frac{2}{8}$		$\frac{2}{4}$		$\frac{6}{8}$		$\frac{4}{4}$
$\frac{0}{8}$				$\frac{4}{8}$				$\frac{8}{8}$

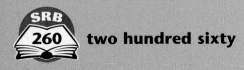

Addend One of two or more numbers that are added. For example, in 5 + 3 + 1, the addends are 5, 3, and 1.

Algorithm A set of step-by-step instructions for doing something, such as carrying out a computation or solving a problem.

Angle A figure that is formed by two rays or two line segments with a common endpoint. The common endpoint is called the *vertex* of the angle. An *acute angle* has a measure greater than 0° and less than 90°. An *obtuse angle* has a measure greater than 90° and less than 180°. A *reflex angle* has a measure greater than 180° and less than 360°. A *right angle* measures 90°. A *straight angle* measures 180°. See also *endpoint, ray,* and *vertex.*

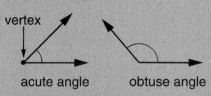

acute angle   obtuse angle

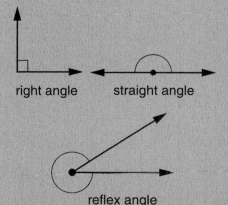

right angle   straight angle

reflex angle

Apex In a pyramid or a cone, the vertex opposite the base. See also *base of a pyramid or a cone.*

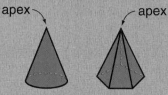

apex   apex

Area The amount of surface inside a closed boundary. Area is measured in square units, such as square inches or square centimeters.

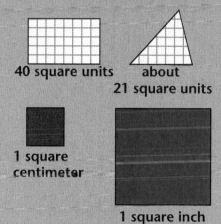

40 square units   about 21 square units

1 square centimeter

1 square inch

Array An arrangement of objects in a regular pattern, usually rows and columns. Arrays can be used to model multiplication. For example, the array below is a model for 3 * 5 = 15. See also *rectangular array.*

column

row {

Associative property A property of addition and multiplication (but not of subtraction or division) that says that when you add or multiply three numbers, it doesn't matter which two are added or multiplied first. For example:
(4 + 3) + 7 = 4 + (3 + 7) and
(5 * 8) * 9 = 5 * (8 * 9).

Average A typical value for a set of numbers. The word *average* usually refers to the *mean* of a set of numbers, but there are other averages. See also *mean, median,* and *mode.*

Axis, *plural* axes (1) Either of the two number lines that intersect to form a *coordinate grid.*

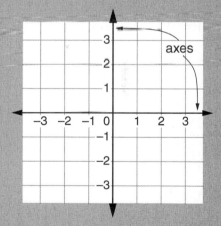

axes

(2) A line about which a solid figure rotates.

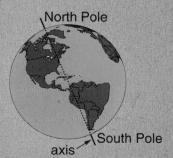

North Pole

South Pole

axis

Glossary

Bar graph A graph that uses horizontal or vertical bars to represent data.

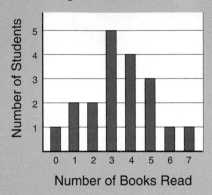

Base (in exponential notation) The number that is raised to some power. For example, in 5^3, the base is 5. See also *exponential notation*.

Base of a polygon A side on which a polygon "sits." The height of a polygon may depend on which side is called the base. See also *height of a parallelogram* and *height of a triangle*.

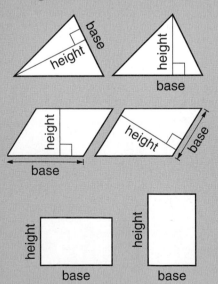

Base of a prism or a cylinder Either of the two parallel and congruent faces that define the shape of a prism or a cylinder.

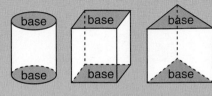

Base of a pyramid or a cone The face of a pyramid or a cone that is opposite its apex.

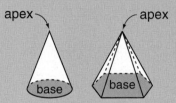

Broken-line graph A graph in which data points are connected by line segments. Same as *line graph*.

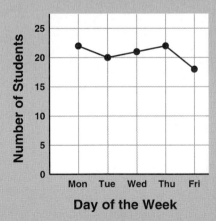

Attendance for the First Week of School

Day of the Week

 C

Capacity The amount a container can hold. Also, the heaviest weight a scale can measure.

Change diagram A diagram in *Everyday Mathematics* used to represent situations in which quantities are increased or decreased.

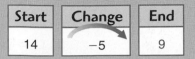

Start	Change	End
14	−5	9

Circle The set of all points in a plane that are a given distance from a given point in the plane. The given point is the *center* of the circle and the given distance is the *radius*.

Circle graph A graph in which a circle and its interior are divided into parts to show the parts of a set of data. The whole circle represents the whole set of data. Same as *pie graph*.

Circumference The distance around a circle or a sphere; the perimeter of a circle.

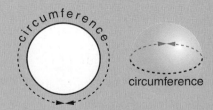

Clockwise rotation A turning in the same direction as that of the hands of a clock.

Column-addition method A method for adding numbers in which the addends' digits are first added in each place-value column separately and then 10-for-1 trades are made until each column has only one digit. Lines are drawn to separate the place-value columns.

100s	10s	1s
2	4	8
+ 1	8	7
3	12	15
3	13	5
4	3	5

Common denominator Any number, except zero, that is a multiple of the denominators of two or more fractions. For example, the fractions $\frac{1}{2}$ and $\frac{2}{3}$ have the common denominators 6, 12, 18, and so on. See also *denominator*.

Commutative property A property of addition and multiplication (but not of subtraction or division) that says that changing the order of the numbers being added or multiplied doesn't change the answer. For example: $5 + 10 = 10 + 5$, and $3 * 8 = 8 * 3$.

Comparison diagram A diagram used in *Everyday Mathematics* to represent situations in which two quantities are compared.

Quantity
12

Quantity	Difference
9	?

Composite number A whole number that has more than two factors. For example, 4 is a composite number because it has three factors: 1, 2, and 4.

Concave polygon A polygon in which at least one vertex is "pushed in." Same as *nonconvex polygon*.

Concentric circles Circles that have the same center but radii of different lengths.

Cone A 3-dimensional shape that has a circular *base*, a curved surface, and one vertex, which is called the *apex*. The points on the curved surface of a cone are on straight lines connecting the apex and the circumference of the base.

Congruent Having exactly the same shape and size.

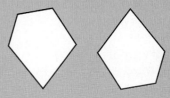

congruent pentagons

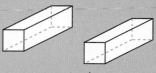

congruent prisms

Convex polygon A polygon in which all vertices are "pushed outward."

Coordinate A number used to locate a point on a number line, or one of two numbers used to locate a point on a coordinate grid. See also *coordinate grid*.

Coordinate grid A device for locating points in a plane using *ordered number pairs*, or coordinates. A *rectangular coordinate grid* is formed by two number lines that intersect at right angles at their zero points. See also *coordinate* and *ordered number pair*.

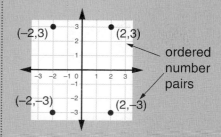

two hundred sixty-three

Glossary

Counterclockwise rotation A turning in the direction that is opposite to that of the hands of a clock.

Cube A polyhedron with 6 square faces. A cube has 8 vertices and 12 edges.

Cubic unit A unit used in measuring volume, such as cubic centimeters or cubic feet.

Curved surface A surface that is rounded rather than flat.

Cylinder A 3-dimensional shape that has two circular or elliptical bases that are parallel and congruent and are connected by a curved surface. The points on the curved surface of a cylinder are on straight lines connecting corresponding points on the bases. A can is shaped like a cylinder.

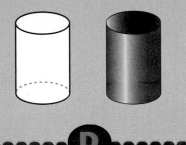

Data Information that is gathered by counting, measuring, asking questions, or observing.

Decimal A number that contains a decimal point, such as 2.54. See *standard notation*.

Decimal point A dot used to separate the ones and tenths places in decimal notation.

Degree A unit of measure for angles based on dividing a circle into 360 equal parts. Also a unit of measure for temperature. A small raised circle (°) is used to show degrees.

an angle measuring 1°

Denominator The number below the line in a fraction. In a fraction where a whole is divided into equal parts, the denominator represents the number of equal parts into which the whole (the ONE or unit) is divided. In the fraction $\frac{a}{b}$, b is the denominator.

Diameter A line segment that passes through the center of a circle or a sphere and has endpoints on the circle or the sphere; also, the length of this line segment. The diameter of a circle or a sphere is twice the length of its radius.

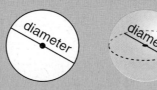

Difference The result of subtracting one number from another.

Digit One of the number symbols 0, 1, 2, 3, 4, 5, 6, 7, 8, 9.

Distributive property A property that relates multiplication and addition or subtraction. This property gets its name because it "distributes" a factor over terms inside parentheses.

Distributive property of multiplication over addition:
$a * (b + c) = (a * b) + (a * c)$
$2 * (5 + 3) = (2 * 5) + (2 * 3)$
$= 10 + 6 = 16$

Distributive property of multiplication over subtraction:
$a * (b - c) = (a * b) - (a * c)$
$2 * (5 - 3) = (2 * 5) - (2 * 3)$
$= 10 - 6 = 4$

Dividend The number that is being divided in division. For example, in $35 \div 5 = 7$, the dividend is 35.

Divisor The number that divides another number in division. For example, in $35 \div 5 = 7$, the divisor is 5.

Edge A line segment where two faces of a polyhedron meet.

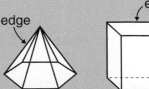

Endpoint A point at the end of a line segment or ray. A line segment is normally named using the letter labels of its endpoints. See *line segment* and *ray*.

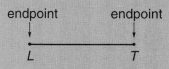

line segment *LT*

Equation A number sentence that contains an equal sign. For example, $15 = 10 + 5$ is an equation.

Equilateral triangle A triangle with all three sides equal in length. In an equilateral triangle, all three angles have the same measure.

Equivalent fractions Fractions that have different denominators but name the same amount. For example, $\frac{1}{2}$ and $\frac{4}{8}$ are equivalent fractions.

Estimate An answer that is close to an exact answer. Also, to calculate an answer that is close to the exact answer.

Even number A whole number that can be divided by 2 with no remainder. The even numbers are 2, 4, 6, 8, 10, and so on. Zero (0) may also be considered even.

Exponent A small, raised number in *exponential notation* that tells how many times the base is to be multiplied by itself. For example, in 5^3, the exponent is 3. See also *base* and *exponential notation*.

Exponential notation A way to show repeated multiplication by the same factor. For example, 2^3 is exponential notation for $2 * 2 * 2$. The small, raised 3 is the exponent. It tells how many times the number 2, called the base, is used as a factor.

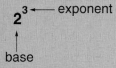

Extended multiplication fact A multiplication fact involving multiples of 10, 100, and so on. In an extended multiplication fact, each factor has only one digit that is not 0. For example, $6 * 70$, $60 * 7$, and $60 * 70$ are extended multiplication facts.

Face A flat surface on a 3-dimensional shape.

Fact family A set of related addition and subtraction facts or related multiplication and division facts. For example, $5 + 6 = 11$, $6 + 5 = 11$, $11 - 5 = 6$, and $11 - 6 = 5$ are a fact family. $5 * 7 = 35$, $7 * 5 = 35$, $35 \div 5 = 7$, and

$35 \div 7 = 5$ are another fact family.

Factor One of two or more numbers that are multiplied to give a product. The numbers that are multiplied are called *factors* of the product. For example, 4 and 3 are factors of 12, because $4 * 3 = 12$. As a verb, *to factor* can also mean to find two (or more) smaller numbers whose product equals a given number. For example, 15 can be factored as $5 * 3$.

$$\underset{\text{factors}}{4 * 3} = \underset{\text{product}}{12}$$

Fair Free from bias. Each side of a fair die or coin will come up about equally often. In a fair game, every player has the same chance of winning.

False number sentence A number sentence in which the relation symbol does not accurately relate the two sides. For example, $8 = 5 + 5$ is a false number sentence.

Flip See *reflection*.

Formula A general rule for finding the value of something. A formula is often written using letters, called variables, that stand for the quantities involved. For example, the formula for the area of a rectangle may be written as $A = l * w$, where A represents the area of the rectangle, l represents its length, and w represents its width.

Glossary

Fraction A number in the form $\frac{a}{b}$ or a/b. Fractions can be used to name parts of a whole, to compare quantities, or to represent division. For example, $\frac{2}{3}$ can be thought of as 2 divided by 3. See also *numerator* and *denominator*.

Frieze pattern A geometric design in a long strip in which an element is repeated over and over again. The element may be rotated, translated, and reflected.

Geometric solid A 3-dimensional shape, such as a prism, pyramid, cylinder, cone, or sphere. Despite its name, a geometric solid is hollow; it does *not* contain the points in its interior.

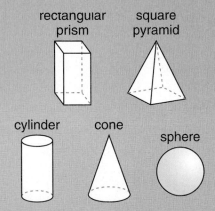

rectangular prism   square pyramid

cylinder   cone   sphere

Geometry Template An *Everyday Mathematics* tool that includes a millimeter ruler, a ruler with sixteenth-inch intervals, half-circle and full-circle protractors, a percent circle, pattern-block shapes, and other geometric

figures. The Template can also be used as a compass.

Height of a parallelogram The shortest length between the base of a parallelogram and the line containing the side opposite its base. The height is perpendicular to the base. See also *base of a polygon*.

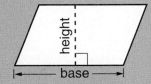

Height of a prism or a cylinder The shortest length from a base of a prism or a cylinder to the plane containing the opposite base. See also *base of a prism or a cylinder*.

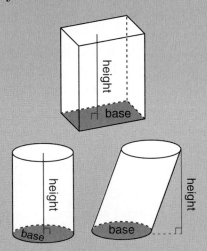

Height of a pyramid or a cone The shortest length from the vertex of a pyramid or a cone to the plane

containing its base. See also *base of a pyramid or a cone*.

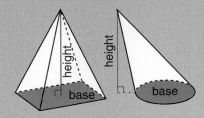

Height of a triangle The shortest length between the line containing a base of a triangle and the vertex opposite that base. See also *base of a polygon*.

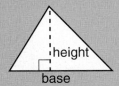

Hemisphere Half of Earth's surface. Also, half of a sphere.

Heptagon A polygon with seven sides.

Hexagon A polygon with six sides.

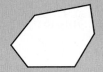

Hexagram A six-pointed star formed by extending the sides of a regular hexagon.

Image The reflection of an object that you see when you look in a mirror. Also, a figure that is produced by a transformation (a reflection, translation, or rotation, for example) of another figure. See also *preimage*.

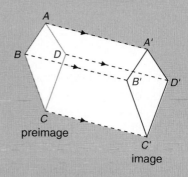

preimage

image

Improper fraction A fraction whose numerator is greater than or equal to its denominator. For example, $\frac{4}{3}$, $\frac{5}{2}$, $\frac{4}{4}$, and $\frac{24}{12}$ are improper fractions. In *Everyday Mathematics*, improper fractions are sometimes called top-heavy fractions.

Inequality A number sentence with >, <, ≥, ≤, or ≠. For example, the sentence $8 < 15$ is an inequality.

Inscribed polygon A polygon whose vertices are all on the same circle.

inscribed square

Integer A number in the set {...−4, −3, −2, −1, 0, 1, 2, 3, 4, ...}; a *whole number* or the *opposite* of a whole number.

Interior The inside of a closed 2-dimensional or 3-dimensional figure. The interior is usually not considered to be part of the figure.

Intersect To meet or cross.

Intersecting Meeting or crossing one another. Lines, segments, rays, and planes can be intersecting.

intersecting lines

intersecting planes

Kite A quadrilateral with two pairs of adjacent equal sides. The four sides cannot all have the same length, so a rhombus is not a kite.

Landmark A notable feature of a data set. Landmarks include *median, mode, maximum, minimum,* and *range*.

Latitude A measure, in degrees, of the distance of a place north or south of the equator.

Lattice method A very old way to multiply multidigit numbers.

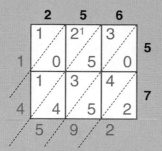

$256 * 57 = 14{,}592$

Left-to-right subtraction A subtraction method in which you start at the left and subtract column by column. $932 - 356 = ?$

```
                    9 3 2
Subtract the 100s.  − 3 0 0
                    ───────
                      6 3 2
Subtract the 10s.   −   5 0
                    ───────
                      5 8 2
Subtract the 1s.    −     6
                    ───────
                      5 7 6
```

Line A straight path that extends infinitely in opposite directions.

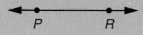

Line graph See *broken-line graph*.

Line of reflection (mirror line) A line halfway between a figure (preimage) and its reflected image. In a reflection, a figure is "flipped over" the line of reflection. See also *reflection*.

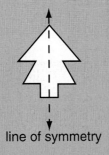

line of reflection

Line of symmetry A line drawn through a figure that divides the figure into two parts that look exactly alike but are facing in opposite directions.

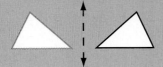

line of symmetry

Line plot A sketch of data in which check marks, Xs, or other marks above a labeled line show the frequency of each value.

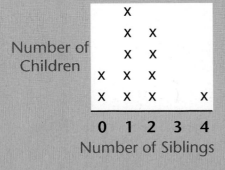

Line segment A straight path joining two points. The two points are called the *endpoints* of the segment.

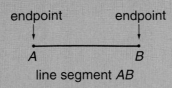

endpoint   endpoint

A   B
line segment *AB*

Lines of latitude Lines that run east-west on a map or globe and indicate the location of a place with reference to the equator, which is also a line of latitude. Lines of latitude are called *parallels* because each one is parallel to the equator.

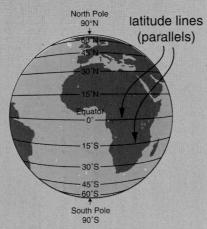

Lines of longitude Lines that run north-south on a map or globe and indicate the location of a place with reference to the prime meridian, which is also a line of longitude. Lines of longitude are semicircles that meet at the North and South Poles. They are also called meridians.

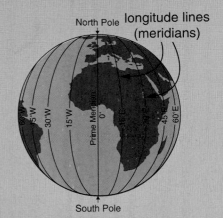

Longitude A measure, in degrees, of how far east or west of the prime meridian a place is.

Lowest terms See *simplest form*.

Magnitude estimate A very rough estimate. A magnitude estimate tells whether an answer should be in the tens, hundreds, thousands, ten thousands, and so on.

Map scale A tool for estimating real distances between places shown on a map by relating distances on the map to distances in the real world. For example, a map scale may show that one inch on a map represents 100 miles in the real world. See also *scale*.

Maximum The largest amount; the greatest number in a set of data.

Mean The sum of a set of numbers divided by the number of numbers in the set. The mean is often referred to simply as the *average*.

Median The middle value in a set of data when the data are listed in order from smallest to largest. If there is an even number of data points, the median is the *mean* of the two middle values.

Metric system of measurement A measurement system based on the base-ten numeration system. It is used in most countries around the world.

Minimum The smallest amount; the smallest number in a set of data.

Minuend The number that is reduced in subtraction. For example, in $19 - 5 = 14$, the minuend is 19.

mixed number A number that is written using both a whole number and a fraction. For example, $2\frac{1}{4}$ is a mixed number equal to $2 + \frac{1}{4}$.

Mode The value or values that occur most often in a set of data.

Multiplication diagram A diagram used for problems in which there are several equal groups. The diagram has three parts: a number of groups, a number in each group, and a total number.

Also called *multiplication/ division diagram*. See also *rate diagram*.

rows	chairs per row	total chairs
15	25	?

Name-collection box A diagram that is used for writing equivalent names for a number.

| 25 | 37 − 12 | 20 + 5 |

~~HHT HHT HHT HHT HHT~~
twenty-five
veinticinco
X X X X X
X X X X X
X X X X X
X X X X X
X X X X X

Negative number A number that is less than zero; a number to the left of zero on a horizontal number line or below zero on a vertical number line.

n-gon A polygon with *n* sides. For example, a 5-gon is a pentagon and an 8-gon is an octagon.

Nonagon A polygon with nine sides.

Nonconvex polygon See *concave polygon*.

Number model A number sentence that models or fits a number story or situation. For example, the story *Sally had $5.00, and then she*

earned $8.00 can be modeled as $5 + 8 = 13$.

Number sentence A sequence of at least two numbers or expressions separated by a relation symbol ($=, >, <, \geq, \leq, \neq$). Most number sentences also contain at least one operation symbol ($+, -, \times, *, \bullet, \div, /$). Number sentences may also have grouping symbols, such as parentheses.

Number story A story with a problem that can be solved using arithmetic.

Numerator The number above the line in a fraction. In a fraction where a whole is divided into a number of equal parts, the numerator represents the number of equal parts that are being considered. In the fraction $\frac{a}{b}$, a is the numerator.

Octagon A polygon with eight sides.

Odd number A whole number such as 1, 3, 5, and so on, that cannot be evenly divided by 2. When an odd number is divided by 2, there is a remainder of 1.

ONE See *whole*.

Open sentence A *number sentence* which has *variables* in place of one or more missing numbers and which is neither true nor false. For example, $5 + x = 13$ is an open sentence. See also *number sentence* and *variable*.

Operation symbol A symbol used to stand for a particular mathematical operation. The most widely used operation symbols are $+$, $-$, $\times$, $*$, $\bullet$, $\div$, and $/$.

Opposite of a number A number that is the same distance from 0 on the number line as a given number, but on the opposite side of 0. For example, the opposite of $+3$ is -3, and the opposite of -5 is $+5$.

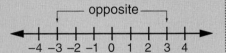

Order of operations Rules that tell in what order to perform operations in arithmetic and algebra. The order of operations is
1. Do the operations in parentheses first. (Use rules 2 through 4 inside the parentheses.)
2. Calculate all the expressions with exponents.
3. Multiply and divide in order from left to right.
4. Add and subtract in order from left to right.

Ordered number pair Two numbers that are used to locate a point on a *coordinate grid*. The first number gives the position along the horizontal axis, and the second number gives the position along the vertical axis. The numbers in an ordered pair are called *coordinates*. Ordered pairs are usually written inside parentheses: (5,3). See *coordinate grid* for an illustration.

Origin The 0 point on a number line or in a coordinate grid.

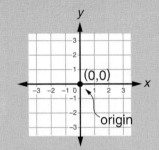

Parallel Never meeting and always the same distance apart. Lines, line segments, and rays in the same plane are parallel if they never meet, no matter how far they are extended. The symbol $\parallel$ means *is parallel to*.

parallel lines   line parallel to a plane   parallel planes

Parallelogram A quadrilateral with two pairs of parallel sides. Opposite sides of a parallelogram are congruent.

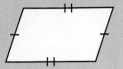

Parentheses Grouping symbols, (), used to tell which parts of an expression should be calculated first.

Partial-differences method A way to subtract in which differences are computed separately for each place (ones, tens, hundreds, and so on). The partial differences are then added to give the final answer.

$$
\begin{array}{r}
9\ 3\ 2 \\
-\ 3\ 5\ 6 \\
\hline
\end{array}
$$

$900 - 300 \rightarrow$	$6\ 0\ 0$
$30 - 50 \rightarrow$	$-\ \ \ 2\ 0$
$2 - 6 \rightarrow$	$-\ \ \ \ \ \ 4$
$600 - 20 - 4 \rightarrow$	$5\ 7\ 6$

Partial-products method A way to multiply in which the value of each digit in one factor is multiplied by the value of each digit in the other factor. The final product is the sum of the several partial products.

$$
\begin{array}{r}
6\ 7 \\
\times\ \ 5\ 3 \\
\hline
\end{array}
$$

$50 \times 60 \rightarrow$	$3\ 0\ 0\ 0$
$50 \times 7 \rightarrow$	$3\ 5\ 0$
$3 \times 60 \rightarrow$	$1\ 8\ 0$
$3 \times 7 \rightarrow$	$+\ \ \ \ 2\ 1$
	$3\ 5\ 5\ 1$

Partial-quotients method
A way to divide in which the dividend is divided in a series of steps, and the quotients for each step (called partial quotients) are added to give the final answer.

```
6)1010
 − 600 │ 100
   410
 − 300 │  50
   110
 −  60 │  10
    50
 −  48 │   8
     2 │ 168
     ↑     ↑
```

Remainder   Quotient

1,010 / 6 → 168 R2

Partial-sums method A way to add in which sums are computed for each place (ones, tens, hundreds, and so on) separately and are then added to give the final answer.

```
                  2 6 8
               + 4 8 3
Add the 100s.  →  6 0 0
Add the 10s.   →  1 4 0
Add the 1s.    → +  1 1
Add partial sums. → 7 5 1
```

Parts-and-total diagram A diagram used in *Everyday Mathematics* to represent situations in which two or more quantities are combined.

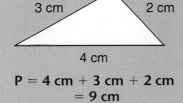

Total	
13	
Part	**Part**
8	?

Pentagon A polygon with five sides.

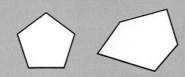

Percent (%) Per hundred or out of a hundred. For example, "48% of the students in the school are boys" means that 48 out of every 100 students in the school are boys.

Percent Circle A tool on the Geometry Template that is used to measure or draw figures that involve percents (such as circle graphs). See also Geometry Template.

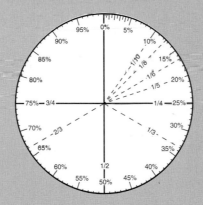

Perimeter The distance around a closed 2-dimensional shape.

3 cm   2 cm

4 cm

P = 4 cm + 3 cm + 2 cm
  = 9 cm

Perpendicular Meeting at right angles. Lines, rays, line segments, and planes that meet at right angles are perpendicular. The symbol ⊥ means *is perpendicular to*.

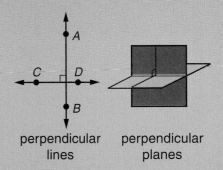

perpendicular   perpendicular
lines   planes

Pi (π) The ratio of the *circumference* of a circle to its *diameter*. Pi is the same for every circle and is approximately 3.14. Pi is the sixteenth letter of the Greek alphabet and is written **π.**

Pie graph See *circle graph*.

Place value A system that values a digit according to its position in a number. In our number system, each place has a value that is ten times that of the place to its right and one-tenth the value of the place to its left. For example, in the number 456, the 4 is in the hundreds place and has a value of 400.

Point An exact location in space. The center of a circle is a point.

Polygon A closed, 2-dimensional figure that is made up of line segments joined end to end. The line segments of a polygon may not cross.

Polyhedron A closed, 3-dimensional figure whose surfaces, or faces, are all formed by polygons and their interiors.

Power of a number Usually, a product of factors that are all the same. For example, 5 * 5 * 5 (or 125) is called "5 to the third power" or "the third power of 5," because 5 is a factor three times. 5 * 5 * 5 can also be written as 5^3.

Preimage A geometric figure that is somehow changed (by a *reflection, a rotation,* or a *translation,* for example) to produce another figure. See also *image*.

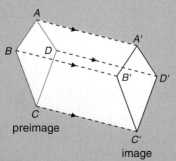

preimage

image

Prime meridian An imaginary semicircle on Earth that connects the North and South Poles and passes through Greenwich, England.

Prime number A whole number that has exactly two *factors*: itself and 1. For example, 5 is a prime number because its only factors are 5 and 1.

Prism A solid with two parallel *faces,* called *bases,* that are congruent polygons, and its other *faces* are all parallelograms. The points on the lateral faces of a prism are all on lines connecting corresponding points on the bases. Prisms are named for the shape of their bases.

triangular prism   rectangular prism

Probability A number from 0 to 1 that tells the chance that an event will happen. The closer a probability is to 1, the more likely the event is to happen.

Product The result of multiplying two numbers called *factors.* For example, in 4 * 3 = 12, the product is 12.

Proper fraction A fraction in which the numerator is less than the denominator; a proper fraction names a number that is less than 1.

For example, $\frac{3}{4}$, $\frac{2}{5}$, and $\frac{12}{24}$ are proper fractions.

Protractor A tool for measuring and drawing angles. A half-circle protractor can be used to measure and draw angles up to 180°; a full-circle protractor, to measure and draw angles up to 360°.

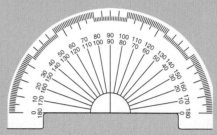

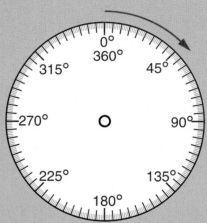

Pyramid A solid in which one face, the *base,* is any polygon, and all the other *faces* are triangles that come together at a point called the *vertex* or *apex.* Pyramids are named for the shape of their bases.

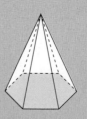 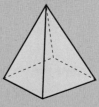

hexagonal pyramid   rectangular pyramid

Quadrangle A polygon that has four angles. Same as *quadrilateral*.

Quadrilateral A polygon that has four sides. Same as *quadrangle*.

Quotient The result of dividing one number by another number. For example, in 35 ÷ 5 = 7, the quotient is 7.

Radius, *plural* **radii** A line segment from the center of a circle (or sphere) to any point on the circle (or sphere); also, the length of such a line segment.

Random number A number that has the same chance of appearing as any other number. Rolling a *fair* die will produce random numbers.

Range The difference between the *maximum* and the *minimum* in a set of data.

Rate A comparison by division of two quantities with unlike units. For example, a speed such as 55 miles per hour is a rate that compares distance with time.

Rate diagram A diagram used to model rate situations. See also *multiplication diagram*.

number of pounds	cost per pound	total cost
3	79¢	$2.37

Ratio A comparison by division of two quantities with like units. Ratios can be expressed with fractions, decimals, percents, or words. Sometimes they are written with a colon between the two numbers that are being compared. For example, if a team wins 3 games out of 5 games played, the ratio of wins to total games can be written as $\frac{3}{5}$, 0.6, 60%, 3 to 5, or 3:5. See also *rate*.

Rational number A number that can be written as a fraction using only whole numbers and their opposites.

Ray A straight path that extends infinitely from a point called its *endpoint*.

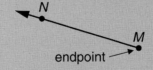

Rectangle A parallelogram with four right angles.

Rectangular array An arrangement of objects in rows and columns such that each row has the same number of objects and each column has the same number of objects.

Reflection The "flipping" of a figure over a line (the *line of reflection*) so that its image is the mirror image of the original. Same as *flip*.

reflection

Regular polygon A polygon whose sides are all the same length and whose angles are all equal.

Regular polyhedron A polyhedron whose faces are formed by a single kind of congruent *regular polygon* and in which every vertex looks exactly the same as every other vertex. There are five regular polyhedrons:

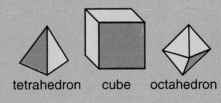
tetrahedron   cube   octahedron

dodecahedron   icosahedron

Relation symbol A symbol used to express a relationship between two quantities.

symbol	meaning
=	"is equal to"
≠	"is not equal to"
>	"is greater than"
<	"is less than"
≥	"is greater than or equal to"
≤	"is less than or equal to."

Remainder An amount left over when one number is divided by another number. For example, if you divide 38 by 5, you get 7 equal groups with a remainder of 3. We may write $38 \div 5 \rightarrow 7$ R3, where R3 stands for the remainder.

Rhombus A quadrilateral whose sides are all the same length.

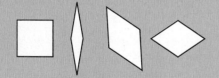

Right triangle A triangle that has a 90° angle.

Rotation A movement of a figure around a fixed point or axis; a *turn*.

Rotation symmetry A figure has rotation symmetry if it can be rotated less than a full turn around a point or an axis so that the resulting figure (the *image*) exactly matches the original figure (the *preimage*).

Round To adjust a number to make it easier to work with or to make it better reflect the level of precision of the data. Often, numbers are rounded to the nearest multiple of 10, 100, 1,000, and so on. For example, 12,964 rounded to the nearest thousand is 13,000.

Sample A part of a group chosen to represent the whole group.

Scale The ratio of a distance on a map, globe, or drawing to an actual distance. See also *map scale*.

Scale drawing A drawing of an object or region in which all parts are drawn to the same *scale*. Architects and builders often use scale drawings.

Scientific notation A system for writing numbers in which a number is written as the product of a *power* of 10 and a number that is at least 1 and less than 10. Scientific notation allows you to write big and small numbers with only a few symbols. For example, $4 * 10^{12}$ is scientific notation for 4,000,000,000,000.

Scroll To move through previous displays using the 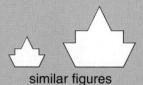 and keys on the calculator.

Side One of the line segments that make up a polygon.

Similar Exactly the same shape but not necessarily the same size.

similar figures

Simpler form A fraction can be put in simpler form by dividing its numerator and denominator by a whole number that is greater than 1. For example, $\frac{18}{24}$ can be put in simpler form by dividing the numerator and the denominator by 2. The result, $\frac{9}{12}$, is in simpler form than $\frac{18}{24}$.

Simplest form A fraction less than 1 is in simplest form if there is no number other than 1 that divides its numerator and denominator evenly. A *mixed number* is in simplest form if its fractional part is in simplest form.

Slide See *translation*.

Solution of an open sentence A value or values for the variable(s) in an *open sentence* that makes the sentence true. For example, 7 is the solution of $5 + n = 12$.

Sphere The set of all points in space that are a given distance from a given point. The given point is the center of the sphere and the given distance is the radius.

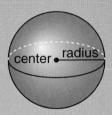

Square A rectangle with all sides equal.

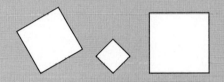

squares

Square number A number that is the product of a whole number multiplied by itself. For example, 25 is a square number because 25 = 5 * 5. The square numbers are 1, 4, 9, 16, 25, and so on.

Square of a number The product of a number multiplied by itself. For example, 81 is the square of 9 because 81 = 9 * 9.

Square unit A unit used in measuring area, such as square centimeters or square feet.

Standard notation The most familiar way of representing whole numbers, integers, and decimals. In standard notation, the value of each digit depends on where the digit is. For example, standard notation for three hundred fifty-six is 356. See also *place value*.

Straightedge A tool for drawing line segments. A straightedge does not have measure marks on it, so if a ruler is used as a straightedge, the marks on it should be ignored.

Subtrahend In subtraction, the number that is being taken away from another number. For example, in 19 − 5 = 14, the subtrahend is 5.

Sum The result of adding two or more numbers. For example, in 5 + 3 = 8, the sum is 8.

Survey A study that collects data.

Symmetric Having the same size and shape on either side of a line or looking the same when turned by some amount less than 360°. See also *line of symmetry* and *rotation symmetry*.

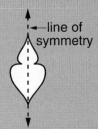

line of symmetry

Tally chart A table that uses marks, called tallies, to show how many times each value in a set of data appears.

Number of Pull-Ups	Number of Children
0	⑇⑇ /
1	⑇⑇
2	////

3-dimensional (3-D) Solid objects that take up volume. 3-dimensional objects have length, width, and thickness.

Trade-first subtraction A subtraction method in which all trades are done before any subtractions are carried out.

Transformation Something done to a geometric figure (the *preimage*) that produces a new figure (the *image*). The most common transformations are *translations* (slides), *reflections* (flips), and *rotations* (turns).

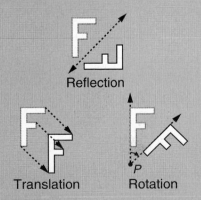

Reflection

Translation

Rotation

Translation A movement of a figure along a straight line; a "slide."

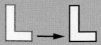

Trapezoid A quadrilateral that has exactly one pair of parallel sides.

Triangle A polygon with three sides.

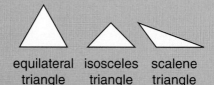

equilateral   isosceles   scalene
triangle   triangle   triangle

Triangular numbers Numbers that can be shown by triangular arrangements of dots. The triangular numbers are 1, 3, 6, 10, 15, 21, 28, ...

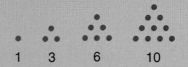

1   3   6   10

True number sentence A number sentence in which the relation symbol accurately relates the two sides. For example, $15 = 5 + 10$ and $25 > 20 + 3$ are both true number sentences.

Turn See *rotation*.

Turn-around facts A pair of multiplication (or addition) facts in which the order of the factors (or addends) is reversed. For example, $3 * 9 = 27$ and $9 * 3 = 27$ are turn-around multiplication facts and $4 + 5 = 9$ and $5 + 4 = 9$ are turn-around addition facts. There are no turn-around facts for subtraction or division.

2-dimensional (2-D) Having length and width, but not thickness. 2-dimensional shapes have area but not volume. Circles and polygons are 2-dimensional.

U.S. customary system of measurement The measuring system most frequently used in the United States.

Unit A label used to put a number in context. In measuring length, for example, inches and centimeters are units. In "5 apples," the word *apples* is the unit. See also *whole*.

Unit fraction A fraction whose numerator is 1. For example, $\frac{1}{2}$, $\frac{1}{3}$, $\frac{1}{8}$, and $\frac{1}{20}$ are unit fractions.

Variable A letter or other symbol that represents a number. A variable can represent one specific number or it can stand for many different numbers.

Vertex The point where the rays of an angle, the sides of a polygon, or the edges of a polyhedron meet.

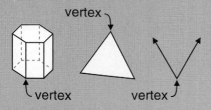

vertex

vertex   vertex

Volume The amount of space inside a 3-dimensional object. Volume is usually measured in cubic units, such as cubic centimeters or cubic inches. Sometimes volume is measured in units of capacity, such as gallons or liters.

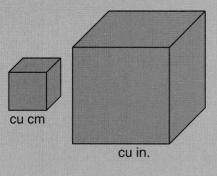

cu cm

cu in.

"What's My Rule?" A type of problem in which you try to figure out a rule for relating two sets of numbers. Also, a type of problem in which you try to figure out one of the sets of numbers, given a rule and the other set of numbers.

Whole (or **ONE** or **unit**) The entire object, collection of objects, or quantity being considered—the ONE, the unit, 100%.

Whole number Any of the numbers 0, 1, 2, 3, 4, and so on.

Page 4
1. 7,000   2. 700,000
3. 70   3. 70,000

Page 6
1. false   2. true   3. true   4. false

Page 7
1. 1, 2, 3, 4, 6, and 12 are the factors of 12.

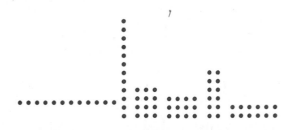

2. 1, 3, 5, and 15 are the factors of 15.

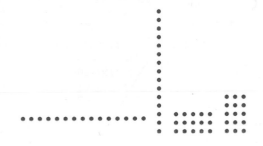

3. 1, 2, 3, 4, 6, 8, 12, and 24 are the
factors of 24.

4. 1 and 13 are the factors of 13.

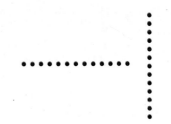

Page 10
1. 688   2. 113   3. 421   4. 1,825
5. 135   6. 82   7. 99   8. 935
9. 1,262   10. 123

Page 11
1. 37   2. 481   3. 449
4. 261   5. 3,146   6. 762

Page 13
1. 198   2. 196   3. 314   4. 569

Page 14
1. 522   2. 138   3. 319   4. 448

Page 16
1. 900   2. 37,000   3. 2,400
4. 24,000   5. 2,100   6. 30,000

Page 17
1. 504   2. 2,400   3. 2,850
4. 1,089   5. 868

Page 18
1.

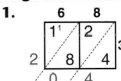

3 * 68 = 204

2.

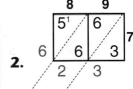

7 * 89 = 623

3.

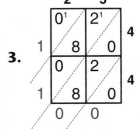

44 * 25 = 1,100

4.

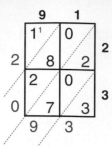

$23 * 91 = 2,093$

5.

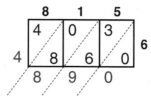

$6 * 815 = 4,890$

Page 20
1. 30   **2.** 36   **3.** 3,000
4. 420   **5.** 60

Page 22
1. 42 R1   **2.** 18 R4
3. 55 R1   **4.** 138 R4

Page 26
1. 0.7   **2.** 0.08
3. 0.42   **4.** $1\frac{36}{100}$ or $\frac{136}{100}$
5. $\frac{9}{100}$ **6.** $9\frac{27}{100}$ or $\frac{927}{100}$

Page 29
1. a. 20   **b.** 0.20 or $\frac{2}{10}$
    c. 0.02 or $\frac{2}{100}$ **d.** 0.02 or $\frac{2}{100}$
2. The value of 9 is 90.
    The value of 8 is 8.
    The value of 7 is 0.7 or $\frac{7}{10}$.
    The value of 6 is 0.06 or $\frac{6}{100}$.
    The value of 5 is 0.005 or $\frac{5}{1,000}$.
3. .248

Page 31
1. $0.79 > 0.3$ **2.** $4.49 < 4.6$
3. $\frac{1}{2} < 0.55$ **4.** $0.999 < 1.1$

Page 35
1. 3.83   **2.** 0.70   **3.** 1.02   **4.** 9.77

Page 37
1. 4   **2.** 90   **3.** 60
4. 9   **5.** 5

Page 46
1. $2\frac{3}{4}$ **2.** $2\frac{1}{2}$ **3.** $\frac{9}{4}$
4. $\frac{5}{3}$ **5.** $\frac{25}{8}$

Page 48
1. a. $\frac{2}{3}$
    b. Sample answers: $\frac{4}{6}, \frac{8}{12}$
2. Sample answers: $\frac{2}{4}, \frac{4}{8}, \frac{56}{112}$
3. Sample answers: $\frac{6}{36}, \frac{1}{6}, \frac{9}{54}$

Page 49
1. a. true   **b.** true   **c.** false   **d.** true
2. a. Sample answers: $\frac{6}{8}, \frac{9}{12}, \frac{15}{20}$
    b. Sample answers: $\frac{36}{48}, \frac{75}{100}$

Page 50
1. A: $\frac{3}{16}$; B: $\frac{7}{8}$; C: $4\frac{1}{4}$
2. a. $\frac{3}{4}$ **b.** $\frac{6}{8}$ **c.** $\frac{12}{16}$

Page 52
1. $<$ **2.** $>$ **3.** $>$ **4.** $<$

Page 54
1. $\frac{5}{6}$ **2.** $\frac{2}{6}$ or $\frac{1}{3}$ **3.** $\frac{2}{12}$ or $\frac{1}{6}$ **4.** $1\frac{1}{6}$ or $\frac{7}{6}$

Page 55
1. $\frac{23}{20}$ or $1\frac{3}{20}$ **2.** $\frac{3}{8}$ **3.** $\frac{2}{12}$ or $\frac{1}{6}$ **4.** $\frac{13}{12}$ or $1\frac{1}{12}$

Page 56
1. $\frac{10}{3}$ or $3\frac{1}{3}$ **2.** $\frac{18}{4}$ or $4\frac{2}{4}$ **3.** $\frac{12}{5}$ or $2\frac{2}{5}$
4. 3   **5.** 4   **6.** 2

Page 57
1. 9   **2.** 16
3. Rita gets $8, Hunter gets $4.

Page 60

1. $\frac{1}{2}$ 0.50 50%   2. $\frac{3}{4}$ 0.75 75%

3. $\frac{1}{10}$ 0.10 10%   4. $\frac{4}{5}$ 0.80 80%

Page 63

1.

Number of Hits	Number of Players
0				
1				
2					
3		
4		

2.

Number of Players

X
X X X
X X X X
X X X X X X

0   1   2   3   4

Number of Hits

Page 64

1.

Number of Points	Number of Games
10-19		
20-29	||||
30-39	|||
40-49	|||

Page 65

1. 0   2. 4   3. 4

4. 2   5. 2

Page 66

1. min = 0; max = 4; range = 4;
   mode = 2, 3 and 4; median = 2.5

2. 14

Page 67

1. 154 miles

2. Mean (average distance per day) = 22 miles

Page 68

1. Italy: about 42; Canada: about 26;
   United States: about 13

2. Canadians take about twice as many
   vacation days per year.

Page 69

Cars in a Parking Lot

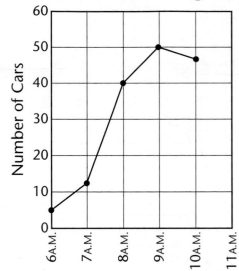

Page 70

It is more likely to snow on Monday.
($\frac{1}{6}$ is about 17%.)

Page 72

1. $\frac{6}{10}$, $\frac{3}{5}$, or 60%   2. $\frac{5}{10}$, $\frac{1}{2}$, or 50%

3. $\frac{6}{10}$, $\frac{3}{5}$, or 60%   4. $\frac{4}{10}$, $\frac{2}{5}$, or 40%

5. $\frac{2}{10}$, $\frac{1}{5}$, or 20%   6. $\frac{3}{10}$ or 30%

Page 77

Sample answer for 1-4:

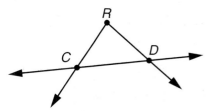

Answer Key

Page 79

1.

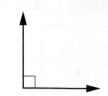

2. Sample answer:

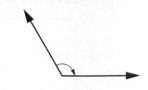

3. a. ∠A   **b.** ∠C, ∠E   **c.** ∠B, ∠G

    d. ∠D   **e.** ∠F

    f. ∠DEF, ∠FED, ∠DEG, ∠GED

Page 80

Sample answers:

1.

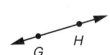

2.

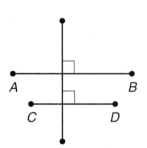

Page 81

1.

   D

2. Sample answer:

Sample answers:

3.

4.

Sample answers:

5.

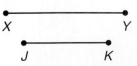

6.

Page 83

1. a. quadrangle or quadrilateral

    b. hexagon

    c. octagon

2. Sample answers: **3.** Sample answers:

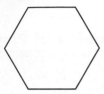 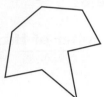

4. The sides of the cover of this book are not all the same length.

Page 84

1. *SCA, ACS, ASC, CSA, CAS*

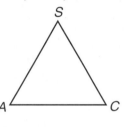

2.

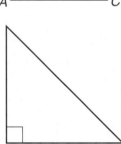

Page 86

Sample answers:

1. All four sides of a square are equal. A rectangle can have two sets of equal sides that are different lengths.

2. All four sides of a rhombus are equal. Two adjacent sides of a kite are one length and the other two sides are a different length.

3. A trapezoid has exactly one pair of parallel sides. A parallelogram has two pairs of parallel sides.

Page 87
Sample answers:
1. **a.** They each have at least one circular face. Each has a curved surface.
   b. A cylinder has three surfaces; a cone has two. A cylinder has a flat top and a flat bottom; a cone has a flat bottom and comes to a point at the top.
2. **a.** They each have one curved surface.
   b. A cone has a flat base, one vertex, and one edge. A sphere has no edges and no vertices.

Page 89
1. **a.** 5   **b.** 1
2. **a.** 6   **b.** 6
3. triangular prism
4. tetrahedron, octahedron, icosahedron
5. **a.** 12   **b.** 6
6. Sample answers:
   a. Their faces are equilateral triangles.
   b. A tetrahedron has four faces. An octahedron has eight faces.

Page 91
a, b, c, d

Page 93
1.

2. C

Page 95
1.

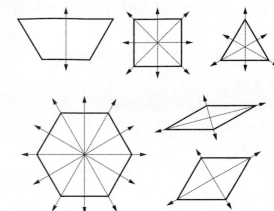

2. infinite; any line drawn through its center is a line of symmetry

Pages 98–104
Answers vary.

Page 107
1. millimeter, gram, meter, centimeter
2. **a.** $\frac{1}{1000}$ **b.** 5,000 mm

Page 108
1. 3 cm; 30 mm
2. 2.3 cm; 23 mm
3. 4.6 cm; 46 mm
4. segment 1: $1\frac{1}{4}$ in.; segment 2: 1 in.; segment 3: $1\frac{3}{4}$ in.

Page 111
1. 15 ft   2. 60 mm   3. 24 m   4. 39 in.

Page 112
1. 21 mm
2. It is slightly more than $3 * 21$ mm $= 63$ mm
3. It is slightly more than $3 * 12$ in. $= 36$ in.

Page 114
1. 6 units^2 2. 22.5 in.^{2} 3. 25 m^2

Page 115
1. 660 ft^2 2. 240 in.^{2} 3. 8.6 cm^2

Answer Key

Page 116
1. 6 in.^{2} **2.** 27 cm^2 **3.** 4.8 yd^2

Page 118
1. 1,000 cm^3 **2.** 1,980 in.^{3}

Page 120
1. 180 grams; 170.1 grams
2. 366 ounces

Page 122
1. 70° **2.** 270°

Page 123
1. 25° **2.** 150°

Sample answers:

3.

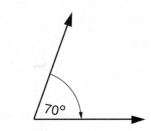

4.

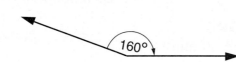

5.

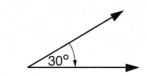

Page 124
1.–4.

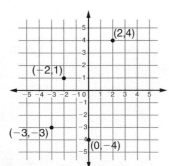

Page 128
1. true **2.** true **3.** true
4. $y = 7$ **5.** $z = 8$ **6.** $w = 6$

Page 129
1. $(2 * 2) + 10 = 14$
2. $0 = (3 - 3)/6$
3. $1,000 = (5 + 5) * (50 + 50)$
4. $10 - (6 + 4) = 0$
5. $1 = (4 * 5)/(4 * 5)$
6. $10 = (4 + 1) * 2$

Page 130
1. $15 - 6/2 + 2 = 14$
2. $5 * 8/(2 + 2) = 10$
3. $3 + 2 * 4 - 15/5 = 8$
4. $4 + 7 * 5 = 39$

Page 131
1. $100 = 55 + 45$ **2.** $\frac{1}{2} = 0.5$
3. $\frac{3}{4} > \frac{1}{4}$ **4.** $3 * 50 > 100$
5. $\frac{1}{2} * 100 = 50$ **6.** $3.2 > 3.05$

Page 133
1.

Total			
?			
Part	Part	Part	Part
5.5	6	3	8

$5.5 + 6 + 3 + 8 = n$
Ella ran 22.5 miles.

2.

Quantity
35

Quantity	Difference
21	?

$21 + n = 35$
The Eagles scored 14 points in the second half.

3.

Quantity
45

Quantity	Difference
38	?

$45 - 38 = n$
Monica had $7 more than Maurice.

Page 135

1. a. $x + 5 = 8$
   b. $3 * n = 15$
2. a. $A = 4 \text{ cm} * 3 \text{ cm} = 12 \text{ cm}^2$
   b. $A = 6 \text{ cm} * 2 \text{ cm} = 12 \text{ cm}^2$

Page 137

1. $8 * (12 + 9) = (8 * 12) + (8 * 9)$
2. $(7 * 23) + (7 * 16) = 7 * (23 + 16)$
3. $5 * (16 - 14) = (5 * 16) - (5 * 14)$
4. $(9 * 3) + (9 * 4) = 9 * (3 + 4)$

Page 139

1. 14: even
2. 25: square   odd
3. 13: prime   odd
4. 15: triangular   odd
5. 17: odd   6. 18: even
7. 22: even   8. 27: odd
9. 1, 4, 9, 16, 25, 36, 49, 64, 81

Page 141

1.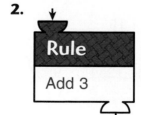

Rule
Subtract 11

99 88 77 66 55

2.

Rule
Add 3

Page 144

1.

in	out
3	24
5	40
7	56

2.

in	out
25	75
75	125
0	50

3.

Rule
+3

in	out
1	4
2	5
3	6
10	13
15	18

4.

Rule
*5

in	out
1	5
2	10
3	15
7	35
9	45

Page 146

1.

in	out
9	3
36	12
1	$\frac{1}{3}$
1.5	0.5
123	41
390	130

2.

in	out
11	7
28	24
0	-4
4	0
54	50
122	118

3.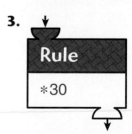

Rule
*30

Page 149

1. The no. of days walked before the first 6- mile walk was $2 + 3 + 4 + 5 = 14$. The next day she walked 6 miles, on day 15.

2. Draw 2 squares of width n touching side by side. Perimeter $= 6 * n = 24$. So, the width n is 4 in. and the length of the original rectangle is 8 in.

Page 151

1. Sample Answer: it took about 3 minutes to count numbers from 100,001 to 100,100. So, it would take about 30,000 minutes to say a million numbers.
$30,000$ minutes $= 500$ hr $= 20.8$ days or about 21 days.

2.  Alternate answer

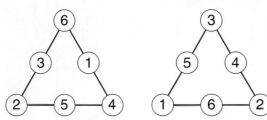

3. The area is 7 cm^2.

Page 152

1.

Start	Change	End
12	+9	21

2.

Quantity
137 cm

Quantity	Difference
78 cm	59 cm

3.

Total
343

Part	Part
218	125

Page 155

1. David is not correct. Using leading-digit estimation gives $500 * 30$ which is 15,000.

2. Caroline is correct. There are 24 hours in a day and 7 days in a week. Using leading-digit estimation gives $20 * 7$ which is 140 hours.

Page 157

1. 90	**2.** 150	**3.** 7,910
4. 14,000	**5.** 5,000	**6.** 90,000

Page 158

1. Hundreds   2. Thousands   3. Hundreds

Page 163

1. 16   **2.** 28   **3.** 63   **4.** 81

Page 169

1. 0.625   **2.** $\frac{175}{1000}$ **3.** 64%   **4.** 2.75

5. 41.67%   **6.** $\frac{45}{100}$ **7.** 0.75   **8.** $0.8\overline{3}$

9. $\frac{556}{1000}$ **10.** $\frac{67}{100}$ **11.** 3.25   **12.** $0.\overline{428571}$ or 0.429

Page 173

1. 8,580   **2.** 8,600   **3.** 9,000

Page 175

1. 500,000   **2.** 0.000000009

3. 0.022   **4.** 51,500

Page 176

1. $8.914 * 10^{11}$ **2.** $6.459 * 10^{12}$
3. $5.387 * 10^{11}$ **4.** $2.994 * 10^{14}$
5. 655,321,000   **6.** 159,000,000,000

Page 179

1. Tip: $15.00   **2.** Tip: $11.15

Page 182

1. 19, 30, 41, 52, 63   **2.** 9, 12, 15, 18, 21

Page 217

Los Angeles: 34°North, 118°West
Philadelphia: 40°North, 75°West
Atlanta: 34°North, 85°West

Index

Z

Zero

    as a counting number, 3

    as a placeholder, 27

    as a rational number, 58

    Celsius freezing point of
      water, 107

    decimals with, 30

    in operations, 16, 20

    negative numbers and, 3, 58

    on calculators, 178

    opposite, 58

    padding with, 30, 32

    points, 3, 119, 121–122, 124

    powers of 10 operations, 16,
      20